The Historical Series of the Reformed Church
in America

No. 5

THE DUTCH REFORMED CHURCH IN THE AMERICAN COLONIES

by

GERALD F. DE JONG

Wm. B. Eerdmans Publishing Co.
Grand Rapids, Michigan

Gerald F. De Jong

Copyright © 1978 by Gerald F. De Jong
All rights reserved

Library of Congress Cataloging in Publication Data

De Jong, Gerald Francis, 1921–
The Dutch Reformed Church in the American colonies.

(The Historical series of the Reformed Church in
America ; no. 5)
   Bibliography: p.
   Includes index.
   1. Reformed Church in America—History.   I. Title.
II. Series: Reformed Church in America. The historical
series ; no. 5.
BX9515.D39   285'.73   78-17216
   ISBN 0-8028-1741-6

Printed in the United States of America

To the Memory of
my father
OTTO DE JONG (1893–1967)
and
my mother
HATTIE DOUMA DE JONG (1894–1965)

Gelijk een hert schreeuwt naar
de waterstromen,
alzo schreeuwt mijn ziel tot U,
o God!

Psalm 42:2

The Historical Series of the Reformed Church in America

This series has been inaugurated by the General Synod of the Reformed Church in America, acting through its Commission on History, for the purpose of encouraging historical research and providing a medium wherein this knowledge may be shared with the academic community and with the members of the denomination in order that a knowledge of the past may contribute to right action in the present.

It is an especial pleasure to present to the church this volume concerning her colonial experience upon the occasion of her 350th anniversary.

Editor

The Rev. Donald J. Bruggink, Ph.D., Western Theological Seminary

Contents

Illustrations

Foreword

In the nineteenth century the Reformed Church in America was in the forefront of historical research through the work of Edward Tanjore Corwin (1834–1914). Not only were the first scientifically researched histories of the Reformed Church in this country the products of his pen, but the collection of all the original documents which he could find and their storage in Gardner Sage Library in New Brunswick (thus creating, in effect, our Reformed Church archives) were largely achieved under his leadership. By the time of his death few churches in this country were in a better position to study their past, especially as it related to colonial times.

The unfortunate fact is that in the next half-century no advantage was taken of this great historical pioneering task which Corwin accomplished. The Reformed Church in America in that period seemed to have little interest in its own history and little historical consciousness, preferring to live with the history that had already been written and the mythology which inevitably developed from it. While there were occasional works of local history which proved to be of value, there was little or no serious work interpreting this history of the church or making use of new discoveries in historical research.

Happily all that has now begun to change. There is no better indication of that change than Gerald F. De Jong's new volume on the story of the Reformed Church from 1628 to 1792. The reader will discover that some of the tensions and differences within the church did not, as is so often supposed, arrive with the mid-western immigrants in 1847 but were actively argued in colonial days. The story of the Americanization of the Dutch Church, a story which has almost never before been studied, is here told by a careful historian whose patient research is balanced by his appreciation of the importance of the church in colonial life.

The need for this book has long been obvious. I hope that it signals the fact that we have once again become aware that only a church which is conscious of its origin can have significant ideas about its destiny.

Howard G. Hageman, President
New Brunswick Theological Seminary

Preface

Three hundred fifty years ago, in 1628, a small gathering of people met in a mill loft in the little wilderness village of New Amsterdam and organized the first Reformed (Dutch) congregation in North America. Little did they dream that their small community would someday become the metropolis that New York is today. Nor could they have imagined that three and one-half centuries later, from this small band of worshippers would develop the Reformed Church in America with its more than nine hundred congregations. They would also have been surprised to learn that this Church in 1978 would be supporting several institutions of higher learning as well as a missionary program that spanned the globe, and would have a maze of special boards and commissions concerned with matters ranging from ecumenical endeavors to social issues and from the role of women to the representation of minorities.

It has been said that a century is but a step in the march of Providence. Considered in that light, the Reformed Church in America has now marched only three and one-half steps. But a great deal has taken place in that period of time, and this study is an attempt to recount only a part of that story, namely, from the founding of the Church in 1628 to 1772. The decision to end this history with 1772 rather than the American Revolution (the usual terminating date for colonial histories) was arrived at for two reasons: first, 1772 is a significant date for the Church because it was in that year that it received ecclesiastical independence from the mother church in Holland; second, the story of the Church in the Revolution has already been well-treated in two other studies: "The Reformed Church and the American Revolution" by John Beardslee III in *Piety and Patriotism*, edited by James Van Hoeven (Grand Rapids: Eerdmans, 1976) and *The Revolutionary War in the Hackensack Valley: The Jersey Dutch and the Neutral Ground, 1775–1783* by Adrian C. Leiby (New Brunswick: Rutgers University Press, 1962).

The writer is patently aware that it is somewhat of a misnomer to use the qualifying adjective "Dutch" when referring to the Reformed Church. The latter never was an ethnic religious body made up exclu-

1

2

sively of Dutchmen and Dutch preachers; from the beginning it included persons from several ethnic backgrounds. On the other hand, as this study will point out, there are many valid reasons for referring to it as a Dutch Church during the colonial period, not the least of which is the fact that it was officially so termed until about the time of the Civil War.

Sources used in this study are quoted as they are found without the use of the Latin word *sic* to indicate archaic spellings, incorrect words and punctuation, or faulty logic. This procedure was followed because the sources span more than three centuries, and a multiplicity of *sics* would at times have to be used—resulting in more of a distraction than a help to the reader.

In writing this history, my labors were of course facilitated by various published documentary materials and numerous monographs. A special recognition is due those scholars of the past, such as Edward T. Corwin, Berthold Fernow, Edmund O'Callaghan, and Arnold J. F. Van Laer, who uncovered materials from dusty archives, deciphered difficult handwriting, and translated documents into English from a Dutch language (as well as German and Latin) that often differed markedly from what is in use today. Although monographs concerned with church history are often eulogistic rather than objective in nature, fortunately there have been exceptions. Writers such as Adrian Leiby and James Tanis have clearly demonstrated that church history and sound scholarship can be compatible. To writers such as these, I am also indebted.

I am grateful to many persons who read parts of the manuscript and offered constructive criticism. Particular thanks in this regard are given to the various members of the Historical Commission of the Reformed Church and to William Coventry, Jonathan Hinkamp, Herman Harmelink III, R. Alton Lee, Joseph Loux Jr., and Henry Zwaanstra. As the manuscript reached the final stages of completion, I profited from the careful editorial pen of Donald J. Bruggink, general editor of the Historical Series of the Reformed Church in America. In addition, appreciation is expressed for repeated courtesies extended by staff members of numerous libraries, especially those at Northwestern College, Rutgers University, Western Theological Seminary, and New Brunswick Theological Seminary, as well as the New York Historical Society Library, the New York Public Library, and the library of the Holland Society of New York. A special word of thanks is due John Beardslee III, archivist at the Sage Library at New Brunswick Seminary, and to his kind and gracious assistant, Miss Elsie Stryker. Several persons assisted me in locating illustrations, but a special word of thanks is in order to Deweese W. DeWitt.

Limited portions of this book have been published in different form in *The New York Historical Society Quarterly*, *Church History*, and *The Dutch in America, 1609–1974* (New York: Twayne Publishers, 1975). I am grateful for permission from their editors to reproduce that material.

Thanks are due my children for tolerating my frequent "absenteeism" during the past few years while I traveled or confined myself to my study to do research and writing. Last, but above all, a special word of gratitude must go to my wife, Jeanne, who typed and retyped the manuscript more times than either of us care to remember, and who by her encouragement and patience has helped make writing this book, too, a labor of love.

Gerald F. De Jong
University of South Dakota

I

The Beginnings In The Old World

The Reformed Church in America, like many religious denominations in the United States, traces its origins to the Old World, particularly to the Netherlands. Indeed, the term Dutch was used in the various offical titles of this denomination until 1867, when its present name was adopted.[1] A history of the Church must therefore begin with a general account of the establishment of the Reformed Church in the Netherlands, together with a review of the events that led to the founding on American soil of a Dutch colony and a branch of the Netherlands Church.

At the time that the Dutch Reformed Church was established in the Old World during the sixteenth century, the term Netherlands encompassed a much larger territory than is the case today.[2] The Netherlands, or *Nederlanden*, meaning "Low Countries," was originally made up of seventeen provinces constituting primarily the present countries of the Netherlands, Belgium, and Luxemburg. The southern or "Walloon" provinces were French-speaking, while those to the north used the Dutch language. Beginning in the late fifteenth century, these seventeen provinces gradually lost their independence, first to Burgundy, then to Austria, and finally to Spain.

Christianity began taking a firm hold among the inhabitants of the Low Countries with the arrival of itinerant Irish missionaries in the southern Netherlands during the seventh century, followed soon after by the great Anglo-Saxon missionaries Willibrord and Boniface, who labored primarily in the northern Netherlands. The people of the Low Countries took their religion seriously as is evidenced by the activities of such "pre-reformers" as Gerard Groote and Wessel Gansfort during the century before Martin Luther. Moreover, the simple piety and practical mysticism of the semi-monastic Brethren of the Common Life were a healthy antidote to the generally sad state of affairs existing in the Roman Catholic Church at the close of the Middle Ages.

In view of the traditional interest of the Low Countries in religious matters, it is not surprising that the Protestant Reformation took root there at an early date. Already in 1523, two Augustinian monks, Henry Voes and John Esch, were put to death in Brussels because of their

Lutheran sympathies. Anabaptism also appealed to the people of the Low Countries, and after 1535 the Anabaptists surpassed the Lutherans in number. One of the most distinguished Anabaptist leaders was Menno Simons, whose followers became known as Mennonites. It was Calvinism, however, that finally became the dominant form of Protestantism in the Low Countries. This came about in part through the proselyting work by Netherlandish students who had studied in Geneva—some of them at the foot of the master himself, John Calvin. Calvinism was also spread by French Huguenots who found refuge from persecution by fleeing to the Low Countries. Calvin's writings, especially the *Institutes of the Christian Religion*, were likewise influential in winning converts.

The Reformation in the Low Countries which led to the founding of the Dutch Reformed Church became inextricably entwined with the revolt against Spain that broke out during the 1560's. Heavy financial demands on the populace together with the centralizing policies of Philip II, king of Spain from 1556 to 1598, produced considerable unrest. Religious causes were also a factor. Philip II was a militant Catholic who was determined to stamp out Protestantism, using whatever means he considered necessary. The unrest finally led to a coalescence of the various political, economic, and religious groups opposing Spanish domination. The Calvinists in particular became closely identified with the movement seeking independence from Spain.

Although most of the Low Countries participated in the revolt, it succeeded only in the north. By the time of the Twelve Years' Truce in 1609, the seven northern provinces had achieved *de facto* independence, which became *de jure* by the Treaty of Münster in 1648. The new state became known by various names, including the Dutch Republic, the United Provinces, and the Netherlands. It also became popularly known as Holland, after the name of its most important province. The failure of the political revolt in the southern provinces meant that the Reformation also ultimately failed there. As a consequence, many Protestants from the south fled to the northern provinces, where they greatly increased the ranks of the Calvinists. The southern provinces remained primarily Catholic and had to wait until the 1830's before finally winning their political independence with the creation of the present state of Belgium.

The Calvinists in the Low Countries began organizing late in the Reformation period.[3] Thus, in 1566, a convention or synod was convened secretly at Antwerp to bring the churches into closer union. Here was adopted, with some minor revisions, the Belgic Confession of Faith. Consisting of thirty-seven articles, it had been composed in 1559 and published in 1561 by the martyr, Guido de Brés, a native of the southern Low Countries and a close associate of Calvinist leaders throughout western Europe. The Heidelberg Catechism was also provisionally adopted by the Antwerp synod of 1566. This document had been drafted in 1563 by two young professors, Zacharias Ursinus and Casper Olevianus, at Heidelberg University, a flourishing center of Calvinist theology in the Palatinate.

The Protestants in the northern provinces, despite their ultimate political emancipation, were frequently hard pressed by Spanish troops during the early years of the revolt and many had to go into hiding or exile. It is therefore not surprising that the Reformed Church during its formative years held several organizational meetings in German towns near the Dutch border. These included Wesel in 1568 and Emden in 1571. The synod at Wesel, sometimes termed the first general synod of the Dutch Reformed Church, was attended by fifty-three delegates representing about twenty congregations. It adopted a provisional form of church government and approved Peter Dathenus' Dutch versification of the Psalms for use in worship. It also gave further acceptance to the Heidelberg Catechism. The synod at Emden confirmed and elaborated on the decisions made at Wesel three years earlier.

As the military situation of the northern provinces improved, the number of Dutch Reformed congregations increased and provincial synods were held in scattered places on Dutch soil. These included, among others, Alkmaar (1573), Dordrecht (1574), Middelburg (1581), The Hague (1586), and Groningen (1595). The first national synod to be held on Dutch soil was at Dordrecht in 1578. Frequently, one synod confirmed, sometimes with modifications, what a previous synod had provisionally approved. Considering the multi-national membership of several of these gatherings and the presence in the Netherlands of Calvinist refugees from other countries, it is not surprising that some leeway was initially granted to congregations in matters of doctrinal standards, orders of worship, and the structure of church government. With the passage of time, however, and as more synods were held on Dutch soil, a more nationalistic and established church developed in the Netherlands. This is not surprising, because Calvinist congregations in Switzerland, France, and elsewhere also developed along national lines and adopted their own special Reformed doctrinal standards. Thus, whereas the Belgic Confession seemed to suit the Dutch frame of mind, the Swiss, Gallican, and Westminster confessions had special appeals for other national groups.

The most significant convention of Reformed divines held in the

Netherlands during the early period was at Dordrecht in 1618–1619. This started out as an ecumenical assembly of eighty-four delegates from England, the Germanies, the Swiss cantons, and the Netherlands. The latter, however, had a preponderance of representatives, including fifty-three ministers and elders and five theological professors. The synod was convened to settle the bitter theological disputes that had been raging for several years within Calvinist circles, particularly over questions concerning divine election, atonement, and reprobation. When these problems were finally dispensed with after one hundred fifty-four sessions, the foreign delegates returned home but those from the Netherlands remained behind to sit as a national synod to deal with other matters. During its twenty-six sessions, resulting in what are usually referred to as the "Post-Acta," it reviewed and adopted what became the official texts of the Belgic Confession and Heidelberg Catechism, and decided on rules for church government as well as liturical forms for use in public worship. It also sanctioned a new translation of the Bible into Dutch, which resulted in the publication in 1637 of the famous *Statenbijbel.*

As was true of the doctrinal standards and the convening of synods, so too the founding of several universities in the Netherlands for training young men for the ministry helped unify the Dutch churches and give them a common theological basis. These schools and the dates of their appearance included Leiden, 1575; Franeker, 1585; Groningen, 1614; and Utrecht, 1636. Until about 1750 most of the Dutch Reformed ministers in the American colonies received their theological training at one of these institutions.

The Belgic Confession, the Heidelberg Catechism, and the Canons of Dort became the cornerstones of the Reformed Church in the Netherlands. As such, they were transplanted to the New World, so that the churches established by Netherlanders in the American colonies became virtually as Dutch Reformed in doctrine as if they had been organized in the Netherlands itself. Even to this day, the Reformed Church in America requires, at least in theory, each minister to cover the contents of the Heidelberg Catechism in his sermons within a specified period of time. Together with these specifically Reformed confessions, the Dutch Reformed churches in the Netherlands and in America accepted the Apostles' Creed, the Nicene Creed, and the Athanasian Creed.

The churches in America also inherited their form of government from the mother church in the Netherlands. As finally established in Holland, church polity consisted of a progression of minor and major assemblies known as consistories, classes, provincial synods, and a national synod. The consistory was the governing body of the local church and was made up of elders, deacons, and the pastor. The elders were charged primarily with enforcing ecclesiastical discipline within the congregation, while the deacons looked after the temporal needs of the church. A classis consisted of a minister and an elder from each congregation located in close proximity to one another within a defined area. It usually met quarterly and exercised general supervision over the churches within its territory, including the licensing and ordaining of new ministers. The provincial synods were made up of two ministers and two elders from each classis in a specific geographical area. Meeting annually, they had general supervision over the proceedings and decisions of the classes. The national synod, made up of selected delegates from each provincial synod, was the highest judicatory body in the Church. Although it had been decided in 1578 that this body should meet triennially, in practice it met rarely and then only in great emergencies. As events turned out, only the consistorial level of church government was established in the American colonies until the latter part of the eighteenth century, when something approaching classes and synods were finally introduced. Until that time, most religious questions of any significance had to be referred to ecclesiastical bodies in the Netherlands, especially the Classis of Amsterdam.

Turning from this brief account of the establishment of the Reformed Church in the Netherlands and its bearing on ecclesiastical developments in America, a few comments must be made about the events that led to the founding of a Dutch colony on American soil and, with it, the establishment of a branch of the Dutch Reformed Church.[4]

One of the striking developments about the Dutch revolt against Spain is that the Netherlands in the midst of its struggle for independence was able to establish itself as the leading commercial country in the world. Netherlanders not only carried on extensive trade with the Baltic region, Russia, and the Mediterranean area, but also established colonies in Africa, Asia, and the western hemisphere. Because the spiritual welfare of Hollanders who lived abroad was a matter of deep concern to the leaders of the Dutch Reformed Church, the expansion of the latter went hand in hand with the establishment of a commercial empire. It is therefore not surprising that during the seventeenth century Dutch Reformed congregations could be found in Japan, Formosa, the East Indies, Ceylon, Turkey, Russia, Africa, Brazil, and the West Indies. Thus it also happened that a Dutch colony together with the Dutch Reformed Church was established in North America. The colony became known as New Netherland and at its height consisted largely of what today makes up the states of New York and New Jersey with parts of Delaware and Connecticut.

The claim to New Netherland was based on various voyages of exploration sent out by the Dutch, particularly that of Henry Hudson in 1609. Although Dutch commercial interests were centered primarily on developing the lucrative spice trade with the Far East, the realization that profits could be made from the fur trade with the Indians gradually caused the Dutch to pay some attention to their claims in North America and to establish a few trading posts there. These posts at first were rather makeshift in appearance and did not represent a serious attempt to colonize New Netherland. This attitude changed somewhat in 1621 when various business interests in Holland combined to form the Dutch West India Company.

The charter obtained by this Company from the government gave it a monopoly on Dutch trade with the west coast of Africa, South America, the Caribbean, and North America, and authorized it to establish and govern colonies within its territories. New Netherland, of course, was included in the area under its jurisdiction. The fact that the claims of the Company ranged over such a large part of the globe was unfortunate. New Netherland was generally looked upon as the least desirable of the Company's holdings and consequently its problems and special needs were often ignored. Its management was placed in the hands of a committee or board of nineteen directors, sitting at Amsterdam, who represented five different chambers located in various cities or parts of the Netherlands.

In order to facilitate the administration of affairs in New Netherland, the directors in 1624 approved twenty articles which were to have the force of law in the colony. A resident governor with the title of director general was appointed as executive officer. To assist him in his work, an advisory council was also appointed, along with a *koopman*, or secretary-bookkeeper, and a *schout*, or sheriff. In the decades which followed, several individuals served as directors general, the most significant of whom was Peter Stuyvesant, whose term of office lasted from 1647 to 1664. Generally speaking, the directors general ran the colony in an autocratic manner.

Although the primary interest of the West India Company was commercial rather than colonization, plans were carried out in the spring of 1624 for occupying New Netherland on a more permanent basis. Thirty families, mostly Protestant Walloon refugees from the Spanish Netherlands, were sent out to settle New Netherland. These families were consigned not as traders but as agricultural colonists, and were provided with livestock and farm implements. Most of the colonists were settled on the Hudson River at Fort Orange near the present site of Albany, but some were located to the south on the Delaware River at Fort Nassau and a few on Nut Island (later called Governor's Island), opposite Manhattan Island. In the months that followed, more settlers and additional livestock and implements were sent out.

In 1626, Peter Minuit was appointed director general of New Netherland and more immigrants arrived. At about this same time, the settlement on Nut Island was moved to Manhattan Island, which had earlier been purchased from the Indians. Here, construction of a fort (Fort Amsterdam) was begun, together with a Company storehouse, a mill, and a number of houses. For purposes of security against Indian attacks, Minuit settled the Delaware colonists at Manhattan, and except for a token force of perhaps a dozen men, did the same with the colonists who had earlier settled at Fort Orange. The Manhattan settlement became known as New Amsterdam and by 1628, when the first Dutch Reformed church was established there, it had about two hundred seventy inhabitants.

Additional settlements were founded during the years that followed. These included: Beverswyck and Schenectady, both near Fort Orange; Pavonia and Vriesendael, on the west bank of the Hudson near its mouth; Esopus (later called Kingston); Breuckelen (Brooklyn), Midwout or Vlack Bos (Flatbush), Amersfoort (Flatlands), Vlissingen (Flushing), Heemstede (Hempstead), and Gravenzande (Gravesend), all on the western end of Long Island; and New Amstel (New Castle) and Swanendael (Lewes) on the Delaware River. At the time of its conquest by the English in 1664, New Netherland had a total white population of about eight thousand.[5]

II

The Formative Years, 1624–1652

The colonists of New Netherland probably enjoyed occasional religious services from the time the first small party of settlers arrived on its shores. Dutch merchant ships frequently carried persons who read prayers and a few chapters from Scripture, and perhaps even a sermon, to members of the crew.[1] When ships called at one of the Dutch colonies or trading posts, these individuals frequently made a visit ashore and held religious services for the colonists. The extent to which these services occurred in New Netherland will never be known, but in 1624, a resident lay pastor, known as a *ziekentrooster*, was sent there. This was done as a result of pressure from the church consistory of Amsterdam on the directors of the West India Company.

The office of *ziekentrooster*, which is generally translated as "comforter of the sick," originated during the sixteenth century in response to the need for persons who could assist ordained clergymen in visiting the sick.[2] With the passage of time, comforters of the sick were attached to hospitals, orphanages, poorhouses, the army and navy, and the merchant fleets of the East and West India Companies. Gradually, too, their duties were expanded to include much more than giving consolation to the sick. They were expected to lead the people in prayers every morning and evening and before and after meals and, on appropriate occasions, read a few chapters from the Bible and maybe a sermon from an approved book of sermons. They were also frequently asked to assist in the catechetical instruction of the youth. Although comforters of the sick were prohibited from administering the sacrament of the Lord's Supper, they were permitted, with special permission from the Church authorities, to administer the sacrament of baptism and to officiate at marriage ceremonies. During the seventeenth century, comforters of the sick were frequently sent overseas because of the shortage of ordained ministers at home and because the Dutch communities in the colonies often numbered only a few families, particularly during the early stages in the development of a colony. If stationed overseas, they were sometimes asked to do missionary work among the natives.

A person interested in becoming a comforter of the sick generally

11

made his wishes known to his local consistory. The latter thereupon made an investigation of the applicant's qualifications and decided whether to pursue the matter further and have him examined by a special committee, which included several ministers. During the examination, the candidate was expected to show a knowledge of the Bible, be able to read and write well, and have a good voice for leading worshippers in singing the Psalms. Candidates were occasionally asked to give an actual demonstration of how they would comfort someone who was critically ill.

Bastiaen Krol was the first comforter of the sick to be sent to New Netherland.[3] Born in Harlingen, Friesland in 1595, he later moved to Amsterdam where he obtained employment as a fabric worker. At some point in his life, the details of which are unknown, he developed an urge to go to the East or West Indies as a comforter of the sick. It was not uncommon for the latter to be drawn from the lower classes and to be persons having only a rudimentary education. At the time of Krol's marriage in 1615, he was still unable to write, having to sign his name to the marriage certificate with a cross. It is also interesting to note that he did not become a baptized member of the church until a year after his marriage.[4]

On October 12, 1623, at the age of twenty-eight, Krol appeared before the consistory at Amsterdam with a request that he be appointed as a comforter of the sick to one of the colonies. It may be assumed that by this time he had learned to write because an illiterate person would not have been considered for such a position. Although his testimonials were good, Krol was not immediately approved. He was examined again on November 30 and on December 7. On the latter date, he was accepted for service to New Netherland. His duties as outlined in his contract were:

First, to read common prayers morning and evening, as well as before and after meals. Secondly, to instruct and comfort the sick as needed. Thirdly, to admonish those who ask for help, or are in need of admonishment, by reading from God's Word. Fourthly, at opportune times, to read chapters from God's Word or from books written by Reformed authors or even a sermon.[5]

Krol probably left Holland for New Netherland in late January 1624. More than likely his initial work as comforter of the sick was centered at Fort Orange, near the present site of Albany, because most of the colonial activity was located there. He returned to the fatherland after being in the colony only a few months. On November 14, 1624, Krol appeared before the consistory of Amsterdam with a request that an ordained minister be sent to the colony soon, and if this could not be done that he be given permission to marry and to baptize. He declared that the colonists were demanding a minister and that there were "pregnant women in the colony and some arrangement must be made for the baptism of their children." After some deliberation, the consistory informed him that the number of inhabitants in New Netherland was too small to warrant sending a minister, but that he would be given permission to baptize and to perform marriages. In carrying out these functions, he was told to study and read the appropriate liturgy, and if he thought it necessary to deliver a sermon on these occasions, to read one from an accepted book of sermons written by Reformed theologians. Krol was specifically instructed not to interject any of his own words into either the liturgical formulas or into the sermons.[6]

Upon receiving these new instructions, Krol returned to New Netherland in January 1625. When New Amsterdam on Manhattan Island replaced Fort Orange as the chief settlement in the colony, it more than likely became the center of his activity. Following Krol's return, he served as comforter of the sick for only about a year and a half. On August 1, 1626, he accepted the position of commissary or agent for the West India Company at Fort Orange to replace David Van Krieckenbeeck, who had been killed by the Indians. He served in this capacity until 1644, when he returned to Holland. He also served briefly from 1632 to 1633 as provisional director general of New Netherland.

Krol was the only comforter of the sick in New Netherland until the arrival of Jan Huygens (sometimes written Huyck) in July 1626. Not much is known about Huygens' early life. He at one time served as a deacon in the Dutch Reformed church at Wesel, Germany, which was a popular asylum for religious refugees of Reformed persuasion from the Low Countries and France. When Wesel fell to the Spaniards in 1624, Huygens probably fled to nearby Cleves. In any case, Huygens was serving as an elder in the church at Cleves when the consistory of Amsterdam recommended him on April 2, 1626 to the West India Company as a comforter of the sick. The employment at about this same time of his brother-in-law, Peter Minuit, as director-general of New Netherland was probably an important factor in Huygens' obtaining this appointment.[7]

Jan Huygens arrived at New Amsterdam on July 28, 1626. His work as comforter of the sick involved the same kind of duties as those of Krol: offering prayers on appropriate occasions, reading from Scripture and from a book of sermons on Sunday, catechizing the children, and, of course, consoling the sick. Within two years after his arrival, Huygens was appointed storekeeper for the West India Company at New Amsterdam. The published records are silent as to whether or not he continued to also serve as comforter of the sick, but he probably did. The salaries of lesser officials in New Amsterdam were low, and it was not uncommon for them to take on added responsibilities in order to supplement their meager incomes. Adam Roelantsen, the first schoolmaster in New Amsterdam, for example, took in washing in order to help support his family.

The religious services conducted by Krol and Huygens were undoubtedly at first held in private homes and sometimes, if the weather permitted, outdoors. In 1626, when a horse-mill was built at New Amsterdam for grinding bark to be used in tanning hides, a spacious room of sufficient size to accommodate a congregation was constructed on the second floor. Divine services were held in this mill until a formal church building was constructed in 1633. Plans were also made to erect a tower near the mill to accommodate several church bells that had earlier been seized by the Dutch during the plundering of a Spanish town in Puerto Rico.[8]

In view of the general lack of theological training among comforters of the sick, it was necessary that they be supplied with good books to help them in their work. One of the most valuable aids had the appropriate title of *Den Sieken Troost; Twelk is een onderwysinge inden gheloove, ende den wech der salicheyt; om ghewillichlich te sterven* ("The Consolation of the Sick; Which is an Instruction in the Faith and the Way to Salvation to Prepare Believers to Die Willingly"), but it commonly went by the shorter designation of *Ziekentroost*. It was written in 1571 by the Reverend Cornelis Van Hille, a refugee pastor from the Spanish Netherlands who eventually located at Rotterdam. The *Ziekentroost* contained numerous texts from scripture, with lengthy explanations, describing man's depravity and inability to save himself, and emphasizing that only through belief in Christ could man be delivered from the cares of this world and be victorious over death.[9]

Comforters of the sick also made use of the very popular *Huysboeck*, a Dutch translation of a collection of sermons written in 1577 by the Swiss Reformer, Heinrich Bullinger, on such subjects as the Ten Commandments, the Apostles' Creed, and the sacraments. According to Johannes Uytenbogaert, a leading Dutch preacher of the early seventeenth century, Bullinger's work was read more often in the Netherlands during the Reformation than any other book except the Bible.[10] Other books helpful to the comforters of the sick included Zacharias Ursinus' commentary on the Heidelberg Catechism and a book of Psalms with notes.

INSTRUCTIE

Voor de

PREDIKANTEN

en de

ZIEKENTROOSTERS

Te AMSTERDAM,

By ADRIAAN WOR, Drukker van de Ed. Ed. Heeren
Reprefentanten van zyne *Doorlugtige Hoogheit* en ver-
dere Heeren Bewinthebberen van de Ooft Indifche
Compagnie. *Met Privilegie.*

*Title page of a set of instructions for ministers and comforters of the sick.
(Courtesy of the Koninklijke Bibliotheek, The Hague)*

Comforters of the sick continued to be an important part of the religious life of New Netherland and remained so even after the colony fell to the English in 1664. It is impossible, however, to estimate their total number because the office was later frequently combined with other positions, including those of schoolmaster, *voorlezer*, *voorzanger*, and even church sexton. The number of comforters of the sick in New Netherland, however, never could have been large and was far smaller than the number sent to several other Dutch colonies. There is a report of April 23, 1640, for example, indicating that fourteen persons had recently been sent as comforters of the sick to the East Indies and seven to the West Indies. By comparison, the entire colony of New Netherland at that time was served by only one minister and probably only one or two comforters of the sick.[11] Fewer comforters of the sick were sent to New Netherland because the directors of the West India Company did not hold it in very high regard; greater profits were expected from the colonial possessions in Brazil and the West Indies. Because the Company had to pay most of the costs for maintaining ministers and comforters of the sick, the directors, in fulfilling their religious obligations in the colonies, were naturally inclined to favor those that held their greatest economic interest.

The contribution made by the first persons who held the position of comforter of the sick in the American colonies has not gone unrecognized by the Reformed Church. In 1900, a large mural tablet of gothic design was erected in the Middle Collegiate Dutch Church of New York City in acknowledgement of the work performed almost three hundred years earlier by Krol and Huygens. The inscription on the tablet reads, in part, as follows:

IN MEMORY OF
The Krankenbezoekers
SEBASTIAN JANSEN KROL
and
JAN HUYCK
Officers of the established church of the Netherlands, who, A.D. 1626, came hither, in advance of the first minister, to perform their sacred office of ministering to the people and consoling the sick.

The inscription concludes with several texts appropriate for individuals who followed the calling of comforter of the sick. These texts include the words of the prophet Isaiah, "The voice of one crying in the wilderness" and "Comfort ye, comfort ye my people," as well as the words of Jesus, "I was sick, and ye visited me."[12]

Although comforters of the sick helped satisfy the religious wants of the settlers of New Netherland, an ordained minister was needed. The population of the colony by 1628 totaled several hundred, some of whom had been there for many years and had attended divine services only of the type presided over by Krol and Huygens. Someone qualified to administer the Lord's Supper was especially needed. Moreover, the behavior of the colonists was such that the disciplinary hand of an ordained clergyman was required. It was in response to these needs that the Reverend Jonas Michaelius arrived in New Netherland in April 1628, and shortly organized a church at New Amsterdam. The Reformed Church in America dates its formal beginnings with the founding of this church.

Jonas Michaelius was born in 1584 at Grootebroeck, a village about four miles from Enkhuizen.[13] At age fourteen, he enrolled at the University of Leiden, where he remained for six years. Upon leaving the university and receiving ordination, he preached the gospel in various village churches in the Netherlands for nearly twenty years, until his offer to serve in one of the Dutch colonies. In deciding to exchange the comforts of a village parish for the problems and uncertainties that went with an overseas post, Michaelius showed some of the same crusading and adventurous spirit exhibited by his father. The latter, also a minister, played an active role in the Dutch revolt against Spain. He served as chaplain for a contingent of so-called Sea Beggars, and occasionally acted as an important messenger for this "sea-going" group of guerrillas.

In March 1625, the Classis of Enkhuizen dispatched Michaelius to San Salvador on the coast of Brazil, which the Dutch had just taken from the Portuguese. Before his arrival there, however, word was received that it had been recaptured by the Portuguese. The fleet with which Michaelius sailed was therefore re-routed to Fort Nassau, a Dutch outpost on the Guinea coast of West Africa. Here, Michaelius remained as the colony's preacher for about two years, apparently returning to Holland in late 1627.

The dominie's[14] next assignment was to New Netherland, for which he set sail, at age forty-three, on January 24, 1628, with his wife and two children. A son was left in Holland to continue his education. The voyage was a trying one, lasting nearly seventy-five days. Not only was the small ship battered by frequent storms, but the crew was a disorderly lot, including the skipper who, if we are to believe Michaelius, was drunk during most of the journey. Quarters for the dominie and his family were cramped and the food was nondescript and stale.

Shortly after his arrival in New Netherland on April 7, 1628, Michaelius organized a church at New Amsterdam.[15] In a letter to the

Reverend Adrianus Smotius, minister in Amsterdam, he wrote the following description of this first service as an organized congregation:

At the first administration of the Lord's Supper which was observed, not without great joy and comfort to many, we had fully fifty communicants, Walloons and Dutch, a number of whom made their first confession of faith before us, and others exhibited their church certificates. Others had forgotten to bring their certificates with them, not thinking that a church would be formed and established here; and some who brought them, had lost them unfortunately in a general conflagration, but they were admitted upon the satisfactory testimony of others to whom this was known, and also upon their daily good deportment, since one cannot observe strictly all the usual formalities in making a beginning under such circumstances.[16]

Besides the minister, the first consistory consisted of two elders—the storekeeper, Jan Huygens, and the director general, Peter Minuit—and one deacon, Bastiaen Krol. The latter, however, could attend services only occasionally because of his work as a West India Company official at Fort Orange. The Collegiate Church of New York City is today the direct lineal descendant of this first congregation.

Michaelius' ministry at New Amsterdam was replete with discomforts and heartaches. Living conditions in New Amsterdam at this embryonic stage of development were crude and harsh. The food was monotonous and costly, consisting primarily of beans, peas, barley, and stockfish; dairy products were scarce and costly. To add to his troubles, Michaelius was frequently at loggerheads with the director general, Peter Minuit, and other Company officials. In a scathing indictment in a letter to a friend in Holland, Michaelius accused Minuit and members of his council of scandalous conduct and dishonesty.

Michaelius' wife died seven weeks after his arrival, leaving him to look after three motherless children. The grief of the dominie over this loss was great and he made no effort to hide his feelings. Nevertheless, his faith in God and in His eternal plan remained steadfast. Following the death of his wife, he wrote a friend in Holland:

Now what shall I say? The Lord has done it. I must bear it. And what reasons have I to object? For all things work together for good to them that love Him. This the physical eye, it is true, can now hardly perceive, but reason believes, and the heart trusts, because of the Lord's promise. Meanwhile the human affections suffer and cannot deny themselves. I pray the Lord that neither through this nor through any other trial I shall lose the courage I need so much in this ministry, in order that my work, or rather His, may be successful.[17]

Michaelius apparently returned to Holland in late 1631 or early 1632, having served a year longer than called for in his appointment. On March 4, 1632, he appeared before the consistory of Amsterdam to give an account of his sojourn in the New World. Although he was warmly received by the Amsterdam divines, the directors of the West India Company, before whom he also appeared, gave him a cool welcome because of his criticism of Minuit and other Company officials. Minuit in the meantime had also returned to Holland and defended himself against the fulminations of the dominie.

A few years after his return from New Netherland, Michaelius on three separate occasions in 1637 and 1638 was recommended by the ecclesiastical authorities for another pastorate in New Netherland. The Company directors, however, never acted favorably on these recommendations, despite the colony's great need for pastors. The directors no doubt were influenced in this action by Michaelius' past criticism of the colonial government. Other than his being recommended for another pastorate in New Netherland, little is known about what happened to America's first Dutch Reformed pastor after his return to Holland.

New Netherland was without a minister for only a short time after Michaelius' departure. In the spring of 1633, there arrived at New Amsterdam the Reverend Everardus Bogardus, a young man of twenty-six.[18] Like the colony's first pastor, he had attended the University of Leiden and had also served on the Guinea coast of Africa, but as a comforter of the sick rather than as an ordained minister. Upon his return from Africa in 1632, he received ordination in June 1632 and soon after was sent by the Classis of Amsterdam to New Netherland, where he served fourteen years, 1633–1647.

The dispatch of Dominie Bogardus under the auspices of the Classis of Amsterdam needs explanation. When Holland was in the process of developing its far-flung commercial empire and Dutch Reformed churches were first being established overseas, no single ecclesiastical body had jurisdiction over the colonial churches. Thus, in the case of New Netherland it was the consistory of Amsterdam that sent over the first two *ziekentroosters*, Bastiaen Krol and Jan Huygens, and it was the Classis of Enkhuizen that sent over the first ordained minister, Jonas Michaelius. Gradually, however, as more churches were established in various areas of the world and as Amsterdam became the commercial center of Holland's overseas trade, the direction of ecclesiastical affairs outside the Netherlands devolved on the Classis of Amsterdam. In 1636, the latter body even went so far as to create a special committee to expedite the handling of overseas matters. This committee was known by various names: *Deputati ad res Exteras*, *Deputati ad res Indicas*, and *Deputati ad res Maritimas*, each of which can be translated simply as the "Committee on Foreign Affairs."

The relations of Bogardus with the secular authorities in New Netherland were even more stormy than were those of Michaelius. In part, this was due to the tactlessness and, at times, incompetence of several of the colonial officials, especially the two governors, Wouter Van Twiller (1633–1637) and William Kieft (1637–1647). Not all of the intense friction, however, that developed between these men and Bogardus can be blamed on the secular authorities. The dominie himself was headstrong and frequently discourteous.

Some incidents of the conflict between the minister and the public officials and the words that were exchanged among them make amusing reading. On one occasion, the young dominie referred to Governor Van Twiller as "a child of the Devil, an incarnate villian, whose buck goats [were] better than he."[19] Remarks such as these caused Van Twiller at one juncture to draw his sword and chase Bogardus down one of the streets of New Amsterdam.[20] With particular reference to Governor Kieft, the dominie in an impassioned sermon preached on December 24, 1645, remarked that "in Africa, in consequence of the excessive heat, different wild animals copulate together, whereby many monsters are created. But in this temperate climate, [he] knew not... whence these monsters of men proceeded."[21] The dominie's opponents, on the other hand, accused Bogardus of being a drunkard and of appearing intoxicated on the pulpit; of abusing many of New Amsterdam's citizens, including his own wife; and of not daring to partake of the Lord's Supper on several occasions because of his bad bahavior. Governor Kieft finally refused to attend church services and encouraged other officials to do likewise. Moreover, at times "he caused annoyance during services by permitting games to be indulged in by soldiers and officers, drums to be beaten, and cannon to be discharged."[22]

The authorities in the Netherlands, both secular and ecclesiastical, were kept informed of these quarrels. Finally, Bogardus and Kieft left for the fatherland to explain their behavior. The two men, however, never had an opportunity to plead their cases. The ship on which they sailed, the *Princess*, was wrecked off the English coast on September 27, 1647. Of the nearly one hundred passengers and crew, eight-one persons lost their lives, including Kieft and Bogardus.

When the Reverend Bogardus had arrived in New Amsterdam in 1633, religious services were still being conducted in the mill loft, but a church and parsonage were soon constructed. According to reports, the church was a rather unsightly building that resembled a barn more than a house of worship, and was the butt of jokes by visitors. For this reason, and because rumors were circulating that Fort Orange was planning to erect a substantial church building, Kieft was anxious to build a new church—which incidentally would also serve as a lasting memorial to the vain governor. The West India Company agreed to furnish some money, but more was needed. This problem was finally solved in a very novel manner, as is shown in the following record written a few years after the event:

It happened, about this time, that Everardus Bogardus, the clergyman, gave in marriage a daughter, by his first wife. The Director [Kieft] thought this a good time for his purpose, and set to work after the fourth or fifth drink; and he himself setting a liberal example, let the wedding guests sign whatever they were disposed to give towards the Church. Each, then, with a light head, subscribed away at a handsome rate, one competing with the other; and although some heartily repented it when their senses came back, they were obliged, nevertheless, to pay; nothing could avail against it.[23]

The new church was seventy feet long, fifty-two feet wide, and sixteen feet high, with a steep roof and a prominent tower. It was built of stone at a cost of twenty-five hundred guilders, and was located inside the fort at the lower end of Broadway. It was called the St. Nicholas Church, after the name of the ancient patron saint of the Netherlands, but was also known as the Church in the Fort. A stone inscription placed in the front wall read as follows: "Anno 1642. Willem Kieft, Directeur General, heeft de gemeente desen temple doen bouwen." It served the Dutch Reformed people of lower Manhattan until 1693, when a new edifice was built on Garden Street. The Church in the Fort was then repaired and used by the Episcopalians as a place of worship. It was destroyed by fire in 1741.

A replacement for Bogardus arrived on May 24, 1647, two months before the latter left for the Netherlands. His name was Johannes Cornelissen Backerus, and he came on the same ship as did the new director general, Peter Stuyvesant, destined to become one of New Netherland's most colorful citizens.[24] Backerus had been serving as a minister on the Dutch island colony of Curacao, where Stuyvesant had been governor, and he intended to remain at New Amsterdam only long enough to catch a ship bound for Holland. Stuyvesant, however, prevailed upon him to delay his homeward journey. As Backerus himself wrote, "I was not able to leave this place so easily with a free and untroubled conscience nor would I like to do it at all until this congregation had first been provided with another able and God fearing teacher."[25] His ministry at New Amsterdam was brief (1647–1649) and rather uneventful, except that, like his two predecessors, he sided with an element of the population that for many years had been urging a liberalization of the colonial government. This attitude naturally caused friction between Backerus and Stuyvesant.

While these developments were taking place at New Amsterdam, a new congregation had been organized at Fort Orange, near the present site of Albany, where settlement had been gradually increasing since the introduction of the patroon system in 1629. Patroonships were large grants of land given by the West India Company to entrepreneurs, or patroons, who agreed to settle a certain number of colonists on the land they received. The only patroonship of any significance was established near Fort Orange by Kiliaen Van Rensselaer, a diamond merchant and wealthy landowner of Amsterdam. It became known as Rensselaerswyck.[26]

The patroons were given certain "feudal" rights and privileges over the colonists who settled on their domains, but they also had certain obligations. Article XXVII of the charter establishing the system, for example, specified that the patroons had to provide for the religious needs of the colonists. It was in fulfillment of this requirement that Van Rensselaer, a devoutly religious person as well as a shrewd businessman, began looking for a "learned and godly" minister. His choice fell upon the Reverend Johannes Megapolensis.

At the time Megapolensis signed a contract with Van Rensselaer in 1642, he was thirty-nine years old and was serving two small village churches near Alkmaar in Holland.[27] According to the terms of the contract, the dominie was to serve as minister at Rensselaerswyck for a period of three years at an annual salary of 1000 guilders; if the patroon were satisfied with his services, he would serve an additional three years at an annual salary of 1200 guilders. Furthermore, the dominie and his family were to be provided with a certain amount of food each year, or sixty guilders in lieu thereof, and a proper house in which to live. Megapolensis was not permitted to engage in any farming or trade, but was to confine himself to "the diligent performance of his duties to the edification and instruction of the inhabitants and Indians . . . besides doing such services and favors for the patroon as he can without interfering with or neglecting his duties."[28]

Megapolensis, accompanied by his wife and four children, arrived in New Amsterdam on August 4, 1642, after a seven-week voyage, and immediately proceeded to his destination. As was true of New Amsterdam when it received its first minister, Fort Orange and Rensselearswyck were quite primitive when the new dominie arrived. This was particularly evident in the accommodations for holding religious services. The patroon for some time prior to Megapolensis' arrival had been contemplating the construction of a church on his estate. Already on August 4, 1639, he had written his agent, Arent Van Curler, regarding its exact location, dimensions, and general appearance, "being mostly like that of an eight-cornered mill" having forty-eight feet as its greatest width. Although Van Rensselaer's later correspondence contains further reference to the building of a church, and he even sent a model of the type he wanted, there still was no church building when the dominie arrived at Rensselaerswyck. Most of the services seem to have been held in the minister's house until about 1647, when the *packhuys*, or storehouse, was remodeled to serve as a church. Willem Frederickssen, a carpenter, was credited at that time with eighty guilders for installing therein a pulpit and sounding board, special benches for the magistrates and deacons, and nine pews for the congregation.[29]

The congregation at Resselaerswyck, as was true of most communities in New Netherland, was not a homogeneous group. Although many of the colonists were of Dutch birth, there were also families of Scandinavian extraction as well as a few of German and English background. There were also, as will be noted in a later chapter, some Indians who attended services now and then, as well as a few Negro slaves. The colonists were for the most part farmers and artisans sent over by Van Rensselaer. When the Jesuit missionary Isaac Jogues visited Rensselaerswyck in 1643, shortly after the arrival of Megapolensis, it was made up of about one hundred persons, residing in some twenty-five or thirty scattered houses.[30] There were also the inhabitants of Fort Orange, which continued to remain in the possession of the West India Company, although eventually the patroonship surrounded it on all sides. It was a rather weak fort and was seldom garrisoned by more than a dozen soldiers. It was also inhabited by a few artisans and fur traders.

When the expiration date for Megapolensis's six-year term at Resselaerswyck approached, he made arrangements to return home. The Classis of Amsterdam pleaded with him to stay on until a suitable replacement could be found, informing him that "otherwise what you have built up may be easily broken down; and the church there, which is now enjoying reasonable growth ... would become demoralized, to the detriment of God's glory and the injury of the colony."[31] Megapolensis, however, was determined to leave, and in late 1648 or early 1649 he sent his wife and four children to Holland. He himself left for New Amsterdam in July 1649 to catch a ship for the fatherland.

The dominie's plans for returning to Holland never materialized. Governor Stuyvesant and his council, in accordance with instructions from the directors of the West India Company, strongly urged him to stay. It was pointed out that because of the recent departure of Backerus, if Megapolensis were to also leave, there would be no Reformed pastor in the entire colony and that someone was needed to baptize the children, who at New Amsterdam sometimes numbered four at a single presentation. These arguments proved too much for the conscientious dominie; he decided to remain, thereby becoming the fourth pastor in twenty-one years to serve New Amsterdam. Stuyvesant wrote the Classis of Amsterdam in August 1649, that it would have been very grievous for the well-being of the people if Megapolensis "had not set the honor of God, the service of the Church, and the saving of human souls, above his own very important business. . . . We hope also, that he may with God's favor, serve this feeble lukewarm and faint hearted congregation for a long time."[32]

Dominie Megapolensis faithfully served the congregation at New Amsterdam until his death in 1670. In addition to his preaching duties, he devoted his attention to catechizing the children, visiting the sick, and at times giving advice to Governor Stuyvesant. In contrast to his three predecessors at New Amsterdam, Megapolensis had few difficulties with the public authorities. This is particularly surprising because of the headstrong and obstinate behavior frequently displayed by Stuyvesant. The congregation of the Church in the Fort numbered about one hundred seventy communicant members when the new pastor began his duties in 1649.[33] As more colonists arrived in New Netherland and scattered themselves and formed new settlements in the Hudson Valley and on Long Island, Megapolensis also took it upon himself to visit them a few times each year to preach and administer the sacraments.

Because of the expanding ecclesiastical responsibilities at New Amsterdam and throughout the colony, the Reverend Samuel Drisius was sent to relieve Megapolensis of some of his duties.[34] The consistory of New Amsterdam had earlier requested the Classis of Amsterdam to send a preacher who could handle both the Dutch and English languages, the latter qualification being important because of the English-speaking people living on the western end of Long Island. The Reverend Drisius could fulfill these requirements because he was of Dutch parentage, had been educated in the Netherlands, and had once served an English-speaking church in England. He was also sufficiently acquainted with the French language to visit Staten Island occasionally and administer to the spiritual needs of the Walloons and Huguenots residing there. Drisius was fifty-two years old when he arrived at New Amsterdam in 1652, and served there for twenty-one years until his death in 1673. During this time he became a close, personal friend of Megapolensis. Many of the communications sent from New Amsterdam to the Classis of Amsterdam bear the signatures of both ministers.

Meanwhile, significant developments were also taking place at Rensselaerswyck. For a brief period after the departure of Megapolensis, his son-in-law, the Reverend Wilhelmus Grasmeer, served the congregation. Unfortunately, however, he was recalled to the Netherlands to answer charges of drunkenness and wife neglect, charges which had been brought against him already before he had left for America. Although "warm testimonials" were given him by the Rensselaerswyck congregation in the hope that the Classis of Amsterdam would permit him to return, the Classis decided otherwise. Shortly after, in 1652, Gideon Schaats arrived as a replacement. He had been a schoolteacher for eighteen years at Beest, in the province of Gelderland, before entering the ministry at about age forty-five. The New Netherland church was his first charge. According to the contract between him and the patroon of Rensselaerswyck, Schaats was "to do everything fitting and becoming a public, honest and Holy Teacher, for the advancement of Divine service and church exercise among the old and young." He was to also act as the village schoolmaster.[35]

When Schaats arrived, the congregation was still using the remodeled storehouse as a church, but a more formal structure was soon erected. A letter written by Dominie Schaats in 1657 to a friend in the Netherlands indicates that the regular communicant membership was nearly one hundred thirty, coming from about one hundred twenty houses clustered around the fort and from about fifteen surrounding farms. The number in attendance was considerably larger, however, during the peak trading season.[36] Dominie Schaats served this church for forty-two years until his death in 1694.

It is difficult to imagine the primitive living conditions that daily confronted the first ministers of New Netherland. When Michaelius arrived at New Amsterdam in 1628, it had only a few dozen houses located at the southern tip of Manhattan Island. Some of the first dwellings were rustic to the point of being shapeless huts in which the people, according to Michaelius, "nestled rather than dwelt."[37] The ministers made frequent references to the primeval appearance of the countryside. Thus, Dominie Michaelius wrote in 1628: "The country produces many kinds of good things . . . [including] fish, poultry, game in the woods, oysters, tree-fruits, fruits from the earth, medicinal herbs and others of all kinds. But all is as yet uncultivated, and remains in a wild state."[38] Similarly, the unspoiled, natural beauty of the region around Fort Orange impressed Megapolensis. He, too, described the variety of trees, the plentitude of blueberries and strawberries, and the abundance of fish and wild game. In August 1644, the dominie wrote that in the spring of the year his sons had no trouble in catching fifty perch, each a foot long, in an hour's time, and that partridges and pigeons flew in such large numbers that sometimes up to fifty could be killed at one shot.[39]

In view of the primitive living conditions of New Netherland and the lack of settlers, it is rather surprising that the colony was able to obtain well-trained and dedicated ministers. Although the comforters of the sick were frequently simple men of limited education, this generally was not true of New Netherland's ordained clergymen, with the exception of Dominie Backerus. His theological training was limited to some private study under a local minister, and he had to appear before the Classis of Amsterdam on six occasions over a two year period before finally being ordained into the ministry. On the other hand, the reverends Michaelius, Bogardus, and Drisius had all attended the University of Leiden. Of these wilderness pastors, Michaelius was perhaps the most learned, as is indicated by the following remarks made by his biographer:

We may . . . conclude that Michaelius was a man of culture and learning. He not only speaks and writes his mother-tongue well . . . but he administers the Lord's Supper to Walloons in the French language, he also uses Greek words, and he also is able to write long letters in praise-worthy Latin. Michaelius had read St. Chrysostom, from which he quotes, and also Horace.[40]

The Reverened Johannes Megapolensis was also a man of learning. His library contained books on history, the classics, philosophy, and theology, and his letters, like those of Michaelius, indicate that he was well-versed in these subjects. Already in 1644, Megapolensis had written a catechetical booklet which he hoped would be helpful for instructing the youth in the doctrines and confessions of the Dutch Reformed Church. It was published in the Netherlands and was still being used by the catechetical classes at Brooklyn in 1661. Before sending his son Samuel to Harvard College in 1653, he personally instructed him for several years in Greek and Latin. Megapolensis is perhaps best remembered today for writing a careful study of the Mohawk Indians which was published in Holland in thirty-two pages.

Because of the lack of funds and the undeveloped condition of the countryside, ministerial salaries in New Netherland were sometimes paid in kind. Dominie Megapolensis, for example, in addition to his annual salary of a thousand guilders at Rensselaerswyk was to receive each year "thirty schepels of wheat and two firkins of butter," or sixty guilders in lieu thereof. In a few instances, a pastor was given some land to help support him and his family. Thus, the West India Company provided Michaelius with six or seven morgens of land in place of free board.[41]

The ministers, almost without exception, complained that their salary contracts were poorly honored, and in some instances it appears that the ministers were the victims of deceit by their employers. Dominie Michaelius accused the officials of the West India Company of deliberate fraud when they provided him with a small farm to help support his family, claiming that they "knew perfectly well" that the land was of little value to him because "neither horses nor cows nor labourers" were available for putting the land to use.[42] The patroons, too, were unreliable paymasters, which is one of the reasons Megapolensis refused to remain at Rensselaerswyck. Dominie Gideon Schaats was also very disappointed with conditions on his arrival in 1652. He was allowed 200 guilders for rent but discovered that a house could not be had for less than 450 guilders. Consequently, he spent the early part of his ministry living in the poorhouse which had just been completed but as yet had no occupants. Schaats also complained that goods were often "four times as dear as in the Fatherland" and advised the Classis of Amsterdam to "see to it, that no other brother be misled into these parts, as I have been." To help support the family, the minister's wife engaged in some private trading.[43]

III

Expansion of the Church, 1652–1664

Although growth was slow during the Church's first quarter century in America, a solid foundation was laid for future development. In the dozen years before the fall of New Netherland to England in 1664, five additional ministers arrived and several more churches were organized. The most extensive growth occurred on western Long Island, where Dutch settlement began about 1636 with the founding of Flatlands, then known as New Amersfoort. This was followed by other Dutch settlements at Brooklyn (Breuckelen) in 1646, Flatbush (Midwout) in 1651, New Utrecht in 1657, and Bushwick (Boswyck) in 1660. In the meantime, English colonists received permission to found towns in the midst of the Dutch settlements. These English towns included Hempstead, founded in 1643, followed by Gravesend and Flushing (Vlissingen) in 1645, Jamaica (Rustdorp) in 1655, and Newtown (Middleburg) in 1656.[1]

Dutch Reformed religious services on Long Island were of a varied nature for about the first twenty years after settlement began.[2] Informal services presided over by one or two laymen were frequently held in houses or barns, and occasionally a preacher from New Amsterdam came to administer the sacraments. The colonists also sometimes took the ferry across the river to Manhattan and worshipped in the "Church in the Fort." The ferry, however, was a makeshift affair and unsafe in times of bad weather or rough water. Even in good weather, the inhabitants of the more distant settlements, such as Flatlands, were about a two or three hour walk from the ferry. The inconvenience of the journey to Manhattan, together with the steady growth in population, made it necessary that the Dutch Reformed settlers on western Long Island have their own minister. In response to this need, the directors of the West India Company on March 12, 1654 sent the following communication to Peter Stuyvesant:

We have been pleased to see the zeal of several of our inhabitants of a new village on Long Island for the Reformed religion and that it may not cool, we have resolved upon their representation to contribute in the beginning 600 fl yearly and are looking about here for a fit and

28

pious teacher or minister: We have also notified the reverend Classis here, so that you and the people may expect him by the first opportunity.[3]

On November 11, 1654, however, the Classis informed the ministers at New Amsterdam that "no one desires to undertake such a journey on such a small salary."[4]

Fortunately, the problem of obtaining a pastor for Long Island was resolved quite simply. Even before the letter arrived from the Classis complaining of the meagerness of the proposed salary, a qualified refugee minister from Brazil arrived in New Netherland. His name was Johannes Theodorus Polhemus, and on October 13, 1654, Stuyvesant issued him a permit to preach at Flatbush and Flatlands, which permission was later approved for an indefinite period by the Classis of Amsterdam and the Company directors. Brooklyn and Gravesend were soon added to this charge.

Polhemus was born in 1598, probably in Switzerland where he perhaps also received his education.[5] Between about 1625 and 1636 he served various churches in western Germany and Holland, after which he ministered to the religious needs of several Dutch trading settlements in Brazil for eighteen years. Because of the Portuguese threat to Brazil, he sent his wife and four children back to Holland, hoping to join them later. Why he himself eventually landed in New Netherland is not known; perhaps he tarried in Brazil too long and finally had to leave on whatever ship was available. All that is known for certain is that Polhemus sailed for New Amsterdam on the *St. Charles* along with numerous other refugees, and arrived in September 1654.

Shortly after the arrival of Polhemus, Stuyvesant appointed a three-man committee, headed by Dominie Megapolensis, to superintend the construction of a combined church and parsonage at Flatbush. The plans called for a building having the form of a cross, sixty-five feet long and twenty-eight feet at the widest point, with a ceiling of about fourteen feet. The rear of the structure was designed to serve as living quarters for the dominie and his family. The actual construction was a joint venture of the towns of Flatbush, Flatlands, and Brooklyn, at a total cost of 4,637 guilders. Some of the funds were provided by the West India Company, but a considerable amount was also collected by voluntary subscriptions in New Amsterdam, Fort Orange, and Esopus, as well as among the settlements of Long Island.[6]

Polhemus' salary was supposed to have been 1,040 guilders per year, to be raised by taxation, but the necessary money was not forthcoming. As a consequence, on February 15, 1656, the magistrates of Flatbush and Flatlands were given permission to seek voluntary contributions from their towns as well as from neighboring Dutch settlements. When the residents of Brooklyn objected to this remedy unless the minister would preach alternately in Brooklyn and Flatbush, some inhabitants of Flatlands and Gravesend disapproved because of the greater distance they would have to travel on those Sundays when services were held in Brooklyn. As a final solution, it was decided that the Sunday morning sermon would always be delivered in Flatbush because of its central location, but the traditional afternoon service would be changed to the evening and would be held alternately at Brooklyn and Flatlands. Services in the last two villages were held either in the open air or in private homes or farm buildings, until Flatlands obtained its own place of worship in 1663 and Brooklyn in 1666.

The inhabitants of Brooklyn were not completely satisfied with the above arrangements, and they also soon began criticizing the quality of Dominie Polhemus' preaching. Their dissatisfaction finally culminated in sending a plainly written protest to Stuyvesant and his council in early January 1657:

The burghers and inhabitants of Breuckelen generally and the neighbors say, that for such meager and unsatisfactory service as they have had hitherto, even if they could, they would not resolve to contribute anything, for during the two weeks he comes here only for a quarter of an hour on Sunday afternoon, gives us only a prayer instead of a sermon, from which we learn and understand little and when we think, that the prayer or sermon, whatever it be called, is beginning, it is already over, so that he gives small edification to the congregation. . . . We maintain therefore, that we shall enjoy the same, if not more edification by appointing someone of our midst to read a sermon from a book of homilies . . . every Sunday, than we have hitherto received by the sermon or prayer of said Domine Polhemus.[7]

The infrequent visits of Polhemus to Brooklyn and the growing criticism of his preaching finally goaded its residents in 1659 to seek a pastor of their own. They requested that Stuyvesant and his council take steps to provide Brooklyn with a minister "for the promotion of the true religion and their edification." Stuyvesant considered the request to be reasonable and forwarded it to the directors of the West India Company in Holland. The directors also approved the request and asked the Classis of Amsterdam to choose a minister for the position. The person chosen was the Reverend Henry Selyns.

Henry Selyns, the second Reformed minister to serve on Long Island, was born in 1636 of an old and respected family of Amsterdam.[8]

His father, Jan Selyns, had served on the consistory of the Reformed Church of that city for thirty-three years. On March 19, 1657, at the age of twenty-one, young Selyns enrolled in the University of Leiden for the study of theology. Three years later, on January 5, 1660, he was recommended for the ministry to New Netherland. Selyns left Holland aboard the *Golden Beaver*, and reached New Netherland on June 11, 1660. Later, in writing about his experiences aboard ship, Selyns had this to say:

While at sea, we did not neglect religious worship but every morning and evening we besought God's guidance and protection, with prayer and the singing of a psalm. On Sundays and Feastdays the Holy Gospel was read when possible. The sacrament was not administered on ship-board, and we had no sick people during the voyage. God's favor brought us all here in safety and in health.[9]

When the residents of Brooklyn discovered they would have difficulty in raising the salary that had been promised Selyns, Stuyvesant offered to pay him 250 guilders a year out of his own pocket on condition that on Sunday evenings the dominie would preach in the chapel on Stuyvesant's bowery or farm on Manhattan Island.[10] This offer was accepted, so that Selyns preached at Brooklyn on Sunday mornings and at Stuyvesant's bowery on Sunday evenings. The bowery chapel was intended primarily for Stuyvesant's family and some forty slaves as well as for a few neighbors. After Dominie Selyns was installed at Brooklyn, Polhemus confined his work to Flatbush and Flatlands. Dominie Selyns proved to be a popular minister. People from several of the Long Island settlements, including far-off Gravesend, often journeyed to Brooklyn to hear him preach. Similarly, his Sunday evening listeners in the "Bowery" were often increased by visitors from New Amsterdam.

Flatlands received its own church building in 1663—the second Dutch Reformed edifice to be built on Long Island. It was octagonal in shape, with a sharply-pitched roof surmounted by an open cupola. The latter was designed to house a bell but the congregation was unable to afford such a luxury until 1686, when one was imported from Holland. In the meantime, the people were summoned to church by the old custom of beating a drum.[11] The interior of the church was designed to hold about one hundred thirty worshippers, with the pulpit shaped like half a wine glass and placed so that the minister could observe everyone of his listeners during the sermon. A massive sounding board was suspended above the pulpit. The worshippers at Flatlands sat in pews, except for a chair for the minister's wife and another for the town magistrate. This quaint little church remained unaltered in its shape until 1762, when three sides were extended in such a way as to create an irregular hexagon, thereby accommodating twenty-eight more worshippers. A new church edifice was built in 1794.[12]

A church was not constructed at Brooklyn until 1666, so that Selyns did most of his preaching in a remodeled granary. At the time of his arrival in 1660, the congregation at Brooklyn consisted of thirty-one families, totaling one hundred thirty-four people, of whom twenty-four were communicant members. The congregation included colonists from the nearby settlements of Wallabout, Gowanes, and the Ferry.[13] After completing the four-year term on Long Island as stipulated in his agreement, Selyns returned to Holland in July 1664.

Selyns' replacement at Brooklyn was Samuel Megapolensis, the youngest son of Dominie Johannes Megapolensis. As early as 1658, the latter had written the Classis of Amsterdam that he would like to have his son Samuel, then attending the University of Utrecht, serve one of the New Netherland churches. He added:

I cherish a strong desire to see him again among us before I die; as I expect that New Netherland, where I have now passed seventeen years of my ministry, will be the place of my burial. It will be a great joy to me to have my son return, qualified by God in doctrine and life, to build up the church in this land. I commit these matters to God's providence and your kindness.[14]

The younger Megapolensis remained at Brooklyn for only four years, leaving for Holland in 1668. The aged Polhemus thereupon once again became a kind of circuit preacher for western Long Island, looking after four churches. In 1670, when the elder Megapolensis died and Drisius was too feeble to preach, Polhemus even included the Manhattan church in his circuit for a brief period. This saintly man of God died in 1676 at age seventy-eight.

When the Reverend Selyns crossed the Atlantic in 1660 to take charge of the church at Brooklyn, he was accompanied by another pastor, the Reverend Hermanus Blom. As a theological student, Blom had earlier visited New Netherland in the spring of 1659, having heard that there was a "lack of preachers in the open country."[15] He stayed for a short time at several communities, including Esopus, a small settlement on the Hudson about halfway between New Amsterdam and Fort Orange. Esopus, also called Wiltwyck, was renamed Kingston after the English took over the colony in 1664. A church had been organized there shortly before Blom's visit. The inhabitants of Esopus were impressed with Blom and asked him to be their permanent pastor. This he agreed to do, but he first had to return to the fatherland for ordination. He was examined and ordained on February 16, 1660, and soon after sailed for New Netherland with a rather ambiguous mandate from the Classis of Amsterdam: "To preach there, both on water and on the land and in all the neighborhood, but principally in Esopus."[16]

Blom was a diligent pastor and well-liked by his flock; church membership increased from sixteen to sixty in three years. In the late summer of 1663, when Esopus experienced a dreadful Indian raid, the dominie played a heroic role in giving comfort to the wounded and bereaved. As he wrote to the authorities in the Netherlands:

There lay the burnt and slaughtered bodies, together with those wounded by bullets and axes. The last agonies and the moans and lamentations of many were dreadful to hear. I have been in their midst, and have gone into the houses, and along the roads, to speak a word in season, and that not without danger of being shot by the Indians; but I went on my mission, and considered not my life my own. I may say with Jeremiah, "I am he who hath seen misery in the day of the wrath of the Lord.".... The houses were converted into heaps of stones, so that I might reflect with Micah, We are made desolate; and with Jeremiah, A piteous wail may go forth in his distress. But in all this, my request to our brethren is to remember us and our suffering Church in their prayers. With Paul I say, Brothers, pray for us.[17]

A Reformed church was also established to the south on the Delaware River during the New Netherland period. At one time, it appeared that the Dutch settlements of this area would be even more important than those along the Hudson, but this interest lasted only a few years.[18] Increasingly, the colonists along the Delaware were neglected by the Dutch West India Company, and little attention was given to looking after their spiritual needs. Not until 1654 was a church organized, and this was done rather preemptorily by the Reverend Polhemus when the ship carrying him from Brazil made a brief stop at New Amstel, the major settlement on the Delaware. New Amstel was renamed New Castle after the English conquest in 1664. At first, the people were served by lay preachers, but in 1657 an ordained minister, the Reverend Everardus Welius, arrived. He was provided with a parsonage, and a house was soon purchased and remodeled into a church. Welius' ministry was cut short by death in 1659. At the time of his death, the New Amstel church had sixty members.[19] Not until 1664 was another minister, the Reverend Warnerus Hadson, appointed, but he died on the voyage. Thus, the Delaware settlements were without a Reformed pastor at the time of the English takeover.

Late during the New Netherland period, two more churches were founded. The first of these was organized in 1660 at Bergen, New Jersey, just across from Manhattan Island. The charter congregation consisted of twenty-seven members and worshipped in a log church. For almost ninety years it was served by lay leaders from within their own midst, with an occasional visit by a pastor from New Amsterdam or elsewhere to administer the sacraments. A similar situation existed on the northern end of Manhattan at New Haarlem, later simply called Harlem, where a church was also organized in 1660. Except for a few brief periods, the Harlem church was dependent upon occasional visits by pastors from New York for almost eighty years. Its congregation in particular was made up of a mixture of ethnic groups, including Frenchmen, Walloons, Englishmen, Danes, Swedes, and Germans, as well as Dutchmen. In addition to these new churches, preaching stations were established at Staten Island, which Dominie Drisius occasionally visited to administer the sacraments, and at Schenectady, which was occasionally supplied by Dominie Schaats of nearby Rensselaerswyck.

The Reformed Church was the only one legally permitted to have public worship services in New Netherland. A regulation of March 28, 1624 declared, "They shall within their territory hold no other services than those of the true Reformed religion, in the manner in which they are at present conducted in this country."[20] Similarly, the first article of Peter Stuyvesant's commission, taken under oath, specified that he was "not to permit any other than the Reformed doctrine."[21] The restrictions on religious freedom, however, were meant to apply only to public and not to private worship. Thus, although a Company decree of 1638 restated the regulation of 1624 concerning religion, it further declared that no person should be "in any wise constrained or aggrieved in his conscience, but every man shall be free to live up to his own in peace and decorum."[22]

The directors of the West India Company about 1650 began advocating restraint in interpreting the restrictions on religious freedom. Disappointed with the slow colonization of New Netherland, they hoped that a more tolerant policy would encourage foreigners and non-Reformed Hollanders to settle there. Even without such encouragement, there were present by this time many colonists who were not of the Reformed persuasion. This is evident from the following observation made by the Jesuit missionary Isaac Jogues when he visited New Amsterdam in 1646:

No religion is publicly exercised but the Calvinist, and orders are to admit none but Calvinists, but this is not observed, for besides the

Calvinists there are in the colony Catholics, English Puritans, Lutherans, Anabaptists, here called Mnistes (Mennonites), etc.[23]

In contrast to the Company directors who favored toleration in the interest of promoting settlement, the ministers were generally desirous of keeping the religious restrictions intact. This was particularly true of the two preachers at New Amsterdam, Megapolensis and Drisius, whose views were strongly supported by the Classis of Amsterdam.[24] Thus, on May 26, 1656, the Classis commended the New Amsterdam pastors and their consistory for their determination to prohibit the right of public worship to the Lutherans, Mennonites, English Independents, and Jews, adding, "Let us then—we here in this country and you there—employ all diligence to frustrate all such plans, that the wolves may be warded off from the tender lambs of Christ."[25]

The New Netherland clergy also had a strong ally in Governor Stuyvesant, son of a preacher and a fiery Calvinist himself. Several times during his early years as head of the colonial government he and his council issued ordinances against "dangerous Heresies and Schisms." Typical was the decree of February 1, 1656, which forbade all

public or private conventicles and meetings, except the usual and authorized ones, where God's Word, according to the Reformed and established custom, is preached and taught in meetings held for the religious service of the Reformed Church, conformably to the Synod of Dort, which is to be followed here, as in the Fatherland, and in the Reformed Churches of Europe.[26]

In 1653, when news reached Megapolensis and Drisius that the Lutherans of New Netherland were planning to call a minister of their own, the two dominies immediately requested the Classis of Amsterdam to do everything possible to forestall such an event. It was pointed out that if the Lutherans were permitted to organize, not only would they absent themselves from Reformed services, but it would "pave the way for other sects, so that in time our place would become a receptable for all sorts of heretics and fanatics."[27] The classis agreed and pressured the directors of the West India Company on February 23, 1654 to pass a resolution not to permit any Lutheran pastors at New Amsterdam "nor any other public worship than that of the true Reformed."[28] Nevertheless, in July 1657, a Lutheran minister from Holland, the Reverend Johannes Ernestus Goetwater (sometimes written

Gutwasser) arrived at New Amsterdam, having been sent by the Lutheran church of "Old" Amsterdam. It is possible that he came with the permission of the directors.

Megapolensis and Drisius, upon learning of Goetwater's arrival, immediately sent a petition to the burgomaster and aldermen of New Amsterdam advising them that measures be taken to "arrest the evil ready to creep in." The town officials, supported by Stuyvesant, honored this petition by informing Goetwater that he was not to hold any Lutheran services until he had received further orders. The two dominies grudgingly agreed with this action, although they would have preferred that he be sent back on the same ship on which he had arrived. On September 4, 1657, about two months after his arrival, Goetwater was ordered to return to Holland, but due to a prolonged illness and to his being hidden for a time by the Lutherans, he did not set sail from New Amsterdam until June of 1659. Following his departure, Megapolensis and Drisius wrote the Classis, "There is now again quietness among the people, and the Lutherans again go to church, as they were formerly accustomed to do." Upon receiving this information, the Classis resolved to thank the "Reverend Brethren" for their "good endeavors put forth."[29]

As a concession to the Lutherans, Megapolensis and Drisius agreed to support a request to revise slightly the wording in the baptismal formula in order to make it more acceptable to the Lutherans. In consenting to the change, the two dominies were under strong pressure from the directors of the West India Company who had informed them that if they persisted in their refusal to change the formulary, the Company would be obliged to allow the Lutheran's a church of their own. The directors in 1659 also informed Stuyvesant that henceforth on examining preachers for New Netherland they would be careful about employing anyone who had "scruples about unnecessary forms, which cause more division than edification."[30] Indeed, before the reverends Blom and Selyns left in 1660 to assume their pastorates in New Netherland, the directors received assurances that they would make no difficulties about using a baptismal form acceptable to the Lutherans.

An exception to refusing permission for the Lutherans to hold public worship services was made in the Delaware Valley where numerous Scandinavians resided. Their presence was due to Sweden's decision in 1638 to found a colony there—to be called New Sweden. The Dutch considered this act an intrusion into territory they claimed was part of New Netherland. After the failure of efforts to reach a settlement by negotiation, the directors of the West India Company ordered Stuyvesant to use military force. In occupying New Sweden, the Dutch naturally found themselves with a significant Scandinavian element on their hands. Even the intolerant Stuyvesant agreed it would be improper to deny the right of the approximately two hundred Swedes and Finns residing there to continue their own Lutheran church which they had earlier organized. According to the surrender terms, therefore, the Scandinavians were permitted to "retain one Lutheran preacher." Considering the bad reputation of this minister, the authorities probably thought that few Dutch Reformed people would join this Lutheran congregation. According to a letter of 1657 from the Dutch ministers of New Amsterdam, the Lutheran preacher, Lokenius by name, was:

A man of impious and scandalous habits, a wild, drunken, unmannerly clown, more inclined to look into the wine can than the Bible. He would prefer drinking brandy two hours to preaching one; and when the sap is in the wood his hands itch and he wants to fight whomsoever he meets.[31]

Concern was also expressed by the New Netherland ministers about the presence of Quakers and Anabaptists, some of whom were found at New Amsterdam but were in greater number on Long Island, particularly in those towns having a significant number of English colonists. These included Gravesend, Flushing, Jamaica, Hempstead, and Oyster Bay. A few examples will illustrate the attitude of the clergy and the public authorities toward these religious groups. On February 12, 1652, Anna Smits, an Anabaptist, was told to appear before the consistory of New Amsterdam to answer charges of using slanderous words against God and His servants.[32] In early 1656, after Megapolensis and Drisius complained to Stuyvesant and his council that Quaker preaching was taking place at Newtown on Long Island, the two ministers were sent there to seek out a qualified layman to act as a reader for divine services.[33] Also, in 1656, two young Quaker women were imprisoned by the authorities of New Amsterdam. Megapolensis and Drisius in writing the Classis about this incident declared: "We trust that our God will baffle the designs of the devil, and preserve us in the truth, and bring to nothing these machinations of Satan."[34] Another Quaker, Robert Hodgson, was arrested in 1657 at Hempstead, Long Island, imprisoned, and severely flogged.[35] On a few occasions, religious dissidents were banned to Rhode Island, which according to the reverends Megapolensis and Drisius was "the receptacle of all sorts of riff-raff people, and is nothing else than the sewer of New England."[36]

The directors of the West India Company disagreed with the strong measures being taken against the Quakers and Anabaptists. As was true of the Lutherans, the directors were fearful that such actions would interfere with colonization. Therefore, with specific reference to the Quakers and "other sectarians," they wrote Stuyvesant on April 16, 1663:

We doubt very much, whether we can proceed against them rigorously without diminishing the population and stopping immigration, which must be favored at a so tender stage of the country's existence. You may therefore shut your eyes, at least not force people's consciences, but allow everyone to have his own belief, as long as he behaves quietly and legally, gives no offence to his neighbors and does not oppose the government. As the government of this city has always practised this maxim of moderation and consequently had a considerable influx of people, we do not doubt, that your Province too would be benefitted by it.[37]

The clergy of New Amsterdam also took an intolerant attitude toward the Jews. The first Jew to come to New Netherland was Jacob Barsimon, who arrived in August 1654. In the following month, twenty-three Jews—men, women, and children—arrived at New Amsterdam aboard the *St. Charles* from Brazil. They had left Brazil to escape persecution after the colony fell to the Portuguese in 1654. They were in a very destitute condition, having left most of their property behind and having used for passage fare what few goods they could take with them. To the credit of the clergy, it must be noted that Megapolensis on several occasions "put his hand into the alms box of the church and gave them at various times sums totaling several hundred guilders."[38] This act of kindness, however, cannot be interpreted to mean that the dominie appreciated the presence of Jews at New Amsterdam. Rather, the contrary is obvious from a communication he sent the Classis on March 18, 1655:

These people, have no other God than the unrighteous Mammon, and no other aim than to get possession of christian property, and to win all other merchants by drawing all trade towards themselves. Therefore we request your Reverences to obtain from the Lords-Directors, that these godless rascals, who are of no benefit to the country, but look at everything for their own profit, may be sent away from here. For as we have here Papists, Mennonites and Lutherans among the Dutch; also many Puritans or Independents, and many Atheists and various other servants of Baal among the English under this Government, who conceal themselves under the name of Christians; it would create a still greater confusion, if the obstinate and immovable Jews came to settle here.[39]

The ministers had no more success in ridding the colony of the Jews than they had in expelling the Lutherans and the Quakers. Some of the Jews who came aboard the *St. Charles* remained and were joined by others from Brazil and Holland. In this instance, too, it seems that the directors were motivated by expediency and economic considerations, including the fact that some Jews in Holland had a large amount of capital invested in the West India Company.[40]

Fears were also expressed occasionally about the Catholics in New Netherland, but this group was never very numerous. Protestant leaders at Fort Orange even interceded on a few occasions in behalf of Catholic missionaries taken captive by the Indians.[41] Despite such generosity, the Dutch Reformed clergy were not particularly fond of the Catholics, as is shown in the exchange of ideas between Megapolensis and the French Jesuit, Simon Le Moyne. The latter spent eight days in New Amsterdam in the autumn of 1657, and met several times with Megapolensis. He informed the dominie that he had heard other Jesuits speak of him and wanted personally to pay his respects and thank him for the kindnesses he had shown in rescuing some Jesuits from the Indians while Megapolensis was pastor at Rensselaerswyck. The conversations were apparently amiable, although at one point Megapolensis asked the good father if "he had taught the Indians anything more than to make the sign of the cross, and such like superstitions."[42]

The following spring, Le Moyne sent Megapolensis three little booklets, one on the succession of the popes, another on councils, and a third on heresies. Le Moyne had written them himself and pleaded with the dominie to read and study them carefully because "Christ hanging on the Cross, was still ready to receive [him] if penitent."[43] Megapolensis wrote a lengthy ten page reply in Latin, the general tone of which was unfriendly. The Jesuit's comments on the succession of the popes, according to Megapolensis, were indefensible, as anyone could see unless he were "blinder than a snake." Only those who had a superficial knowledge of history would deny that among the popes there had been "atheists, Epicureans, sorcerers, sodomists, and the like." Le Moyne, he wrote, should be ashamed to give such Dagons and Belials a place alongside of Christ! On the matter of the church councils, Megapolensis admitted that there were some in which the presence of the Holy Spirit was manifested, but there were also those in which "the devil had been the leader." In conclusion, Megapolensis declared that he would pray to God "the Father of all grace and to His Son Jesus Christ" that Le Moyne would be "released from the snare of his errors."[44]

The determination to favor the Reformed Church in New Netherland did not mean that such partiality was shown exclusively to the *Dutch* Reformed. Two English pastors, for example, the reverends Francis Doughty and Richard Denton, were permitted to preach on western Long Island where a significant number of Englishmen had settled. Doughty resided at Newtown and Denton at Hempstead, but as itinerant preachers they served a wide area. The theology of these two men was considered close enough to Presbyterianism to make them acceptable to Dutch Reformed pastors. Thus Dominie Megapolensis once referred to Denton as a "pious, godly and learned man, who is in agreement with our churches in everything,"[45] and when Doughty left for Virginia, the Dutch ministers at New Amsterdam expressed sorrow at this loss. The Huguenots and Waldenses, because of their close affinity to Calvinist theology, were also left unmolested by the authorities of New Netherland.

Like the first ministers who served in New Netherland, the later arrivals were also generally well-educated men. Thus, Selyns and Welius had studied at Leiden, while Blom and the younger Megapolensis had studied at both Leiden and Utrecht. Also, as was true in the past, and continued to be true long after New Netherland fell to England in 1664, ministerial salaries often included payment in kind, such as grain and firewood, as well as some rent-free farmland. The salary arrangement between Blom and his congregation at Esopus is particularly interesting because it clearly reflects the rural character of most parishes. Among other pledges made to him, the inhabitants of Esopus promised:

> to treat him decently and in order that his Reverence shall be able to sustain himself and be more encouraged in his work . . . to make a good bouwery for him, provide it with a house, barns, cows, and other cattle as proper, to tend the land . . . plough it, and bring the whole in good order, so that he may cultivate it himself, or hire it out advantageously, as long as he shall fill the position of preacher here, but in case he should leave or die, then this bouwery shall always remain for the support of the minister, then being here.[46]

It was fortunate that the ministers often received a part of their payment in kind, or had the use of some rent-free land, because salaries were generally poorly paid. Although the West India Company continued to be lax in meeting its financial obligations to the pastors in its employ, even greater difficulties were experienced by ministers who were dependent on the commonalty for their salaries. For example, although the inhabitants of the Dutch towns on Long Island in 1654 had promised Dominie Polhemus 1,040 guilders per year and a parsonage, Polhemus seldom received more than a fraction of his promised salary. Moreover, the construction of the parsonage, which was to be located within the church, proceeded at a snail's pace; two years after Polhemus had accepted his new post, the pastor and his family were still living in unfinished rooms in the back of the church. To complete these rooms and to make them more liveable for the approaching winter, Governor Stuyvesant in September 1656 sent a hundred hemlock planks to be used primarily for the ceiling and wainscotting. Few of these planks, however, were used for their intended purpose but instead were carried off by the villagers. The dominie complained in December 1656 to Stuyvesant that the parsonage "remains open as it was and I with my wife and children must live and sleep on the bare ground and in the cold."[47]

Dominie Selyns also discovered there was a wide gap between the salary of 1200 guilders per year that had been promised him in 1660 and what he actually received. On August 30, 1660, two of the magistrates of Brooklyn appeared at New Amsterdam before Stuyvesant and his council, declaring they had recently convened the townspeople in an attempt to determine exactly how much salary they could actually pay Dominie Selyns. As a result of this gathering, the magistrates informed Stuyvesant and his council that "after much trouble they could discover and bring together not more than 300 guilders yearly, to be paid in grain at beaver evaluation, and besides they would provide a suitable lodging for said D. Selyns." The governor reminded the magistrates that the dominie had accepted the call on the promise of a salary of 1200 guilders. When they answered that such a large amount could not be raised, Stuyvesant replied that the people of Brooklyn "should have considered that before they asked for and gave a call to a clergyman."[48]

As was noted, Stuyvesant came to the assistance of the Brooklyn congregation by employing Selyns on a part-time basis for 250 guilders a year as a visiting preacher for his farm on Manhattan Island. The two combined salaries of the dominie, however, did not equal half the amount that had been promised him. When Selyns, who was one of the colony's most learned and respected ministers, returned to Holland in 1664, the salary problem was one of his primary reasons for leaving.

The general attitude and behavior of the people contributed to the difficulty the ministers had in collecting their promised salaries—the proverbial Dutch capacity for hard work and thriftiness being often lacking among the early colonists. In 1626, Isaac De Rasière, the chief commercial agent in the colony, declared that many people showed a "lazy unconcern" about bettering themselves.[49] Dominie Michaelius wrote in August 1628, that "many among the common people would have liked to make a living, and even to get rich, in idleness, rather than by hard work, saying they had not come to work, that as far as working is concerned, they might as well have staid at home."[50] Remarks made in 1658 by Vice-Director Jacob Alrichs of the Delaware settlements and in 1660 by Stuyvesant indicate that, in their views, this problem still existed at the close of the New Netherland period.[51]

Other records of New Netherland also show that many of its residents were far from being model citizens. An examination of biographical sketches of the residents living in Rensselaerswyck between 1630 and 1658, for example, indicates an unusually large number of persons who were fined or reprimanded for thievery, brawling, excessive drinking, and failure to pay debts.[52] Nor was the situation any better at New Amsterdam. Drunkeness, street brawls, name-calling, and the like were quite common, as was fornication with the Indians, although the latter was prohibited by law. Stuyvesant declared in 1648, that one-fourth of the town was made up of "Brandy shops and Tobacco or Beer houses."[53] Even the ministers were the victims of crime. Thus, Dominie Megapolensis was once threatened with a knife and on another occasion suffered great loss as a result of theft.

The behavior of the colonists did not make the work of the pastors any easier. In reference to the seventeen taphouses in New Amsterdam, Dominie Backerus wrote the Classis of Amsterdam on August 15, 1648:

What bad fruits result therefrom, your Reverences will easily understand. . . . If you could obtain from the Hon. Directors an order for closing these places, except three or four, I have no doubt, the source of much evil and great offense would be removed. . . . In order to best help the Church of God here, and to resist a bad world, I think we must begin with the children; for many of the older people are so far depraved, that they are now ashamed to learn anything good.[54]

Dominie Schaats, writing on June 27, 1657, made similar observations about the situation at Resselaerswyck:

About the church and congregation here: Much could be said about the indiscreet walk of many. There are many hearers, but not much saving fruit . . . we have been also considerably deceived by certain ones, so that on account of their inconsistent walk . . . I have been obliged to suspend them from the Lord's Table. The people are rather reckless . . . [and] the taverns and villainous houses have many visitors . . . the Company says that the congregation must pay the preacher. But they prefer to gamble away, or lose in bets, a ton of beer at twenty-three or twenty-four guilders, or some other liquor. I will say nothing against the better class; but of these there are too few to make up the salary.[55]

It is thus obvious that the austerity, hard work, and high moral principles preached by the stern Calvinist ministers had only a limited effect on the inhabitants of New Netherland.

The frequency with which governmental decrees were issued on the matter of Sunday observance also indicates that puritanical sabbaths were far from being a reality. A decree of October 26, 1656, is particularly interesting because it shows that the Dutch Reformed were not always a solemn, pious people, but found much to enjoy in this life on earth. The decree, in addition to prohibiting on Sunday "any ordinary labor, such as Ploughing, Sowing, Mowing, Building, Woodsawing, Smithing, Bleaching, Hunting, [and] Fishing," also forbade the people from "frequenting Taverns or Tippling Houses, Dancing, playing Ball, Cards, Tricktrack, Tennis, Cricket or Ninepins, [and] going on pleasure parties in a Boat, Cart or Wagon before, between or during Divine Service." On September 10, 1663, several items were added to the list of prohibited Sunday activities. These included "roving in search of Nuts and Strawberries and . . . too unrestrained and excessive Playing, Shouting and Screaming of children in the Streets and Highways."[56]

Any discussion of religion in New Netherland would be incomplete without some mention of developments in education.[57] This is so because of the semi-ecclesiastical character of education at this time. Several synods of the Reformed Church in Holland had emphasized the need to provide schools so that not only the basics of education could be provided, but also that the teaching of religion and good morals might be enhanced. As a consequence, education in the old Netherlands was widespread at the elementary level during the seventeenth century. These developments in New Netherland, however, were slow in getting started.

Various declarations were made from time to time about the need for schools in New Netherland and their importance for the spiritual development of the children. For example, the charter providing for the patroon system in 1629 stipulated that the patroonships should be provided with ministers and schoolmasters "as quickly as possible . . . that thus the service of God and zeal for religion may not grow cool and be neglected."[58] Despite such pronouncements, there is no evidence of a schoolmaster residing in New Amsterdam before 1638 or in Rensselaerswyck before 1648. As late as 1657, the reverends Megapolensis and Drisius of New Amsterdam informed the Classis of Amsterdam that unless more was done for education, one could "expect nothing else than young men of foolish and undisciplined minds."[59] By 1664, however, all but two of the eleven chartered towns of New Netherland had common schools, and New Amsterdam also had a Latin school. Formation of the latter was particularly urged by the ministers so that the colony's youth would not have to journey to Boston to obtain a classical education.

Of the schools that were eventually founded in New Netherland, the one established at New Amsterdam in 1638 exists to this day. Known as the Collegiate School, it has become one of America's most prestigious secondary schools.[60] Its beginnings, however, were not auspicious. The first schoolmaster, Adam Roelantsen, had a checkered career. He was a party to numerous lawsuits, most of which were not to his credit, including suits arising from slanderous remarks, assault, adultery, and failure to pay debts. Throughout the New Netherland period, the school had no permanent home of its own, being usually held in private houses. Salaries were low and, like those of the ministers, were seldom paid in full. As a consequence, schoolmasters had short tenures and classes were held irregularly.

As was true in the mother country, church and state in New Netherland were co-partners in matters of education. The local ministers and consistories, and on occasion also the Classis of Amsterdam, joined with the secular authorities in examining and approving schoolmasters and the curricula. Several examples can be given to illustrate the close ties existing between religion and education. Morning and afternoon school sessions were opened and closed with prayer. Twice a week, the schoolmaster instructed his pupils in the common prayers and in the Heidelberg Catechism, while the Bible, the Book of Psalms, and the Proverbs of Solomon served as textbooks. Even the basic elementary readers contained such items as the Ten Commandments, the Lord's Prayer, and the creeds of the Church.

As was noted in the previous chapter, the schoolmaster's duties in time frequently became indistinguishable from those of the *ziekentrooster* and *voorlezer*. According to one set of instructions, for example, the schoolmaster of New Netherland was obliged not only to teach "reading, writing and ciphering" to the youth but was also expected

to promote Religious Worship, to read a portion of the Word of God to the people, to endeavor as much as possible to bring them up in the ways of the Lord, to console them in their Sickness and to conduct himself with all diligence and fidelity in his calling, so as to give others a good example, as becometh a devout, pious and worthy Consoler of the Sick, Church Clerk, Precentor and Schoolmaster, in which capacities all persons, without distinction, were commanded to acknowledge him.[61]

In view of the close alliance that often existed between the offices of teacher and preacher, it is understandable why the ecclesiastical authorities thought they should have a voice in the examination and appointment of schoolmasters.

IV

Trials and Difficulties under English Rule, 1664–1714

The English for some time had begrudged the Dutch position in New Netherland because of its strategic location between the English settlements of New England to the northeast, and Virginia and Maryland to the south. It was therefore only a matter of time before England would try to annex the Dutch colony. This step was taken on August 28, 1664, when four British men-of-war with soldiers aboard appeared off New Amsterdam, and were soon joined by additional forces from New England and eastern Long Island. In alarm, Governor Stuyvesant sent the reverends Johannes and Samuel Megapolensis and two of the town magistrates to determine from the English commander, Richard Nicolls, why a hostile fleet had anchored off the town. The younger Megapolensis, who had just arrived in the colony a few weeks earlier as a replacement for Dominie Selyns, was probably sent along because of his knowledge of the English language. Nicholls informed the delegation that the English were demanding the surrender of the town and the colony.

Defense was hopeless: the walls of Fort Amsterdam were weak from lack of upkeep, less than a third of the gunpowder was serviceable, the soldiers in the fort numbered only about one hundred fifty, and only about two hundred fifty civilians were capable of bearing arms. In addition, because of a shortage of food stuffs, the settlement could withstand a siege of only a few days. The arrival of the West India Company slaveship *Gideon*, with two hundred ninety black slaves on board, a few days before the appearance of the British fleet, added to the food problem of New Amsterdam. Perhaps most important of all, the people had no will to resist.

Despite these weaknesses, the fiery Stuyvesant was determined to fight to the bitter end; fortunately, wiser and cooler heads prevailed. Much of the credit for convincing the governor of the futility of resistance must go to the reverends Johannes and Samuel Megapolensis. On one occasion, according to testimony later given by a sergeant serving in the fort at the time of surrender, when two small British frigates passed close to the fort and it appeared that Stuyvesant was about to order one of the gunners to open fire on the vessels, the elder Megapolensis and his son "led him away and prevailed on him to retire."[1] On the morning of Friday, September 5, the governor was presented with a petition signed by ninety-three of New Amsterdam's most prominent citizens. Although Johannes Megapolensis' name was not among the signatures, he was one of the chief promoters of the petition.[2] It pointed out the hopelessness of the situation and urged capitulation. Stuyvesant agreed to honor the petition and surrendered the town.

Although New Amsterdam was in no condition to defend itself, the officials of the West India Company in Holland were greatly upset over the town's surrender. Much of their wrath was directed against Stuyvesant and the elder Megapolensis. Along with other accusations, Stuyvesant was reprimanded for "lending an ear to preachers and other chicken-hearted persons"[3] and for being "moved by the flattering tongues of Preachers and others who were troubled about their private property, without regarding the interest of State and Company."[4]

Stuyvesant was eventually exonerated for his actions but Dominie Johannes Megapolensis was never that fortunate, despite many attempts to intercede in his behalf. In August 1668, for example, four years after the surrender, the following affidavit was presented to the Company by Stuyvesant and five other former officials of New Amsterdam:

We the undersigned... attest and declare as truth that the Rev. Domine Johannes Megapolensis (having been a minister here about 19 years at the time of the capitulation of this place), has not as far as we know, behaved in any other manner, than was becoming to a faithful subject of the States-General and of the W. I. Company and to a pious and godly minister. In everything he has appeared to us to exhibit these traits.[5]

The dominie himself defended his action in letters to the Classis of Amsterdam and to the Synod of North Holland, and requested their help in collecting his back salary which he claimed amounted to two thousand guilders. Their efforts in this respect and similar attempts by his son Samuel, following his return to Holland in 1669, proved unavailing. As late as 1676, the widow of the elder Megapolensis was still trying to collect from the West India Company the arrears in salary due her late husband.[6]

After the surrender, New Amsterdam was renamed New York—a

name that was also applied to the colony—in honor of the new proprietor, James, duke of York, who was a brother of Charles II, king of England. A few weeks later, the settlement at Fort Orange was renamed Albany in honor of another of the new proprietor's titles. New Amstel, on the Delaware, was also occupied by the English; it was renamed New Castle. In this way, New Netherland, which had been a Dutch colony for about a half century, became an English possession.

Several perplexing questions were raised after the fall of New Netherland concerning the status of the Dutch Reformed Church. What, for example, would be its relationship to the Classis of Amsterdam? Could its members, especially the ministers, be subjects of the British government, but owe ecclesiastical obedience to a religious body in Holland? Would the Dutch Reformed people of New York and New Jersey be expected to contribute to the financial support of an established English Church? Who would pay the salaries of ministers formerly paid by the West India Company? These and other problems troubled the Church for many years after 1664.

The concern that the ministers expressed for the future of the Church during the years immediately after the English conquest can be gathered from a letter of September 7, 1668, sent by Dominie Samuel Megapolensis to a friend in the Netherlands:

Abominations and scandalous sins are daily committed. . . .The labors of the ministry are now much more burdensome than they ever were before under the Dutch government; for there are now five separate places in which we must render services. Some of these are as much as three (Dutch, nine English) miles distant. These services must be rendered in both hot and cold weather. . . .We have frequently hitherto complained to our rulers in relation to our small salaries . . . [which] small amount is irregularly paid . . . In reference to the church, and ecclesiastical matters generally, little that is good can be said. . . .We are also threatened by the Indians. . . .It appears as if God were punishing this land for its sins. Some years (ago) there appeared a meteor in the air. Last Year we saw a terrible comet in the west, a little above the horizon, with the tail upward, and hanging over this place. It showed itself for about eight days, and then disappeared. So we fear God's judgements, but supplicate his favor.[7]

During the first two decades after the English conquest of New Netherland, relations between the Dutch Reformed churches and the new English government were prescribed by two sets of laws: the Articles of Capitulation and the so-called Duke's Laws.[8] The Articles of Capitulation applied to those areas that were predominantly Dutch, and initially were signed by the leading citizens of New York City. Later, they were also approved by the residents of the upper Hudson Valley at Albany and by those on the Delaware River at New Castle. Article Eight, in particular, pertained to religion. By it, the Dutch were guaranteed not only the right to private liberty of conscience but also the right to worship publicly according to their own customs and church discipline. This was a greater concession than the Dutch had given to those of the non-Reformed faith during the New Netherland period.

The Duke's Laws, drawn up in 1665, were a special set of regulations that at first applied only to Yorkshire, an administrative unit that was established shortly after the surrender and included Long Island, Staten Island, and the Bronx peninsula. Because most of the English population of New York colony was located in this area, these laws were based in part on English practices that were followed in other American colonies. The regulations, however, did contain special concessions to the Dutch because of their large numbers on western Long Island. In 1675, the Duke's Laws were made applicable to the entire province of New York.

Like the Articles of Capitulation, the Duke's Laws also provided for religious toleration. The right of private judgment in religious matters was allowed and congregations were assured freedom of public worship. This, of course, led to a multiplicity of sects, a development that did not please all the Dutch pastors. Thus, Johannes Megapolensis in April 1669 informed the Classis of Amsterdam: "There is still another difficulty. The Lutherans here have obtained a preacher from Amsterdam and received him with great kindness."[9] The fact that the Lutheran pastor took up residence only a few doors from Megapolensis' home undoubtedly added to his bitterness. Dominie Wilhelmus Van Nieuwenhuysen, Megapolensis' successor, made a similar complaint in 1674, declaring that the Lutherans were allowed "too much liberty."[10]

According to the Duke's Laws, each community or town would be provided with a church supervised by wardens entrusted with the task of building and maintaining churches, providing for the poor, and maintaining the minister. The costs for the community churches were to be met by public taxation. Thus, as one writer has stated, "establishment was allowed, but it was to be a local matter."[11] This could prove advantageous to members of the Dutch Reformed churches because they were in a majority in numerous places in New York and remained so for many years.

A recent study of the make-up of the New York City Common Council, based on such matters as the occupational, family, and religious background of its members, sheds considerable light on the favorable representation that the Dutch Reformed Church sometimes had in political bodies elected by the people. During the period 1689–1733, one hundred twenty-three individuals were elected as councilmen, and each had an average length of service of about four and a half years. An examination of the religious background of these men shows that thirty-nine (32%) were lay officials in the Dutch Reformed Church, the major denomination in the city at this time, whereas only nineteen (16%) held lay positions in the Anglican Church, the second most important denomination. As the author of the study states, "The predominance of the leaders associated with the Dutch Reformed Church reflected the numerical superiority of that denomination within the city and continued a pattern which had prevailed since the first days of settlement on the island." In the following period, 1734–1775, the numerical superiority of Dutch Reformed laymen in the Common Council actually increased, and did not come to an end until after the Revolution.[12]

It is thus obvious that if the letter of the Duke's Laws were followed, it would mean that many of the community churches would be Dutch Reformed in faith, but that minority groups, such as Lutherans and Quakers, although allowed their own houses of worship, would have to contribute financially to the locally established church. Despite refusals now and then by the public authorities to honor this part of the Duke's Laws, several examples can be given to illustrate the favored status that the Dutch Reformed churches sometimes enjoyed in matters of public financial support. In 1670, when a new Dutch Reformed pastor was needed in New York as a replacement for Dominie Megapolensis, the governor approved a request that the town's inhabitants, including Lutherans, Anglicans, and others, be taxed to assure that the salary of a thousand guilders promised to the new Dutch preacher would be paid. Similarly, in 1672, five hundred guilders in public money was allowed the town's Dutch Reformed congregation for the repair of their house of worship.[13]

In the Albany area, too, where the Dutch Reformed element remained in a decided majority for many years after 1664, the Dutch church enjoyed a privileged position for a time. Thus, in 1670, the governor informed some of the commissioners there that the Dutch Reformed church, as the "parochial church" of that place, should be given public support. As an extreme example of this favored position, it can be noted that the Lutherans of Albany for a time even had to use the sexton of the Dutch Reformed church for the burial of their dead. If they insisted on using their own sexton for this purpose, they still had to pay the stipulated fee to the Dutch Reformed sexton.[14]

The Duke's Laws also stipulated that certain public buildings, including churches, in use before 1664 would not change ownership. The Dutch Reformed colonists could therefore continue to use their church in the fort, although the fort itself would henceforth be British-owned. As a gesture of goodwill, the Dutch Reformed permitted the British chaplain of the garrison forces to hold Anglican services in this church each Sunday at the conclusion of the Dutch Reformed services. A similar concession was made to the French Reformed congregation.

The first English governors of New York—Richard Nicolls (1664–1668), Francis Lovelace (1668–1674), Edmund Andros (1674–1681), and Thomas Dongan (1683–1688)—generally tried to be tolerant in religious matters. Even the reconquest of New Amsterdam in 1673 by the Netherlands during the Third Anglo-Dutch War, and its return to England by the Treaty of Westminster in 1674, did little to alter this basic policy of religious toleration. The instruction of 1674 of the duke of York to his new governor, Edmund Andros, for example, directed him to "permit all persons of what Religion soever, quietly to inhabit within ye precincts of yor jurisdiccôn, without giveing ym any disturbance or disquiet whatsoever, for or by reason of their differring opinions in matter of Religion," provided they keep the peace.[15]

In 1683, the duke of York permitted the colonists to have their own elected assembly. One of its first official acts was the passage of the Charter of Liberties and Privileges which set forth the principles that the government would henceforth follow in administering the colony. On religious matters, it differed little from the Duke's Laws except that the provision for religious freedom was stated more succinctly. When the Catholic duke of York ascended the English throne in 1685 as James II, he revoked this charter and dissolved the Assembly. Although these actions caused alarm among the colonists, freedom of worship continued as before.

The policy of religious toleration was not entirely the result of preference on the part of the English authorities. James, as duke of York and later as king of England, was deeply interested in New York's economic development as a source of revenue. In view of the many diverse religious groups in the colony, including Dutch Reformed, Presbyterian, Lutheran, Quaker, Jewish, and others, a policy of intolerance would have hurt the colony's growth. Moreover, James could hardly have advocated an arbitrary religious policy because of the limited choices that were open to him in this matter. Had he sought to impose conformity to a particular religion it would have been either the Anglican, which was the state church of England, or Roman Catholicism, which was the religion with which the duke was most sympathetic. To impose either of these would have been foolhardy because the Anglicans and Roman Catholics were very small minorities in New York for many years after 1664.[16]

Although religious toleration was practiced in New York during the period that James owned it as a ducal proprietorship and later as a royal colony, this does not mean that friction never occurred between the Dutch Reformed Church and the secular authorities. An incident in the autumn of 1675 illustrates one of the problems faced by a Church that owed ecclesiastical obedience to authorities in one country but civil obedience elsewhere. It centered around the attempt to force a Dutch Episcopalian, Nicholas Van Rensselaer, upon the Dutch Reformed congregation at Albany. Van Rensselaer had been licensed to preach by the Dutch Reformed Church in Holland but was never fully ordained by that body.[17] As a son of the great patroon, he was a man of social distinction. He became acquainted with Charles II, king of England, during the latter's exile and after the Restoration in 1660 he went to England to serve as chaplain at the Dutch embassy and as preacher to the Dutch congregation at Westminster. Later, in 1665, he was ordained a deacon in the Anglican Church. When Edmund Andros arrived in New York in 1674 as the new governor, Nicholas Van Rensselaer accompanied him, having been recommended by the duke of York for a position in one of the Dutch Reformed churches.

When Governor Andros arbitrarily decided to induct Van Rensselaer into the church at Albany as a colleague of Dominie Gideon Schaats, the Dutch Reformed churches strongly protested. Schaats and his consistory complained that this was an infringement on the prerogative of the Dutch congregations to call their own ministers. Under the leadership of the Reverend Van Nieuwenhuysen of New York City, other Dutch Reformed churches made common cause with the Albany body. Thus, when Van Rensselaer came to New York to deliver a sermon, Van Nieuwenhuysen forbade him to baptize any children who might be brought to the service. Van Rensselaer thereupon complained to Governor Andros who held a hearing on the matter, at which time various attestations were made regarding the qualifications of Van Rensselaer. To these, Van Nieuwenhuysen replied that although the ordination of the Church of England did not disqualify a person from serving a Dutch Reformed congregation, such ordination did not necessarily qualify him to serve in full capacity, particularly in the matter of administering the sacraments. The Dutch Reformed churches in America, he declared, were governed by the constitution of the Reformed Church of Holland and therefore, according to Article 53 of that constitution, Van Rensselaer could not serve fully "without having previously solemnly promised, as is usual in the admission of ministers in the Netherlands, to conduct himself in his services, comformably to their Confession, Catechism and Mode of Government." Van Nieuwenhuysen added that he doubted very much whether a minister who had been ordained by the Dutch Reformed Church would be permitted to administer the sacraments in any of the Anglican churches in England "without previously promising to maintain and follow the Canons, Articles and Rules" of the Anglican Church.

The matter was finally solved when Van Rensselaer promised, in writing, to conduct himself "as minister of Albany and Rensselaerswyck according to the Dutch Church, conformably to the public Church service and discipline of the Reformed Church of Holland." During the following years, questions were raised about Van Rensselaer's behavior and in 1677, Governor Andros himself had to depose him because of scandalous conduct.[18]

In addition to occasional difficulties with the secular authorities, other problems also faced the Dutch Reformed churches after the English conquest. Particularly troublesome were the frequent difficulties the ministers had in collecting their salaries. Most Dutch pastors had already confronted this problem during the New Netherland period, and the situation worsened during the early years under English rule. For example, according to one account, Dominie Blom's difficulties in collecting his salary at Kingston after 1664 were triple what they had been under Dutch rule.[19]

Although, as was noted, provisions had been made in the Duke's Laws for church wardens to compel compulsory support of a church in each parish, these regulations were not always observed. As one writer has stated, "the governors were loath to press non-Dutch to pay taxes for the Dutch Reformed Church."[20] Moreover, this requirement, which was so obnoxious to the "minority" churches, was eventually removed. The ministers therefore sometimes had to rely on the free-will offerings of their congregations for support, but these offerings were usually small. Although the colonists generally were not poor and a few of them were comparatively well-to-do, it would take time for the people to become accustomed to contributing freely to the support of their ministers.

The problem facing the dominies on the matter of salaries is clearly illustrated in a communication sent to the Classis of Amsterdam by the Reverend Johannes Megapolensis in April 1669; "On Sundays we have many hearers. People crowd into the church, and apparently like the sermon; but most of the listeners are not inclined to contribute to the support and salary of the preacher. They seem to desire, that we should live upon air and not upon produce." Megapolensis believed that the public authorities could have resorted to some coercion, but when he spoke with the English governor about the matter, he was told that "if the Dutch will have divine service their own way, then let them also take care of and support their own preachers."[21]

The churches also had to contend with a shortage of ministers. When New Netherland fell in 1664, there were six Dutch Reformed ministers in the colonies, but two of these, Samuel Megapolensis and Hermanus Blom, soon returned to Holland. This meant that only four ministers remained in 1668: Johannes Megapolensis and Samuel Drisius in New York City, Johannes Polhemus on Long Island, and Gideon Schaats in Albany. These clergymen carried on their work in poverty. Moreover, none of them were young men, three of them being over sixty and the fourth very near that age. By 1676, three of these ministers had died, namely, Megapolensis, Drisius, and Polhemus. Meanwhile, only one replacement had been sent out, Dominie Wilhelmus Van Nieuwenhuysen, who arrived at New York in 1671. Because of the shortage of ministers, one pastor frequently had to serve two or more churches. In other instances, churches had to rely almost exclusively on a *voorlezer*, or lay reader, with an occasional visit from an ordained pastor to administer the sacraments.[22] As will be explained in detail in the following chapter, the number of ministers gradually increased so that by 1714, there were ten Dutch Reformed pastors in the colonies, but meanwhile the number of congregations had grown to about thirty-five.

One of the most serious crises facing the church during the first half century under English rule was the so-called Leisler Troubles of 1688–1691. This incident was a confusing period in New York history but, in summary, this is what happened.[23] When the news reached the English colonies that William of Orange had landed in England in 1688 for the purpose of deposing the Catholic king James II, the citizens of Boston arrested the governor of the Dominion of New England, Edmund Andros, an appointee of James II. The province of New York was affected by the arrest because it was a part of the Dominion. Rumors also circulated about a French invasion and a Catholic plot to take over the English colonies in America. To add to the confusion, in June 1689, Francis Nicholson, Andros' young and inexperienced lieutenant-governor in New York, fled the country. In the absence of any legal government, Jacob Leisler, a captain in the militia of New York, was appointed as a kind of *pro tem* governor by a citizens' committee.

Not everyone acknowledged Leisler, and the province of New York soon became divided into two highly antagonistic factions. Although there were exceptions, the aristocratic and more wealthy elements among the population opposed Leisler, while the lower classes supported him in the hope that a more representative government would be established. Leisler managed to maintain himself in office, frequently by arbitrary means, for twenty months. When the government in England finally dispatched a new legal governor to New York in 1691, Leisler hesitated in relinquishing his authority. He was thereupon arrested, found guilty of treason, and executed on May 16, 1691.

The Leisler Troubles had a bearing on the Dutch Reformed Church because of the strong support given to the anti-Leislerian faction by the clergy, including Henricus Selyns of New York, Rudolphus Varick of Long Island, and Godfriedus Dellius of Albany. This action frequently brought the wrath of Leisler's government down upon the clergy. The attitude of the ministers also caused disharmony within the congregations because of the support Leisler enjoyed among many lay people. Some of the latter went so far as to withhold their financial support from the churches.

The question must therefore be asked: Why did the ministers react to Leisler in the manner they did? The reasons are difficult to perceive accurately, but three factors perhaps influenced their decision. First, they probably saw less need than others to support him because they did not believe the rumors that were circulating, such as the story about a Catholic plot to take over the colonial government. Secondly, the dominies undoubtedly questioned Leisler's executive ability. Judging from some of his actions, they must have thought that he lacked several qualifications for office, including experience as well as tact and tolerance. Finally, the ministers were perhaps influenced by social considerations. They tended to consider themselves on the social level of the "aristocrats" and people of influence, such as Nicholas Bayard, Stephanus Van Cortlandt, and Frederick Philipse of New York and Peter Schuyler of Albany, all of whom were opponents of Leisler and had been councillors of Lieutenant-governor Nicholson. Leisler, on the other hand, was unlettered and was considered a commoner because of his social background, although he had acquired some wealth since arriving in the colony from Germany in 1660. The fact that some of Leisler's chief opponents were also elders in the Dutch churches would tend to make the ministers even more sympathetic toward the anti-Leislerian faction, although it should be noted that Leisler was a deacon in the Dutch church. [24]

On September 14, 1690, Dominie Selyns wrote the Classis of Amsterdam: "Domine Varick and myself have suffered more than can be believed and are forced to cultivate patience."[25] In the case of Varick, however, patience was not enough to withstand the pressure and anxiety he had to endure. Consequently, on June 7, 1690, he fled from Long Island to the old Dutch settlement of New Castle on the Delaware. When he returned in the autumn of 1690, he was arrested and imprisoned for five months. Similarly, Dominie Dellius of Albany, who had also preached against Leisler, was summoned to New York, but he instead went into hiding: first in New Jersey, later on Long Island, and then for a time in Selyn's house in New York City. He finally fled to Boston.

Although Selyns had also denounced Leisler from the pulpit, he was permitted to continue his work and for a time was virtually the only Dutch Reformed minister preaching in the colonies.[26] Perhaps Leisler thought it prudent to retain one minister at his post, even one who was in sympathy with the opposition. Selyns was closely watched, however, by Leisler's men. His house was searched and his correspondence with the Netherlands was censored. On one occasion, Leisler himself, who was a member of Selyn' congregation, interrupted the worship service and openly threatened to silence him.

The plight of the ministers is illustrated in the following communication sent to the Classis of Amsterdam by the reverends Selyns, Varick, and Dellius:

Our ministers have been cast under suspicion through slanders against them; while the populace, ever ready for any change, were advised not to contribute for the support of religious services or for ministers' salaries. Choristers and schoolmasters have been encouraged to perform ministerial duties. Members of the Council (of former Governors), who were also mostly Elders of the church, have been saluted by the unheard of titles . . . of traitors and papists. Church officers and other members have been imprisoned and maltreated, put in irons, and confined to darkness. And not satisfied with doing such things, even the Sanctuary has been attacked with violence and open force.[27]

The execution of Leisler in 1691 did not quell the passions which had disturbed New York politics during the previous four years. Many of the people for a long time continued to look upon him as a hero and martyr who had championed the cause of democracy. As a consequence, the antagonistic and bitter relations that the controversy created between the pastors and some members of their flocks continued for several years after Leisler's death. In April 1693, for example, almost two years after Leisler had been executed, Dominie Varick wrote:

for two years now I have not reached the fourth part of my former hearers. . . . I have received but little of my salary in four years, and that only from a few special friends in my congregation: I do not yet see how I am to obtain my back pay. Ministers who serve here will have to live on their own fat.[28]

The Synod of North Holland, meeting at Amsterdam in August 1694, went so far as to draw up plans for laying the plight of the colonial churches before the king of England himself. Such a course of action had been urged as early as October 1692 by Selyns, Varick, and Dellius.[29] Perhaps they thought that the new English king, William III, having been born and raised in Holland, would lend a sympathetic ear and try to improve their plight.

Varick finally became so discouraged that he requested a transfer to one of the Dutch churches in the Caribbean or East Indies. Before this could be done, however, he died on September 24, 1694, leaving behind a wife and four children to mourn him. His early death was perhaps hastened by the suffering and discouragement he had experienced during the previous six years. Selyns, too, thought seriously of giving up the ministry in New York and returning to Holland if his arrears in salary were not paid. The Classis of Amsterdam tried hard to mediate the dispute. Thus, in a letter of April 20, 1693, it urged the clergy in New York to be patient and forgiving, and "strive to calm the minds of those church members who have been provoked and alienated, and thus win them to fellowship once again." The Classis also dispatched letters to the consistories, urging everyone to treat one another in love and peace, "for where the stroke of the hammer is heard, the temple is not built." Nevertheless, as late as October 1698, several members of the Dutch Reformed congregation of New York City sent a lengthy letter to the Classis of Amsterdam complaining about the role that the Dutch ministers had played in the Leisler episode.[30]

The behavior of the clergy in the Leislerian Troubles is a stain upon their otherwise admirable record. This is especially true of Selyns, whose action in the matter was, as one authority has stated, "in the mildest view of the case, most injudicious and unwise."[31] It is unfortunate that the clergy did not pursue a more neutral policy during the episode and use the dignity of their office to quiet the passions of the opposing factions. Actually Leisler's conduct had not been that bad and certainly not treasonable.[32] Later, the whole affair was reviewed by the government of England. Leisler's property which had been confiscated was returned to his heirs and Parliament passed a bill removing the attainder of treason and legalizing his brief period of authority. In 1698, the relatives of Leisler and of his son-in-law, Jacob Milbourne, who had also been executed, were given permission to exhume the bodies, which had been buried near the gallows, and give them a Christian burial under the floor of the city's Dutch Reformed church. This was carried out with considerable joyful fanfare among the people but against the protests of Dominie Selyns and the consistory. In 1702, the New York Assembly voted a large indemnity to his heirs.[33]

Meanwhile, the ministers found themselves threatened from another quarter, namely, the colonial governors. Except for a few incidents, such as the installation of Nicholas Van Rensselaer at Albany, the English governors for many years after the fall of New Netherland made no determined effort to promote the Anglican Church among the Dutch Reformed colonists. Beginning with the administration of Henry Sloughter (1691–1692), however, the governors, on orders of the English crown, tried to advance the interests of the Anglican Church and to assume the right of approving and disapproving the appointment of ministers for other denominations. Fortunately, the elective Assembly had been reintroduced into New York politics in 1691, giving the colonists a forum in which to make their wishes known. Members of the Dutch Reformed Church, who for a long time constituted an important element of the Assembly, used it to voice their opposition to the pro-Anglican policy.

In 1693, the Assembly passed the so-called "Ministry Act," which was largely a restatement of the Duke's Laws. It provided for the support of ministers by public taxation and for annual elections of vestrymen and church wardens who would assist in the calling of ministers to fill vacancies. Governor Benjamin Fletcher (1692–1698), an ardent and overbearing Anglican, had pressured the Assembly into passing this legislation. He hoped to use it as a means for establishing the Anglican Church in New York, but the act fell short of his expectations. It made no specific mention of the Anglican Church, and it was applicable only to the city and county of New York and some surrounding counties—Westchester, Queens, and Richmond.

Governor Fletcher next attempted to get the Assembly to amend the Ministry Act. Failing in this, he began interpreting it as though it gave him the authority he had asked. In particular, he claimed it authorized him to approve or disapprove the appointment of ministers in the above four counties. Most church leaders opposed this interpretation, because not to do so might have meant that Fletcher would approve only Anglican clergymen to fill vacancies.[34]

In its dealings with the public authorities, the Dutch Reformed church in New York achieved a major goal in May 1696 when it received its own charter, something that a special committee of the congregation had been striving to achieve for several years. By it, the

New York church was given "the free exercise and enjoyment... of worshipping God according to the constitutions and directions of the Reformed Church in Holland, approved and instituted by the National Synod of Dort," as well as the right to own and manage its property and exemption from the governor's collative power over ecclesiastical appointments.[35] Dominie Selyns, pastor of the New York congregation and a leader in the effort to gain independence for the Dutch church, explained the contents of the charter to the Classis of Amsterdam in a letter of September 30, 1696:

Its contents are in respect to the power of calling one or more ministers; of choosing elders, deacons, chorister, sexton, etc.; and of keeping Dutch-schools, all in conformity to the Church-Order of the Synod of Dort, Anno, 1619; also, the right to possess a church, a parsonage and other church property as our own, and to hold them in our corporate capacity, without alienation. Also the right to receive legacies of either real or personal property, and other donations, for the benefit of the church, etc. This is a circumstance which promises much advantage to God's church, and quiets the formerly existing uneasiness.[36]

The charter established a precedent because several other Dutch Reformed churches later received similar privileges, including the Kingston church in 1719, Albany in 1720, Schenectady in 1734, Hackensack in 1750, the five churches of the Raritan Valley unitedly in 1753, Hillsborough in 1755, and Bergen in 1771. The charter that was granted to the New York church in 1696 was thus an important victory for the denomination as a whole. Requests for similar charters by other denominations were repeatedly refused, except for the Anglicans. As a token of its gratitude to Fletcher for granting the charter, the consistory of the Dutch church of New York on July 26, 1696, resolved "to make him a present of silver plate, to the value of seventy-five or eighty pounds, in the currency of this province."[37]

The gains made by the Dutch Reformed Church made it less necessary for its leaders to henceforth side with the Dissenters and other non-Anglican groups that had been opposing the governor on various religious issues. Indeed, it is very probable that this was the intention of Fletcher when he allowed the Dutch church of New York to incorporate.[38] Events of the following months indicate that if this was Fletcher's aim, it succeeded quite well. Already in late 1696, the Anglicans of New York purchased a plot of ground on Broadway and began building their own place of worship, to be known as Trinity Church. The Anglicans made another significant step forward when Trinity Church in 1697 obtained a charter of its own.

In commenting on the Anglican charter, which followed within a year after the incorporation of the Dutch church, one authority has stated that "the two charters had all the earmarks of an accommodation between Anglicans and the Dutch."[39] The friendship existing between the two groups at this time was particularly evidenced by the fact that two Dutch Reformed dominies, Selyns of New York and Nucella of Kingston, assisted in the installation of the first Anglican rector, William Vesey, on Christmas Day 1697. Moreover, the installation was performed in the new Dutch church on Garden Street, as the construction of Trinity Church had not yet been completed.

The Charter of 1696 and the replacement in 1697 of the overbearing Fletcher as governor by Richard Coote, the earl of Bellomont, resulted in more peaceful relations between the Dutch Church and the colonial administration. Bellomont showed less inclination than previous governors to advance the Anglican Church and even seemed to favor Dissenters over Anglicans in making appointments. Moreover, he tended to side with the pro-Leislerian faction which was still creating a stir in New York politics at this time. Unfortunately, the moderate Bellomont was succeeded in 1701 as governor by Edward Hyde, Lord Cornbury, whose name, as one writer has said, has often been "associated with all that was bad in English rule."[40] In contrast to his predecessor, Cornbury allied himself with the old anti-Leislerian faction and followed a strong pro-Anglican policy.

The formation in 1701 of the Society for the Propagation of the Gospel in Foreign Parts, commonly called the SPG, caused additional worry at this time among the Dutch Reformed and other non-Anglicans in the colonies. With headquarters in England, the SPG became the missionary arm of the Church of England, with a special interest in promoting Anglicanism in the American colonies, not only among the Indians and Negro slaves but also among the whites, including the Dutch. Between 1702 and the American Revolution, it sent nearly sixty missionaries to the colony of New York.

An indication of the troubles that the Dutch churches could expect from Cornbury came almost immediately. In 1702, a delegation of consistory members from the Dutch churches in Kings County, Long Island, notified the governor of their intention of calling the Reverend Bernardus Freeman of Schenectady as their pastor. The custom of notifying the governor of such matters had been done in the past merely as a matter of courtesy, but this time some church members objected because it might give Cornbury an inflated view of his prerogatives. These fears proved justified when the governor denied Freeman permission to preach in Kings County on the grounds he had "not behaved well in the continuation and encouragement of the dissensions among the people of this province."[41] Although Cornbury later reversed himself on this decision, it left behind some bitter feelings.

The above incident was followed by another crisis in 1704, when Cornbury arbitrarily tried to foist an Anglican, the Reverend Samuel Hepburn, on the Dutch Reformed congregation of Kingston, following the departure of its former pastor, Dominie John Nucella. When members of the congregation, supported by their co-religionists at New York, objected, they were merely told that this was a prerogative of the governor. Meanwhile, some members of the Kingston congregation had sent a request to the Classis of Amsterdam for a new pastor. The man chosen was the Reverend Henricus Beys, and his arrival in 1704 was the cause for further strained relations between the Dutch Reformed clergy and the governor.

Out of courtesy but not obligation, a new preacher on his arrival in the colonies usually went to the governor, accompanied by one or more members of his consistory, to pay his respects before beginning his preaching duties. When the newly arrived Beys called on Governor Cornbury, however, his reception was anything but cordial. He was told he had to have a written license from the governor before he could undertake his pastoral duties, and was threatened with banishment if he attempted to preach without such special permission. In later describing the meeting that he and a member of his consistory had with Cornbury, Beys declared that "stinging words were hurled at us by his Excellency as if we were the lowest negroes or heathens."[42] Another new Dutch Reformed minister, the Reverend Vincentius Antonides, who had just arrived from Holland to serve Brooklyn, was similarly treated by Cornbury.

In explaining his actions, Governor Cornbury claimed that instructions he had received from the English crown gave him the right to induct new ministers. After repeated urgings, he finally showed these instructions to members of his council who were also members of the Dutch Reformed Church. When these councillors pointed out that a careful reading of the instructions indicated that the right of induction pertained only to the Anglican Church, Cornbury refused to accept such an interpretation. Similarly, when told what the practice of his predecessors had been in these matters, he replied that he was not concerned about what others had done.

It was not only the Dutch Reformed churches that felt the heavy hand of the governor's wrath. In 1703, for example, a Presbyterian minister was ejected from his parish at Jamaica, in Queens County, and replaced by an Episcopalian, an incident that set off a near riot. Four years later, in 1707, two Presbyterian pastors, the reverends Francis Makemie and John Hampton were arrested at Newtown, also in Queens County. Cornbury ordered their arrest on the grounds they were preaching without a proper license from the governor. The charges against Hampton were later dropped, but Makemie was brought to trial. Despite a jury that was packed in favor of the governor, Makemie won his case in a trial that has become celebrated in the annals of man's struggle for religious freedom.

Meanwhile, several Dutch Reformed pastors as well as members of their consistories wrote letters to the Classis of Amsterdam informing that body of what had transpired and proposing certain remedies. In particular, they suggested that protests be sent to the English government through the Netherlands ambassador in London and also to the bishop of London, who had general jurisdiction over the Anglican Church in the colonies. When news of these plans reached Governor Cornbury, he prudently relented and adopted a more conciliatory policy. The bad press that he received in England about the Makemie trial undoubtedly also contributed to his change of heart.[43]

In 1708, Cornbury was replaced by John Lovelace who, like Bellomont, followed a moderate policy on religious matters. The successors of Lovelace also followed a more conciliatory policy and were less prone to push Anglican interests. No doubt the dynastic change that occurred in England in 1714, also contributed to this more conciliatory mood. The first two Hanoverians, George I (1714–1727) and George II (1727–1760), because of their ancestry, were more interested in German affairs than those of England, including the promotion of the Anglican Church.

V
The Ministry, 1664–1714

Despite problems over salaries, a shortage of ministers, and differences
with the secular authorities, the Dutch Reformed Church not only sur-
vived but expanded during the years 1664 to 1714. Very little of this
growth was due to Dutch immigration, which came to a virtual stand-
still after the English conquest and remained small during the remainder of the colonial period. Rather, the expansion came primarily from
natural increase: colonial families were generally large, and Dutch families were no exception. Dominie Selyns wrote from New York City
in 1682 that children "multiply more rapidly here than anywhere else
in the world."[1] Similarly, William Penn, in a letter written in 1683
following a visit to his lands in America, reported that the Dutch residing on the Delaware River "have fine Children, and almost every
house full; rare to find one of them without three or four Boys, and
as many Girls; some six, seven, and eight Sons."[2]

Although Dutch immigration was negligible after the fall of New
Netherland in 1664, the arrival of two other groups of Europeans did
contribute to the growth of the Dutch Reformed Church during the
period 1664–1714. These were the French Huguenots and the German
Palatines. The coming of the Palatines and their relationship to the
Reformed Church will be discussed in a following chapter because they
continued to arrive in increasing numbers throughout the eighteenth
century; only the Huguenots will be discussed here.

The Huguenots left France because of religious persecution, and
some of them came to New Netherland at an early date. Staten Island,
in particular, became a favorite asylum for early Hugenot refugees.
Dominie Michaelius, the colony's first ordained minister, and Dominie
Drisius occasionally preached in French for the benefit of both
Huguenots and Walloons. The frequent fusion of the Huguenots with
the Dutch Reformed is understandable because both groups were Calvinists with a similar theology and polity. Moreover, many Huguenots
had lived in Holland for a time before going to America.

When religious persecution increased in France under Louis XIV,
the Huguenots came to America in increasing numbers, especially
after the revocation of the Edict of Nantes in 1685. The largest number

settled in South Carolina, but many of them located in or near Dutch settlements in New York, including Manhattan Island, Long Island, and Kingston. Some also located at New Castle on the Delaware and at Hackensack in New Jersey. According to one authority, "every Dutch community contained a minority, sometimes a large proportion of Huguenots."[3]

One of the largest French settlements was located at New Paltz, about fifteen miles from Kingston. A French Reformed church was organized here about 1683. As happened in several instances, these Huguenots were in time assimilated into the prevailing Dutch society. In commenting on this, one writer states:

For some time the Huguenots of New Paltz used the French language. But as the Dutch was spoken at Kingston, Poughkeepsie and New York, and also in schools and in churches, it was determined in public council to speak Dutch to their children and domestics. In time, the Huguenots in Ulster county adopted the language of the Dutch, together with their habits and customs, and those have been preserved with peculiar perseverence.[4]

Replica of the Huguenot Church built in 1717 at New Paltz. (Courtesy of the Huguenot Society, New Paltz, New York)

The New Paltz church substituted Dutch for French in 1733, and did not switch to English until 1800.[5]

Although many of the Huguenots were ultimately absorbed by Dutch Reformed churches, this was not universally true. Some joined with the Presbyterians or Anglicans, and a few maintained their own pastors and congregations throughout the colonial period—using the French language and retaining French Reformed confessions and liturgy. One of the largest French congregations was located on Manhattan Island. Another was organized about fifteen miles from New York at New Rochelle on Long Island Sound.

Cordial relations were maintained between the Huguenots and the Dutch Reformed. Thus, Dominie Selyns in a letter of 1683 to the Classis of Amsterdam refers to the Reverend Pierre Daillé of the Huguenot church of New York as his colleague, adding that he "is full of zeal, learning, and piety. Exiled for the sake of religion, he now devotes himself here to the cause of Christ with untiring energy."[6] Similarly, when the Reverend Louis Rou, of the same Huguenot congregation, was married in 1713, the ceremony was performed by Dominie Gualtherus Du Bois, Selyn's successor. Until the French Reformed on Manhattan Island built their own church in 1688 on Marketfeld Street, the Dutch allowed them to conduct Sunday services in the Church in the Fort, following the Dutch services.[7]

The growth in population, whether from natural increase or from immigration, contributed not only to the growth in membership of the older Dutch Reformed churches, but it also led to the formation of new congregations. When families grew in size and sons reached adulthood, and as more settlers arrived, it became increasingly difficult to obtain good land at reasonable prices in the older communities. As a consequence, individuals, and even entire families, would sometimes leave a community to find land elsewhere. Soil exhaustion also led some to look for new homes. These migrants would soon be joined at their new location by other settlers, with the result that the countryside, which a few years earlier had been wilderness, gradually became dotted with farms and farm buildings. Now and then, a cluster of dwellings in these newly-opened lands would take on the appearance of a village, with facilities to make pioneer life more bearable—a general store, a blacksmith shop, a tavern, a market, a school, and a place of worship.

As a consequence of the pattern of settlement outlined above, many new communities arose during the period 1664–1714 which had significant Dutch Reformed elements in their population. These included not only new settlements along the Hudson River but also several in New Jersey. Thus, Dutch Reformed elements from western Long Island moved to Monmouth County, while others from Manhattan and along the Hudson Valley settled in the Hackensack, Passaic, and Raritan valleys. A few colonists even moved as far as Pennsylvania.[8]

With the development and growth of these settlements, new Dutch Reformed churches were established. In New York, for example, congregations were organized at Schenectady about 1680, Tappan in 1694, Tarrytown in 1697, Rochester in 1701, and Kinderhook in 1712. Similarly, in New Jersey, Dutch Reformed churches were established at Hackensack in 1686, Acquackanonck (now called Passaic) in 1693, Freehold (Marlboro) and Raritan (Somerville) in 1699, Second River (Belleville) in 1700, Three Mile Run in 1703, and Six Mile Run (Franklin Park) in 1710. In Pennsylvania, three Dutch Reformed churches were organized in 1710: one at Germantown and two in Bucks County. An examination of the manner in which each of these churches arose lies beyond the scope of this study, but an inquiry into

Sleepy Hollow Church at Tarrytown, New York, built in 1699. (Courtesy of Sage Library, New Brunswick Seminary)

the formation of the Schenectady church can shed light on the others because their historical development was often similar.[9]

The region around Schenectady had long been admired by colonists at Fort Orange and Rensselaerswyck for its rich soil. In 1661, Arent Van Curler, who had served for many years as the capable agent for the patroon Kiliaen Van Rensselaer, and several residents from Fort Orange received permission from Governor Stuyvesant to purchase land from the Indians with the intention of starting a new settlement. In the following year, a small band of farmers and fur traders took the next step by laying out farms and a town. The fertile soil of the region soon led to the arrival of additional colonists.

According to an early report, the village was never "entirely destitute of the exercises of Christian education."[10] Almost from the beginning, the community had a *voorlezer*, or lay reader, and Dominie Schaats of Albany occasionally visited there to preach and administer the sacraments. A committee of Schenectady residents was soon created to organize a church, and already in 1679 a petition was sent to two merchants in Holland asking them to use their influence with the Classis of Amsterdam in obtaining a preacher for the village. His qualifications as spelled out in the petition were simple: he must be "a bachelor, who understands notes and psalms." The petitioners agreed to pay the equivalent of "one hundred beavers, in wheat, as yearly salary," but added that they would be "well pleased" if the salary could be "beat down somewhat."[11] Schenectady did not obtain its own pastor, however, until 1684, when Peter Tesschenmaeker arrived. He was killed in an Indian raid in 1690, after which lay readers and ministers from Albany again supplied the pulpit until the arrival of the Reverend Bernardus Freeman in 1700.

An examination of the early history of most other new churches during this period would indicate developments similar to those of Schenectady, that is, newly-formed communities that were too small to establish churches, frequently became preaching stations looked after by a *voorlezer* with occasional visits from a neighboring pastor until they could support preachers of their own. The Reverend Laurentius Van Gaasbeek of Kingston in a letter of 1679 gives us the following interesting information about the manner in which he looked after two small neighboring communities: "I divide my preaching services as follows: I preach two Sundays at Kingston, the third at Hurley, the fourth and fifth again at Kingston, the sixth at Marbletown, and so on."[12]

In some instances ministers remained at the same charge for a number of years, while on other occasions the rate of replacement was high. Although six ministers were serving New Netherland's eleven churches when it fell to the English in 1664, only two Dutch Reformed pastors could be found in the American colonies in 1676: Van Nieuwenhuysen at New York and Schaats at Albany. The former had arrived in 1671 as a replacement for Johannes Megapolensis, who had died in 1670, and for Drisius, who was becoming feeble. Van Nieuwenhuysen's ministry was cut short by death in 1681, and in the following year Henricus Selyns replaced him. Selyns, who had served at Brooklyn from 1660 to 1664 but had returned to Holland shortly before the English conquest, served as sole pastor of New York until 1699, when the Reverend Gualtherus Du Bois arrived as an assistant. This was fortunate, because two years later Selyns passed away. Du Bois' ministry was a fruitful one, lasting until 1751.

At Albany, Dominie Schaats, who began serving there in 1652, carried on alone until 1683, when the Reverend Godfriedus Dellius came to assist him. This was welcomed by all, considering that Schaats was then seventy-six years old. Following Schaats' death in 1694, Dellius served as sole pastor. When he returned to Holland in 1699, neighboring pastors served at Albany until the arrival of Johannes Lydius in 1700. After his death in 1709, an Episcopal minister, the Reverend Henry Barclay, preached in Dutch until 1712, when the Reverend Petrus Van Driessen arrived.

Kingston, too, had a succession of ministers during this period. These included Hermanus Blom to 1667; Peter Tesschenmaeker, 1675–1676, 1678; Laurentius Van Gaasbeek, 1678–1680; John Weekstein, 1681–1687; Laurentius Vandenbosch, 1687–1689; John Nucella, 1695–1704; Henricus Beys, 1706–1708; and Peter Vas, 1710–1756.

Although not quite as apparent as at Kingston, the Long Island churches, too, had several different pastors during the first half-century of English rule. When the Reverend Polhemus, who began serving there in 1654, died in 1676, the Reverend Casparus Van Zuuren replaced him. He returned to Holland in 1685, and in the following year Rudolphus Varick took over the care of the Long Island congregations. Following Varick's death in 1694, Wilhelmus Lupardus arrived in 1695. When he returned to Holland in 1702, the Long Island churches were left vacant for the next three years, but in 1705 the reverends Bernardus Freeman and Vincentius Antonides became joint pastors of these churches, the former serving until 1741 and the latter until 1744.

The Reformed Churches of Brooklyn, Flatbush, Flatlands, and New Utrecht were eventually referred to as the "Collegiate Churches of Kings County." It is impossible to give an exact date when this association developed, but it was there when the Reverend Polhemus died in 1676. At that time, the four churches had a total membership of about three hundred, with Brooklyn having one hundred sixteen members; Flatbush, about one hundred; Flatlands, about sixty; and New Utrecht, about twenty.[13] In the collegiate system, representatives of each congregation had limited powers of a local nature, but all matters of substance were handled by union meetings of the collegiate consistory, usually consisting of two elders and two deacons from each congregation. In 1681, the delegates from the Flatbush church were enlarged by one elder and one deacon to accommodate the people of New Lotts, a new settlement which developed adjacent to Flatbush.[14] The four congregations shared and jointly supported a common minister, a practice which continued to be true even when there was a plurality of ministers, with each minister preaching in turn among the churches and drawing his salary in certain fixed proportions from the various congregations. When a church was not being served by a minister on a particular Sunday, as happened frequently because of the itinerant nature of the arrangement, the local schoolmaster generally read to the congregation from an approved book of sermons. When Reformed churches were organized at Bushwick about 1702 and at Gravesend in 1715, they too were incorporated into the collegiate system. This collegiate association of churches continued to function until the early part of the nineteenth century, being formally dissolved in 1824.[15]

It should be noted that the turnover among the ministers during the period 1664 to 1714 came about primarily because of the deaths of ministers and because of decisions to return to the Netherlands. Ministers at this time generally did not move from pastorate to pastorate *within* the colonies, but there were a few exceptions, most notable of whom was Peter Tesschenmaeker. During his brief ministerial career of about fifteen years, he served several charges, including Kingston (as ministerial candidate), 1675–76; Dutch Guiana, on the coast of South America, 1676–78; Kingston, 1678; New Castle, on the Delaware River, 1679–82; and Schenectady, 1682–90. He also served occasionally at Staten Island and Bergen, 1679–82, and at Hackensack, 1686–87.

Vacant churches added greatly to the duties of neighboring pastors. The extra responsibilities that for a time fell on the shoulders of Van Zuuren of Long Island can be taken as a case in point. When the Reverend Van Nieuwenhuysen died in 1681, Van Zuuren, in addition to looking after his regular charge, journeyed across the East River to preach in New York every other Wednesday for almost twelve months until the arrival of Selyns. He also looked after the churches on Staten Island and at Bergen, New Jersey. According to the Long Island dominie's own testimony, for a time he had about a thousand church members under his care, all widely scattered.[16]

When churches had been vacant for several years, a newly arrived minister was kept particularly busy getting matters back into a normal routine. A letter of Dominie Van Gaasbeek of Kingston written to the Classis of Amsterdam shortly after his arrival from Holland in 1678 can shed light on this problem:

At first I had much trouble to get everything in good order, and in conformity to the government of the Netherland churches. There was but little order in ecclesiastical matters and government, because it was ten years, since Dominie Hermanus Blom... had left, and no preacher had been here since. But I have improved the condition of affairs, as well as I could, and what remains to be done, I hope to accomplish in the future. At present I hold catechetical classes not only on Sundays, after the discourse on our Christian Catechism, but also twice in the week, on Tuesdays and Friday evenings, in my own house. I consider this to be very necessary on account of the very small amount of knowledge which I discovered in many.[17]

In view of the above considerations, it is not surprising that strenuous efforts were made to fill vacant pulpits promptly, although usually with only limited success. Not only did consistories of pastorless churches work hard to obtain replacements, but neighboring ministers often gave assistance in these matters. Thus, when the Long Island churches were vacant in 1676, following the death of Dominie Polhemus, Van Nieuwenhuysen of New York wrote the Classis of Amsterdam: "May the love of Christ incline you to consider how wretched it is to see so many sheep without a shepherd. It is well known to you that trees grow miserably wild if not trimmed and pruned in their season."[18] Similarly, in 1684, when Van Zuuren returned to Holland, Selyns of New York advised the Long Island congregations concerning a replacement.

What procedures were followed in calling a minister to fill a vacancy in the colonies? And on what terms did the ministers accept such calls? The process varied and could be a long, drawn-out affair, as is shown by what transpired after a call was sent to Dominie Selyns, the former pastor of Brooklyn, to serve the church at New York. On February 25, 1681, about a week after the death of the Reverend Wilhelmus Van Nieuwenhuysen, the consistory sent the following communication to the Classis of Amsterdam:

We want you to assist us with your everready help and good counsel, and send us as soon as possible, a minister, pious and faithful, learned and sound in doctrine, and of a blameless life....We remember Dominie Henricus Selyns. His faithful services, his pious life, his peculiar zeal, his amiable conversation, his pleasing and ready speech, left a deep impression upon many hearts. If his Reverence were inclined to come over again, this would be very agreeable to our congregation.[19]

The letter was read at a meeting of the Classis on July 21, after which the classical committee on foreign lands was instructed to deliver a copy to Selyns. Selyns, who had also been contacted directly by letter from the New York church, stated that he would "take counsel about it with God, and with good friends." He was interested in the call but, according to the Classis, he had some "well-grounded objections" for not accepting immediately. He undoubtedly remembered some of the difficulties that occurred during his pastorate at Brooklyn about twenty years earlier.[20]

During the following months, several letters were exchanged between Selyns and the New York consistory regarding terms under which he might assume the pastorate there. Finally, on December 10, 1681, Selyns and various witnesses for both parties appeared before a notary public in Amsterdam, and a contract was duly drafted. Selyns was promised a salary of one thousand guilders per year, payable in quarterly installments, beginning on the day of his departure from the Netherlands. This salary was for preaching twice on Sundays and for performing normal pastoral duties; compensation for holding mid-week services on Wednesday evenings and assisting occasionally in neighboring churches at Bergen and Harlem was to be negotiated after his arrival in New York. A parsonage and sufficient firewood were also promised. Free passage was to be provided for the dominie and his family, as well as for his household goods and books. In the event of the dominie's death, the custom of the churches in the Netherlands would be followed: his widow would receive the full salary of the quarter in which her husband died, together with the salary of the "entire half year following;" thereafter, she would receive the "ordinary widow's pension of one hundred guilders per year," or, in lieu thereof, the sum of one thousand guilders to be paid within a year after her husband's death.[21]

Even after all this groundwork had been laid, it was not until March 16, 1682, three months after the meeting with the notary public, before Selyns finally assured the Classis that he would accept the call. A few weeks later, he received an honorable dismissal from his pastorate at Waverveen, along with a letter of recommendation for the New York consistory. On April 6, 1682, Classis informed the church of New York about Selyns' decision, adding that it was their prayer that "the Lord of the Harvest" would bless his labors among them so that "many souls may be won to Christ."[22] Selyns left the Netherlands for America in late April or early May, but because of a brief sojourn at Dover, England and because of calms and contrary winds, he did not arrive at his destination until August 6, about a year and a half after the New York consistory had first issued him a call.

Of course, not all negotiations over ministerial contracts were as prolonged as was the case with Selyns. In a few instances, when a pastor appeared before the Classis of Amsterdam and indicated a willingness to serve in the colonies, he was sent there without any particular church being designated for him. Thus, Varick was dispatched in 1685 "with the proviso that he shall have the choice of such churches as shall be vacant."[23] Upon arrival, he was contacted by an official delegation from the church at Albany, which told him that the departure of Dominie Dellius was anticipated and the position would then be offered to him. Varick was not attracted by this proposal and signed an agreement with the Dutch churches on Long Island.[24]

Ministers who had once served in the colonies but had returned to Holland were occasionally asked to return to America to serve their former or other congregations. Thus, Dominie Selyns, who went back to Holland in 1664 after serving Brooklyn for four years, was asked in 1677 to return to his former congregation, and in 1670 and again in 1682 calls were sent to him by the New York City church. He accepted the call of 1682. Similarly, Van Zuuren was asked to return to Long Island in 1695, as was Dellius to Albany in 1699.

Requests for ministers were usually "blank calls" in which it was left to the discretion of the Amsterdam divines to make the selection. Most calls, however, were specific in outlining the minister's duties, prescribing such matters as the number of sermons to be delivered each Sunday, how often the Lord's Supper had to be administered, how frequently house visitations should occur, and the number of times that catechism classes should be held. Calls were also specific as to salary arrangements and such "fringe" benefits as the use of a parsonage, garden, orchard, pasture land, and so forth. Although suggestions were often made as to the qualifications desired in a minister, these were generally couched in lofty and sublime phrases. Thus, the request sent in May 1695 by the Kings County churches asked that the Classis of Amsterdam please

take care that only such a one be sent over, who is of good habits and sound doctrine, and who has the proper abilities to build up the

Church of God; who will shine before it by a good example, and edify and watch over it. . . . Also, let him be one who lives according to God's teachings, and who, therefore, teaches also by his life.[25]

The calling of ministers sometimes led to bitter feelings within a congregation. Such a situation occurred when the consistory of the New York church, after consultation with some members of the congregation, issued a call in 1698 to the Reverend Hieronymous Verdieren of Bruynesse, the Netherlands, asking him to serve as an assistant to the aging Dominie Selyns. A segment of the congregation and one of the elders objected to the call on the grounds that not enough of the church members had been consulted, and that the "ancient custom of consulting members of the former Consistory" had not been followed. One sees in this controversy a reminder that the Leisler episode had not yet been forgotten, as the opposition to Verdieren came primarily from the pro-Leislerian faction. When Verdieren heard about the party strife that his nomination had rekindled, he declined the call. A committee of the Classis was thereupon asked to look for another dominie, using great care to find someone with a "pacific character, in order, if possible, to quench the disturbances which have arisen." Out of several candidates who were nominated, Classis finally chose the Reverend Gualtherus Du Bois, who arrived in late 1699. The choice was excellent: Du Bois proved to be a popular preacher who served with distinction until his death in 1751.[26]

The calling of pastors for Albany in 1700, as well as for the Long Island churches in 1705 and for the churches in Bucks County, Pennsylvania in 1710, also resulted in controversies. In some instances, it took many years before such problems were finally settled. Disputed calls were frequently associated with questions about proper ordinations and with debates over evangelical versus doctrinal approaches to preaching. Both of these problems will be explained in a following chapter.

As was true during the New Netherland period, salary arrangements with the ministers sometimes involved more than monetary payments. The agreement by which Wilhelmus Lupardus was engaged to fill the Long Island churches in 1695 was typical: nine hundred guilders annually, a parsonage, free firewood, a garden, and pasturage sufficient for three animals. The contract also had the usual provisions of free passage from Holland for Lupardus and his family as well as their personal belongings. The articles of agreement were particularly specific about the nature of the salary payments, stipulating that these were to be given Lupardus in quarterly installments and in "Holland currency, payable in silver and not in grain, or merchandise, or wampum."[27] This exact specification was included because pastors on arriving in America sometimes discovered that salaries, when converted to Holland currency, were as much as a fifth less than what had been promised.[28]

With the passage of time, promises concerning salaries and fringe benefits were better observed than had been the case immediately after the English conquest of New Netherland in 1664. Nevertheless, problems still occasionally arose. This is clearly shown in a letter of admonition sent in 1680 to the churches of Long Island by the Classis of Amsterdam on the matter of Dominie Casparus Van Zuuren's salary:

> Most Worthy Brethren, we learn from other parties that his stipulated salary is not promptly paid him, and that he receives three hundred guilders less, in Dutch currency, annually, than was promised him, besides the perquisite of free fuel; also that the building of a parsonage for him has hitherto been hindered by strifes, by which a neutral third party, although innocent, always suffers....Such care and domestic anxiety lead to the injury of his ministerial services, grieves his spirit, quenches his gifts, or at least darkens and beclouds them; and as the apostle saith, it redounds to the detriment of the church, if he must perform his duty with sighs.[29]

Most of the ministers who served in the colonies during the first half-century of English rule were well-trained and dedicated men. Of the approximately twenty new ministers who arrived in the American colonies between 1664 and 1714, at least half of them had attended universities in the Netherlands, usually Leiden. Information is difficult to obtain on the remainder, but it is likely that several of them also had strong academic backgrounds. For example, although it cannot be determined for certain if Gualtherus Du Bois attended a university, the minutes of the Classis of Amsterdam make several references to Du Bois' excellent academic qualifications when he was being considered for service at New York. Similarly, soon after his arrival, the New York consistory thanked the Classis for sending someone whose "learning and virtues have justly become an ornament to our church."[30]

One of the most capable and learned ministers of this period was the Reverend Henricus Selyns. Indeed, one of his biographers, writing about a century ago, stated that Selyns "may be justly regarded as one of the founders of the Dutch church in America, who did more to determine its position in the country than any other man."[31] Reference has already been made to his dealings with colonial governors and to his contribution in obtaining a charter for the Dutch church in New York. As pastor at this church from 1682 until his death in 1701, he maintained a busy schedule for himself, preaching twice on Sundays and once on Wednesday evenings to his own congregation, and teaching catechism classes to the young people. In view of his large congregation, which in 1686 totalled about 550 communicant members drawn from over 300 households, the task of visiting the sick and making other pastoral calls also kept him very busy.[32] Nevertheless, he took time to officiate occasionally in the surrounding churches. Three times a year, on Mondays, he journeyed across the Hudson to Bergen, New Jersey, which was without a minister during his term at New York. On these visits, he delivered two sermons and administered the sacraments. Selyns also made occasional visits to pastorless flocks at Harlem, Staten Island, and communities on Long Island.

Despite his busy work schedule, Dominie Selyns found time to write poetry, versifying in both Dutch and Latin. Almost any significant event seemed to encourage him to write a poem. When the occasion called for it, his verses could be quite witty. When Aegidius Luyck, schoolmaster of the local Latin school, for example, married, Selyns wrote a humorous nuptial poem in honor of the occasion. At other times, his poetry could be more serious and philosophical, as was the case following the massacre of some settlers at Esopus in 1663, the death of Johannes Megapolensis in 1670, and the dedication of the new Garden Street Church in 1693. The distinguished Puritan divine, Cotton Mather, said that Selyns

had so nimble a faculty of putting his devout thoughts into verse that he signalized himself by the greatest frequency, perhaps, which may ever be used, of sending poems to all persons, in all places, on all occasions; and in this, as well as upon greater accounts, was a David unto the flocks of our Lord in the wilderness.[33]

One of Selyn's longest Latin poems, written in 1697, was seventy-six lines in length; it was written in praise of Cotton Mather's important work, *Magnalia Americana*, and was prefixed to some editions of this work.

Of a completely different background and training from Dominie Selyns, but just as dedicated to the ministry, was the Reverend Guiliam Bertholf.[34] Born in Holland of humble background, he came to America with his wife and three children about 1683. He settled first at Bergen, New Jersey, but soon moved to Acquackanonck (now called Passaic). Largely self-educated but having a natural talent for preaching and an overwhelming desire to serve the people in a spiritual way, he became a lay minister—first at Harlem and later at Acquackanonck and nearby Hackensack. His hearers were so impressed by his ability and dedication that they persuaded him to go to Holland at their expense to be examined and ordained as their regular pastor. This he did, but he by-passed the Classis of Amsterdam, which probably would have disapproved him, and went instead to the Classis of Walcheren to be licensed as a preacher.[35]

Upon returning in early 1694, Bertholf plunged zealously into his work as pastor of the churches at Hackensack and Acquackanonck. His ministry lasted until 1724, during which time he also occasionally preached and administered the sacraments at Raritan, Ponds, Pompton Plains, Schraalenburgh, and Second River in New Jersey and at Tappan, Tarrytown, and Staten Island in New York. After preliminary work was done by the early settlers themselves, Bertholf helped organize churches at several of these places, including Tappan (1694), Tarrytown (1697), and Raritan (1699). In other instances, such as at Pompton Plains and Schraalenburgh, he laid the groundwork for the organization of churches later, following his ministry.

Bertholf's work, as aptly stated by one writer, "was done as noiselessly as it was done faithfully."[36] Unlike ministers like Selyns and Du Bois, who lived in more populous and cosmopolitan communities, Bertholf had few occasions to mingle in higher society or to exchange repartees with the colonial governors and the like; nor was he expected to deliver deep philosophical sermons or write poetry in Latin. Nevertheless, in looking after the spiritual needs of simple farmers and small artisans and in organizing and guiding new churches, Bertholf's place in the annals of the Dutch Reformed Church is fully as significant as that of his more sophisticated colleagues.

Through forest and stream, over rugged hills and broad plains, up quiet valleys, wherever a group of Dutchmen had cleared for themselves homes in the wilderness, he went comforting the sick and troubled, baptizing children, bringing into the hard and lonely lives of the settlers the cheer of his kindly presence and longed-for news of distant relatives and friends.[37]

Until 1709, Bertholf was the only Dutch Reformed preacher in the colony of New Jersey. In view of his extensive labors there, it is no wonder that he has been called the "Itinerating Apostle of New Jersey" and the real founder of the Dutch Reformed Church there.

Bernardus Freeman, one of the few pastors of this period who was not born in Holland, was another minister who did not have a strong academic background but nevertheless made an important contribution to the colonial church. He was born in Westphalia near the Dutch border and was a tailor by trade. When Freeman appeared before the Classis of Amsterdam in 1699 with a request to be examined for the ministry, he was told that his education was insufficient. He then bypassed the Amsterdam divines and received ordination from the Classis of Lingen. Shortly after, in 1700, he was sent to America and became pastor of the church at Schenectady. Although the Classis of Amsterdam remained disconcerted over the manner in which Freeman received the appointment, his natural gifts as a preacher made him a popular minister. After five years at Schenectady, he became pastor on Long Island, where he served until becoming emeritus in 1741. He is best remembered today for his missionary work among the Indians while serving at Schenectady and his translating several religious works into the Mohawk tongue. He also had a number of sermons published in Dutch.[38]

Of course, not every Dutch Reformed minister of this period was of such a high order as Selyns, Bertholf, and Freeman. It would appear, for example, that Dominie Wilhelmus Lupardus, who served the Kings County churches on Long Island from 1695 to 1702, was not a particularly inspiring preacher. At his ordination into the ministry, the Classical examiners told him they expected "further diligence and stirring up of his gifts."[39] Since the published documents of this period make practically no mention of Lupardus, it would appear that his "gifts" never received the desired "stirring" that Classis had hoped for. Dominie Schaats of Albany also apparently lacked ability to excite and stimulate his listeners. The Labadist missionary, Jasper Danckaerts, in describing his visit to America in 1679–1680, made the following entry in his *Journal* after hearing Schaats preach on a Sunday morning:

He had a defect in the left eye, and used such strange gestures and language that I think I never in all my life have heard anything more miserable; . . . As it is not strange in these countries to have men as ministers who drink, we could imagine nothing else than that he had been drinking a little this morning. His text was, "Come unto me all ye," etc., but he was so rough that even the roughest and most godless of our sailors were astonished.[40]

There were also at least two preachers of this period who had to be relieved of their duties because of misbehavior. Michiel Zyperus, a ministerial candidate who had formerly served in the Dutch colony of Curacao, was obliged to terminate his pastoral duties at Harlem in 1664 because of bad conduct. According to Drisius, he had behaved "most shamefully... drinking, cheating and forging other peoples writings."[41] Similarly, Laurentius Van den Bosch, who had been compelled earlier to leave his Huguenot congregation at Boston for acting "haughtily," had to be suspended in 1689 from Kingston by Selyns and others because of drunkenness and unchastity.[42]

There were also ministers of the "average sort" who did their work of preaching and catechizing and visiting the sick in a routine manner without distinguishing themselves either as public-minded citizens and ardent defenders of church privileges, such as Selyns, or as evangelical ministers, like Bertholf. Dominie Casparus Van Zuuren of Long Island would probably fit into this category. Danckaerts' *Journal* describes the following interesting encounter that took place on May 9, 1680 between Van Zuuren and some of his parishioners:

> While we were sitting there Domine Van Zuuren came up, to whom the boors, or farmers called out as uncivilly and rudely as if he had been a boy. He had a chatting time with all of them....Indeed he sat prating and gossiping with the boors, who talked fouly and otherwise, not only without giving them a word of reproof, but even without speaking a word about God or spiritual matters. It was all about houses and cattle, and swine, and grain; and then he went away.[43]

To Van Zuuren belongs the dubious honor of writing the longest letters to the Classis of Amsterdam but which at the same time contained the least substance. He seems to have been a chronic complainer, and his letters of concern about his salary ran as much as ten pages in length. He also found fault with several prominent people in the colony, including Dominie Van Nieuwenhuysen of New York, the widow of the saintly Reverend Polhemus, the schoolmaster of Flatbush, the governor of New York, the judges of the courts, and the elders in his consistory.[44]

Despite his constant murmuring about his salary and his disparaging remarks about various notables in the colony, Van Zuuren did not shirk his clerical duties. As was noted above, in addition to his regular pastoral work at Flatbush, New Utrecht, Brooklyn, and Flatlands, he also preached occasionally at Bushwick and Gravesend and made periodic visits to churches elsewhere when they were without a pastor. It was undoubtedly this kind of hard work that caused his old congregations on Long Island to overlook his faults and ask him to return in 1695 and again serve as their pastor following the death of Dominie Varick, a request that Van Zuuren turned down.

The increase in membership among the older congregations and the founding of new congregations resulted in the construction of several new houses of worship during the period 1664–1714. The need for a larger church building was felt early in New York where the Church in the Fort, built in 1642, soon became too small to accommodate the expanding congregation. By 1682, its membership numbered about six hundred. It is therefore not surprising that Dominie Selyns shortly after his arrival in that year wrote the Classis of Amsterdam, "as the number of inhabitants here, together with the people coming in from the vicinity, is too great for the size of the church building, they are contemplating the building of a new church, or else of increasing the accommodations in this one by a large gallery."[45]

Rather than remodel the old structure, the decision was made to build a new one. The congregation was influenced in this decision partly because it seemed impractical to go through the expense of enlarging a building that was in a state of decay,[46] but also because the old church was no longer as conveniently located—the center of population having moved farther northward on the island. The site chosen for the new church was on Garden Street, adjacent to the orchard belonging to the widow of Dominie Samuel Drisius. Construction was started in 1691, and the church was dedicated in 1693. The cost was slightly over 64,000 guilders, a substantial sum at the time, especially because this amount does not include donated materials and donated labor. The new edifice has been described as follows:

It was an oblong square, with three sides of an octagon on the east side. In the front it had a brick steeple, on a large square foundation, so as to admit a room above the entry for a consistory room. The windows of the church were small panes of glass set in lead. The most of them had coats of arms of those who had been elders and magistrates, curiously burnt on glass by Gerard Duyckinck. Some painted coats of arms were also hung aginst the walls.[47]

Only New York could afford such an elaborate structure during this period. More typical was the church constructed at New Utrecht in 1700 at a cost of less than 7,500 guilders. It was constructed of field stone and was octagonal in shape, with a steep, eight-sided roof surmounted by a belfry. Located on the southeast corner of the old burying ground on the edge of the village, it was so situated that the road had to pass around the building, thus creating the impression that it was in the center of the road. Charlotte Bangs in her *Reminiscences of Old Utrecht* describes the interior of this quaint church as follows:

There were no pews in this queer little structure, each worshipper providing a chair. On each side of the middle aisle, near the pulpit,

Garden Street Church, built 1693. Later called the South Dutch Church.

Octagonal church at New Utrecht. From a watercolor by Benson Lossing.
(Courtesy of the New York Historical Society, New York City)

places were provided for forty-five women's chairs, while nearer the door were forty-five chairs for men. The high dignitaries of the village and town . . . were assigned an honored place, a bench being placed on the right of the pulpit. No fires were known, and in the winter women carried "warming pans" to church, placing them underfoot and at back. The pulpit was extremely high and shaped like a goblet. The minister climbed to it by way of a winding staircase.[48]

Despite its primitive appearance, this church was not torn down until 1828, one hundred twenty-eight years after it was built. It did, however, undergo some remodeling in 1774, when pews were installed.

Octagonal churches of the type built at New Utrecht was one of the most prevailing styles of Dutch Reformed architecture during the half-century after the fall of New Netherland, at least six of these having been built as well as two shaped like a hexagon.[49] They were patterned after similar churches built in Holland at about this time, such as the one at Willemstad in the province of Zeeland in 1595 and another at Leidschendam near The Hague in 1647.[50] In addition to the New Utrecht church, two other eight-sided churches were constructed on Long Island: Flatlands in 1663 and Bushwick in 1705. The latter was popularly called "The Beehive." Like most others of their type, these churches lasted for many years with few alterations. The Flatlands church was not demolished until 1794 and that at Bushwick not until 1829—in both instances to make way for more imposing edifices. The church that was built at Bergen, New Jersey, in 1680, to replace the log church of an earlier date, was also octagonal in shape, as was the house of worship constructed at Hackensack, New Jersey in 1696.[51]

VI

Expansion of the Church, 1714–1776

The Dutch Reformed Church continued to expand during the eighteenth century so that by 1776, there were nearly one hundred congregations in the colonies. This meant a threefold increase since 1714. As had been true during the half century after the fall of New Netherland to the English in 1664, this growth was due primarily to the natural increase of the Dutch Reformed population already in the colonies. This is clearly evident from the large number of baptisms found in the church records. Natural increase led not only to the growth of existing congregations but also to the founding of new churches as population pressure and soil exhaustion led many people to migrate in search of new lands.

Some of the growth also resulted from the arrival of non-Dutch immigrants who became associated with the Dutch Reformed Church. In the previous period, many of these arrivals were French Huguenots and some of them continued to appear during the eighteenth century. The largest number of non-Dutch immigrants, however, who contributed to the Church's growth after 1714 were Germans. Because most of them came from the Palatinate, a principality in the Rhine Valley, they are often referred to collectively as the Palatines, even though some came from other districts in Germany as well as from Switzerland.[1]

The Palatines left their homelands for a variety of reasons, including tyrannical princes, disgust over the perennial wars that devastated their lands, crop failures, famines, high rents, and religious persecution. Propaganda put out by shipowners and land agents, together with glowing letters of praise from relatives and friends in America, added to their desire to leave their homes and being a new life elsewhere. Most of the Palatines emigrated to Pennsylvania, but a significant number of them went to New York. It was primarily members of the latter group who were attracted to the Dutch Reformed Church.

A small body of about fifty-five German refugees arrived in New York in 1708, after a brief sojourn in England. They were given some land on the Hudson River about sixty miles above New York, where they laid out the town of Newburgh. Two years later, nearly three thousand Germans set sail in ten British ships, the largest single immigration of the colonial period. Perhaps as many as a sixth of their number died before reaching their final destination—a small tract of land on each side of the Hudson River about twenty miles above Kingston. Here they were employed by the British government in cutting down pine trees and manufacturing naval stores, such as pitch, tar, and masts. Seven small settlements were established, including three on the west bank, called West Camp, and four on the east bank, called East Camp but later known as Germantown.

Life was difficult for the refugees. Most of them were farmers and vinedressers by profession, not lumberjacks. Housing was poor and the food was far from adequate. When their subsistence was cut due to a governmental financial crisis, the lot of the refugees became particularly critical. Deceived by government officials, cheated by local landed magnates, and victimized by poor management, some of the disillusioned Germans began migrating to Rhinebeck, Kaatsbaan, Old Catskill, and elsewhere in the Hudson Valley, while others went to New York City and to Hackensack, New Jersey, or filtered down the Delaware and Susquehanna rivers into the wilderness of Pennsylvania. The largest number, however, went to the Schoharie and Mohawk valleys.

The Palatine immigrants who came to New York comprised members of both the Reformed and Lutheran churches, "with the Reformed group doubtless in the majority."[2] As Calvinists, the German Reformed and the Dutch Reformed were often attracted to one another because of similarities in church polity and doctrine. Both groups, for example, adhered to the Heidelberg Catechism. But there were other factors too that drew them together, including long and close political and economic ties between the Netherlands and the Palatinate and similarities in language. Moreover, from an early date, the Reformed Church in Holland counseled refugee Palatine churches in America, and Dutch Reformed ministers in the colonies assisted in looking after neighboring pastorless German congregations. The Dutch churches also gave material aid to their co-religionists. A report of July 7, 1713, for example, mentions the church of New York as having sent eighty bushels of corn, fifty shanks of smoked pork, and one hundred pounds of bread to a group of destitute Palatines who had migrated to the Schoharie Valley.[3]

The assimilation of the Germans into the Dutch Reformed Church was not always uniform. In areas where the Dutch were in a decided majority, the process of assimilation was often striking and plainly visible. As described by Wertenbaker, the Germans residing in these localities often "intermarried with the surrounding Dutch, worshipped at the same church, sent their children to the same school. It was in vain that they appealed for preachers and teachers who could speak both German and Dutch. Eventually they were absorbed into the Dutch population and so lost their identity."[4] This description is not applicable, of course, in all instances and, as will be explained later, was least true in the Schoharie and Mohawk valleys where large numbers of Germans resided.

Even in places where Dutch inhabitants were numerous, German-born pastors sometimes played significant roles. George Wilhelmus Mancius, for example, labored for thirty years (1732–1762) with great success in the Kingston area. His successor, Hermanus Meyer, was also of German birth. The Swiss-born John Henry Goetschius also had a successful career, serving in Queens County, Long Island from 1741 to 1748, followed by a twenty-six year pastorate at Hackensack and Schraalenburgh, New Jersey (1748–1774). Several young men studied theology under him and went on to become distinguished ministers. The German-born Peter Henry Dorsius, pastor of two Dutch Reformed congregations in Bucks County, Pennsylvania (1737–1748), became for a time an important link with the German Reformed churches of that colony.[5]

Although it was not unusual in the eighteenth century for German-born pastors to serve in areas where Dutch influence was particularly strong, such ministers were often expected to do considerable preaching in Dutch. Thus, Mancius' call to Kingston specifically stated that if he could not preach satisfactorily in Dutch within two years, the consistory would be absolved from paying him any further salary. Similarly, John Gabriel Gebhard, who was born in Germany and educated at Heidelberg and Utrecht, was instructed to improve on his Dutch following his call to Claverack and the surrounding area in 1776. Although there was a large German element among his congregations, by 1788, according to the record, he was preaching three services in Dutch to one in German and one in English.[6]

The natural increase of the colonial population and the arrival of immigrants such as the Palatines contributed to the denomination's steady growth. Between 1701 and 1737, forty-two new Dutch Reformed congregations were organized, or an average of more than one per year, making a total of sixty-seven. By 1776, this number had increased to about one hundred. New churches were established not only in the vicinity of the older settlements dating from the previous century, but they also appeared in regions being opened for settlement for the first time. Growth was particularly pronounced in the Schoharie and Mohawk valleys in New York and in northeastern and central New

Jersey. A few churches were also established in Pennsylvania and the groundwork for another was laid in far-off Kentucky.

It is impossible to describe each new congregation that was organized during the eighteenth century. This circumscription is necessary in part because of their large numbers, but also because of lack of definite information about the early history of many congregations. Records are often scanty and some Dutch Reformed churches became extinct within a short time or merged with neighboring Dutch Reformed congregations, while some became affiliated with other denominations. The presence of a mixture of Dutchmen, Germans, and others among some congregations also makes it difficult at times to ascertain their denominational affiliation. The problem is further complicated because different groups sometimes shared church buildings. The Lutherans and the Reformed among the Palatines, for example, used the same buildings for worship services at Rhinebeck from 1716 to 1729, at Kaatsbaan from 1732 to 1737, and at Stone Arabia from about 1734 to 1744. In most instances, such groups met at different hours on the sabbath, but sometimes they met together as one congregation. Finally, the situation is often confusing because the communities in which the churches were located frequently went by several different names.[7]

As was noted, some of the growth of the Dutch Reformed Church during the eighteenth century took place among the older settlements. These included two new churches organized on Manhattan Island, bringing the total there to four. Those existing before 1714 were the Garden Street Church, which replaced the old "Church in the Fort" in 1693, and the church in Harlem, which had been established in 1660 near what is now Second Avenue and 121st Street. The first of the new churches was organized in 1729 on Nassau Street. For a time thereafter, the Garden Street Church became known as the Old Dutch Church, and the one on Nassau Street was designated the New Dutch Church. These two churches had a common consistory and also shared ministers, with the pastors rotating each Sunday, marking the beginning of the Collegiate Church. In 1769, another church was organized, this one on Fulton Street. Because of its location, it became popularly known as the "North Dutch Church," while the one on Nassau Street was called the "Middle Dutch Church," and that on Garden Street, the "South Dutch Church." The North Church was organized especially for services in the English language, hence the preaching by the ministers in rotation did not take effect here until about 1800 when English replaced Dutch in the other churches.[8]

The antiquity of the New York City churches and the fame of such

North Dutch Church, dedicated in 1769.

past ministers as Megapolensis and Selyns prompted other churches and pastors to look to them for guidance. The Classis of Amsterdam, too, showed a special deference toward the ministers of New York, as is clearly evident in a communication sent October 5, 1733 to the Reverend George Mancius of Kingston, New York, a German Reformed pastor who had just become associated with the Dutch Reformed Church:

We would kindly advise you . . . to make request for [counsel and advice to] . . . the Rev. Ministers in New York, who are our confidential friends, to address yourself to them, should you need any light in ordinary cases. For they, by long experience, and an uninterrupted correspondence with the Rev. Classis of Amsterdam are thoroughly versed with former actions of Classis.[9]

The fifty-two year pastorate (1699–1751) of the venerable Gualtherus Du Bois added further to the high respect shown the New York ministers during the eighteenth century. He corresponded regularly with the Classis of Amsterdam and rendered invaluable assistance in looking after the needs of pastorless churches. Thanks to his pacific disposition, he not only succeeded in calming the factional strife still lingering in his own congregation from the old Leisler Troubles, but he also helped mediate disputes elsewhere. In view of these efforts, it is not surprising that the contemporary historian, William Smith, described the work of Dominie Du Bois as being more like that of a bishop among all the Dutch Reformed churches than that of a pastor of a single congregation.[10]

The growth of the Collegiate Church on Manhattan Island during the eighteenth century is indicated by the arrival from the Netherlands of a third minister, Johannes Ritzema, in 1744, and of a fourth, Lambertus De Ronde, in 1750. Although two of the older pastors soon died, Du Bois in 1751 and Boel in 1754, another minister, the Reverend Archibald Laidlie, was called in 1763 to take charge of English services which had just been introduced. In 1770, another pastor, the renowned John H. Livingston, was called to assist in English preaching. Thus, at the outbreak of the American Revolution, there were four Dutch Reformed ministers serving on Manhattan Island, in addition to the Reverend Martinus Schoonmaker who had been ministering to the Harlem church since 1765.

A letter written by the Reverend Laidlie in 1764, a year after his arrival, contains a good description of the religious situation in New York at this time:

The congregation among whom I labor in holy things are kind beyond expectation, and thanks be to God, I do not labor in vain. . . . Here we have people of almost all denominations except Papists. The Dutch congregation is the most numerous and the richest. The Episcopalians are next in numbers and the greatest in power, though all the magistrates are Dutch. The Presbyterians are also numerous, but poor. The Seceders have a meeting. The Lutherans, Quakers, High Dutch [i.e., Germans], Anabaptists, Moravians, etc., all have congregations, some of them pretty numerous.[11]

Like Manhattan Island, Long Island too had a strong Dutch Reformed presence dating from the New Netherland period. By 1714, seven churches had been organized there, including Flatbush, Flatlands, Bushwick, Gravesend, Brooklyn, New Utrecht, and Jamaica. Unfortunately, during the next one hundred years only three new churches were established: Newtown in 1731, and Success and Oyster Bay in 1732. These three new churches, together with Jamaica, all of which were located in what was then Queens County, shared a common ministry until 1802, just as did their sister churches in Kings County, with each parish in the system paying a fixed proportion of the ministerial salaries.

The chronic internal strife among the Long Island churches hampered their growth.[12] The eighteenth century opened with a long, drawn-out quarrel between two factions in Kings County, each led by one of the collegiate preachers, Vincentius Antonides and Bernardus Freeman. Although a reconciliation was worked out between them, disputes broke out anew under their successors, the reverends Ulpianus Van Sinderen and Johannes Arondeus. The latter was deposed in 1752, but still managed to preach for a year or two before returning to Holland. The arrival of the petulant Johannes Rubel in 1759 as a colleague of Van Sinderen did little to calm the situation. His strong Tory feelings, together with reports about mistreating his wife and appearing in a drunken condition on the pulpit, placed him at odds with many of his parishioners. Questions about the validity of the ordination of John Henry Goetschius, pastor from 1741 to 1748 of the four churches in Queens County, also disturbed the tranquility of the churches on that part of Long Island. His successor, Thomas Romeyn, though a quiet and prudent man, also found his position untenable and finally left in 1760 to serve churches in New Jersey. The internal strife among the Long Island churches and the consequent lack of growth prompted the distinguished Reverend Jacob Brodhead to declare in a memorial sermon delivered in Brooklyn in 1851 that the events of the eighteenth century were "painful remembrances."[13] By contrast, the nineteenth century saw considerable growth, so that there were forty-nine Reformed churches on Long Island by 1900.

On nearby Staten Island, too, there was only limited growth. The so-called North Side Church at Port Richmond, organized in 1680, continued to exist, and about 1714 several scattered organizations, including the churches known as Fresh Kills (organized in 1663 primarily for the French Reformed) and South Side or Stony Brook (organized in 1665 primarily for the Waldenses) were joined together to form a single church at Richmond. Until the arrival of the Reverend Cornelius Van Santvoord from the Netherlands in 1718, the Staten Island churches were served primarily by local *voorlezers* and by visiting preachers from New York, Long Island, and New Jersey. Van Santvoord left for Schenectady in 1742 and for the next fifteen years Staten Island was again without a resident pastor, except for the brief pastorate in 1751 of Peter De Wint who was deposed after a few months because of forged credentials. Beginning in 1757 and lasting until 1789, the Staten Island churches shared a minister, the Reverend William Jackson, with the church at Bergen, New Jersey.

The Kingston congregation, which also dates from the New Netherland period, exhibited significant growth during the eighteenth century. For example, in 1667, when the church was rebuilt following an Indian raid, the congregation consisted of one hundred eighty members; by 1753, when a more substantial building of stone was constructed, the congregation had grown to fourteen hundred members and was served by two pastors.[14] The Kingston church made its

Church at Kingston. Built 1679, improved 1721, rebuilt 1752, burned by the British 1777. (Courtesy of Deweese W. DeWitt)

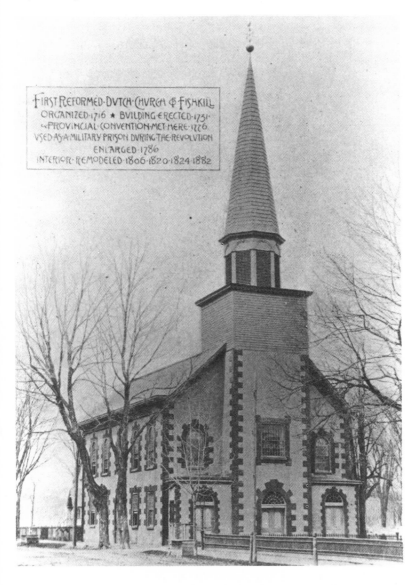

First Reformed·Dutch·Church ⊕ Fishkill
Organized·1716 ★ Building·Erected·1731·
«·Provincial·Convention·met·here·1776
Used·as·a·military·prison·during·the·revolution
Enlarged·1786
Interior·Remodeled·1806·1820·1824·1882

Church at Fishkill, New York. Erected 1731, enlarged 1786. (Courtesy of Sage Library, New Brunswick Seminary)

greatest contribution, however, by serving as the mother church of several new congregations in the area. From an early date, her ministers visited surrounding communities to preach the gospel, administer the sacraments, and perform marriages. When the number of people attending these preaching stations became sufficiently large, steps were taken to organize them into congregations. Sometimes this did not occur until after an interval of many years. Thus, although Dutch preachers from Kingston visited Marbletown as early as 1679, a church was not organized there until 1737.

The Reverend Peter Vas, pastor at Kingston from 1710 to 1756, was particularly helpful in organizing new churches, including Poughkeepsie (1716), Fishkill (1716), Rhinebeck Flats (1731), Montgomery (1732), Shawangunk (1737), Marbletown (1737), Warwarsing (1745), and New Hurley (1770). Poughkeepsie and Fishkill did not acquire their own pastor until 1731, after which they too assisted in establishing and supplying new churches, including Hopewell in 1757 and New Hackensack in 1758.

In view of Kingston's serving as an overseer of so many daughter churches, it is not surprising that an associate pastor was soon called to assist Dominie Vas. His name was George Wilhelmus Mancius and he arrived in 1732. The choice was an excellent one. An accomplished

George Wilhelmus Mancius. (Courtesy of Deweese W. DeWitt)

Kaatsbaan Church, built 1732. (Courtesy of Deweese W. DeWitt)

linguist, he was able to preach in Dutch, German, French, and English. His knowledge of German was particularly beneficial because of the many Palatines who had settled in the Kingston area during the early eighteenth century. Congregations in this region which had large German memberships but became associated with the Dutch Reformed Church included Kaatsbaan (1710), Rhinebeck (1715), and Germantown (1728).

A sharing of duties was worked out between the two Kingston pastors enabling Vas, when he was not in charge of the services at Kingston, to preach to the outlying communities that were primarily Dutch, and permitting Mancius, when not needed at Kingston, to visit neighboring churches that were heavily German. Mancius also served as an itinerant preacher in the Minisink Valley of New Jersey, where he assisted in founding several new churches. Considering the territorial scope of his ministry, it is not surprising that one authority has stated that, "No one in colonial days extended the Reformed Church more persistently than he."[15]

The church at Albany, the second Dutch Reformed church to be organized in North America, also grew during the eighteenth century. Its first church building, erected in 1643, was a small, plain structure of wood. In 1656, just thirteen years later, it gave way to a more substan-

Albany Church, completed 1715. (Courtesy of Sage Library, New Brunswick Seminary)

tial edifice, which in turn was replaced by a larger house of worship in 1715. The new church, which served the congregation until 1799, was an imposing structure of stone with a steep, pyramidal roof and a belfry surmounted by a weathercock. The oaken pulpit which came from Holland in 1656 was retained for use in the new church. In 1797, less than a generation after the Revolution, an even larger house of worship had to be built for the Albany congregation, and in 1815, a second church was organized, followed by a third in 1834.

In the same manner that Kingston became the mother church to several new congregations in the mid-Hudson Valley area, so too Albany helped supervise new churches farther up the Hudson. Kinderhook, for example, had been a mission station of the Albany church for more than thirty years before it was organized in 1712. A listing of some of the services that Albany performed for Kinderhook illustrates the kind of relationship that existed between a mother church and a mission station. These services included the selection of *voorlezers*, assistance in the construction of its first house of worship, contributing to the building's upkeep, sending sacramental wine when needed, and of course, occasional visits by the preacher. Despite its dependence on Albany, the Kinderhook congregation did what it could on its own to ease the financial burdens she imposed on Albany, as is indicated by her collecting one hundred fourteen guilders in 1684 for the mother church.[16]

Even after the Kinderhook congregation was formally organized in 1712, it remained dependent on the Albany preachers until it obtained a pastor of its own in 1727. An agreement signed between the two consistories on January 21, 1720, in behalf of the Albany pastor, Peter Van Driessen, sheds light on the type of work that a visiting pastor did for such churches. By this accord, the signatories agreed that

the Consistory of Kinderhook shall pay to Domine Petrus Van Driessen aforesaid, or his order at Albany, the sum of four pounds and four shillings within two months from today, which is for services performed last January, to wit: visits to the homes here, three sermons, administration of the Lord's Supper and baptism, besides catechism.[17]

Other churches that the Albany ministers looked after (sometimes assisted by neighboring pastors) and the dates for their organization, included Schaghticoke (1707), Claverack (1716), Schodack (1756), Bethlehem (1763), Beaverdam (1765), Helderberg (1767), Hillsdale (1769), and Ghent (1775). In addition, ministers from Albany assisted in looking after several preaching stations on Livingston Manor, some of which later became formally organized churches, including Livingston Manor (1700), Linlithgo (1722), Ancram, also called Gallatin (1746), and West Copake (1758). Albany also gave financial assistance to churches farther away. For example, a memorandum by the churches of Poughkeepsie and Fishkill dated April 2, 1734, mentions "money of the Albany people given to us for our Minister's coming from holand."[18] As was true of several churches in the Kingston area, some of the new churches in the Hudson Valley below Albany had sizeable German memberships, including Claverack, West Copake, Hillsdale, and Ghent.

The Schenectady church, founded about 1680, also exhibited considerable growth during the eighteenth century. It is therefore not surprising that the new church built there in 1732 was nearly the same size as the Middle Dutch Church constructed at New York at about the same time. Dominie Gualtherus Du Bois, senior pastor at New York, after having visited Schenectady in early 1739 as pulpit supply minister, remarked that the inhabitants there were not only "very civilized people" but also "very desirous after God's word." According to Du Bois, these attributes, together with the size of the congregation, made the pastorate there "one of the most notable and advantageous in these parts."[19] The Schenectady church received its own charter in 1734, giving it corporate powers to manage its own property. This was highly desirable because of the large amount of real estate it owned—the equivalent of twelve square miles by 1740.[20] In addition to looking after the religious needs of the local community, the Schenectady church, through financial aid and ministerial supply, also became the mother church of several other congregations in the area.

Church growth in the Hudson and Mohawk valleys was due in no small part to a high birth rate. As an example, one can cite the large number of baptisms recorded during the eighteenth century by the Schenectady ministers. Thus, during the pastorate of the Reverend Thomas Brouwer (1714–1728), 505 baptisms were recorded, while under his successor, Reinhardt Erickzon (1728–1736), 350 baptisms were registered. But the record was set by Dominie Barent Vrooman who during his twenty-nine year pastorate (1754–1783) baptized 3,521 children.[21]

The high quality of many of the ministers who served among the Hudson Valley churches during the eighteenth century also contributed to their growth. The success achieved by the reverends Vas and Mancius at Kingston has already been noted. Another distinguished preacher at Kingston was Hermanus Meyer, who arrived in 1763 as a replacement for Mancius who died the previous year. Meyer was undoubtedly called because his knowledge of German (he was born in Germany but educated at the University of Groningen) would enable him to preach to the numerous Germans residing in the Kingston area—as Mancius had been doing for thirty years. Another distinguished minister of this area was Isaac Rysdyck, pastor at nearby Poughkeepsie and Fishkill from 1765 to 1789. A graduate of the University of Groningen, he became one of the most learned Dutch Reformed ministers of his day. He was also accomplished in ancient languages and helped found a classical school at Fishkill.

Albany and Schenectady were also singularly blessed with having several outstanding preachers. These included the reverends Cornelius Van Schie, Theodorus Frelinghuysen, and Eilardus Westerlo, whose combined ministry at Albany covered fifty-seven years, and the reverends Reinhardt Erickzon, Cornelius Van Santvoord, and Barent Vrooman, whose pastorates at Schenectady covered the period from

1728 to 1783. All but one of these men, Frelinghuysen, had studied at universities in the Netherlands. Not only were they eloquent preachers, but Westerlo and Van Santvoord were also men of sound scholarly attainments. Ezra Stiles, president of Yale College, for example, once remarked that Westerlo "wrote Latin in greater purity than any man he had ever known."[22] Similarly, Van Santvoord, in addition to publishing a stirring defense of the evangelistic preaching of Theodorus Jacobus Frelinghuysen, distinguished himself with his translation of some of the Latin works of his former teacher at Leiden, the renowned Professor Johannes à Marck. The translation was published in Holland along with copious notes by Van Santvoord and was widely acclaimed.

Dutchmen and others continued to push up the Hudson River and its tributaries during the eighteenth century, resulting in the founding of more Dutch Reformed churches. Peter Kalm, a Swedish traveler and an acute observer of the American scene, reported in 1749 that "the whole region about the Hudson River above Albany is inhabited by the Dutch; this is true of Saratoga as well as other places."[23] A Dutch Reformed Church was established at Saratoga, later called Schuylerville, in 1770 and at Waterford in 1771. There was also heavy migration westward from Schenectady up the Mohawk River, a tributary of the Hudson, and along the Schoharie River, a tributary of the Mohawk. A letter of July 27, 1787 states that "the whole [Mohawk] river from Schenectady to Herkimer and the Flats is Dutch and German."[24]

The presence in this area of Germans, many of whom became associated with the Dutch Reformed Church, requires a brief explanation. As was noted in the early part of this chapter many of the Palatine refugees who settled on the lower Hudson began migrating because of unsatisfactory living conditions. In 1712 and 1713, more than a hundred of these families settled in the fertile Schoharie Valley, and after 1722 large numbers moved into the Mohawk Valley beyond Fort Hunter. In the Schoharie Valley, the towns of Schoharie and Middleburgh emerged and became heavily German, as did Herkimer, German Flats, St. Johnsville, and Manheim in the Mohawk Valley.[25]

Not long after the appearance of the Palatines, Dutch farmers also began moving farther westward up the Mohawk Valley and into the Schoharie Valley. As was true in the Hudson Valley, several factors helped draw the German Reformed and Dutch Reformed together. Churches in the Schoharie Valley that were established as Dutch Reformed or eventually became so, with the dates for their organization, include Schoharie (ca. 1730); Middleburgh (1732); Beaverdam (1765);

and Sharon Springs (1771). In the Mohawk Valley, Dutch Reformed churches with sizeable German memberships (sometimes a majority) included Herkimer (1723); Stone Arabia (ca. 1725); German Flats, also called Fort Herkimer (1725); Canajoharie (1750); Niskayuna (1750); Caughnawaga, later called Fonda (1758); Palatine, later called St. Johnsville (1770); and Manheim (1770).

Although in some instances, the Germans were simply overwhelmed by larger numbers of Dutchmen, this was less true here than in the Hudson Valley. The church at Herkimer, for example, retained the German language until well into the nineteenth century, and among some churches, records were kept alternately in Dutch or German, depending on which language the clerk knew best. Occasionally, as in the case of the church at Schoharie in 1762, pastoral calls sent to the Netherlands asked for ministers who were proficient in both "High and Nether Dutch." A few congregations, including those at St. Johnsville and Manheim, did not become officially associated with the Dutch Reformed Church until many years after they were organized. [26]

Stone church constructed at Caughnawaga, later called Fonda. (From Fort Herkimer Church: A Historic Structure Report)

The churches at first were little more than preaching stations supplied by pastors who had been with the Palatines since the beginning of their migrations. Dutch Reformed ministers from Schenectady, Albany, and elsewhere also occasionally visited the area. As was true with the new churches in the Hudson Valley, these churches too sometimes had to wait many years before obtaining their own pastors. Niskayuna, for example, waited forty years, as did Manheim. Sharing ministers was also common. Thus, Herkimer and German Flats, on opposite sides of the river, had a common ministry for almost a century. When a community acquired a resident pastor, he in turn looked after neighboring churches. Thus, Johannes Schuyler, pastor at Schoharie from 1736 to 1755, visited several churches in the vicinity on an itinerant basis. So too did Abraham Rosencrantz, whose residence was usually at Canajoharie but who served as a kind of missionary pastor to most of the white population in the western Mohawk Valley from 1752 to 1796, except for a brief sojourn in New York.

As might be expected because of their location along the outer fringe of the frontier, the first church buildings in the Schoharie and Mohawk valleys were frequently log structures. Because of small memberships and no settled ministry, some of them were built several years before a congregation was formally organized. Some of the log structures were later replaced by fortress-like churches with thick stone walls, such as those at Stone Arabia, German Flats, and Fonda, which also served as places of refuge in the event of attacks from hostile forces. Because some of these communities had large Lutheran populations, places of worship were sometimes shared by Calvinist and Lutheran inhabitants.

Although the region could not have held much attraction for many ministers, considering its location on the border of the white man's civilization and the itinerant nature of the preaching duties, several well-trained ministers served there. Reinhardt Erickzon, for example, founder of the Reformed church at Schoharie, was educated at the University of Groningen. George Michael Weiss, pastor at Schoharie from 1731 to 1732 and later at German Flats from 1736 to 1742, studied at Heidelberg University. Abraham Rosencrantz, who served several churches in the Mohawk region for nearly a half century, was also born and educated in Germany. He has been described by Corwin as "a man of much learning" and "the foremost divine west of Schenectady."[27]

The church in New Jersey also made steady progress during the eighteenth century, increasing by almost twenty congregations between 1714 and the end of the colonial period. This expansion came about in part because of the continued arrival of new settlers from

Dutch Reformed communities in the Hudson Valley and on Long Island and because of a high birth rate. For example, during the brief three-year pastorate of Reinhardt Erickzon at Hackensack (1725–1728), sixty-six new members were added. Similarly, the Reverend Henricus Coens, during his nine-year pastorate (1726–1735) at Acquackanonck, Ponds, and Pompton Plains, received one hundred thirty-five new communicant members and baptized two hundred twenty-two children. Reverend Joseph Morgan topped this by baptizing nearly six hundred children during his pastorate at Freehold and Middletown between 1709 and 1731.[28]

The expansion of the church in New Jersey must also be attributed to the presence of several distinguished and zealous pastors during the eighteenth century. One of the most capable, albeit controversial, of these ministers was the Reverend Theodorus Jacobus Frelinghuysen, pastor of several churches in the Raritan Valley from 1720 to 1747. A worthy successor to the itinerant preacher Guiliam Bertholf, Frelinghuysen was one of the precursors of the Great Awakening, which will be discussed later. Other New Jersey preachers of note included Johannes Leydt, who served churches in the New Brunswick area for thirty-five years from 1748 to 1783, and Jacob Rutsen Hardenbergh, who labored in central New Jersey from 1758 to 1781. Leydt also served as one of the first trustees of Queens College, while Hardenbergh became the first president of that institution. The renowned Dirck Romeyn, who later helped establish what became Union College at Schenectady, also served in New Jersey for a time—he was pastor at Hackensack and Schraalenburgh from 1775 to 1784. Mention should also be made of Benjamin Du Bois, whose sixty-three year ministry from 1764 to 1827 in one place (at Freehold and Middletown) must be close to some kind of a record.

Church growth during the eighteenth century was especially evident in the Hackensack, Passaic, and Raritan valleys.[29] Here, as in the Hudson Valley, the settlers generally retained the customs of their forefathers, which for many meant a continuation of the old Dutch ways, including allegiance to the Dutch Reformed Church. Thus, in commenting on the inhabitants of the Hackensack Valley on the eve of the American Revolution, Adrian Leiby states that they

spoke Jersey Dutch most of the time and English when they had to, just as many New Yorkers did. They listened to Dutch sermons on Sunday and gave their children Dutch names, and the women and children wore clothes having more than a hint of Holland in their style. Certainly no one could have confused the Dutch community in and around Hackensack with English settlements in middle Jersey or the Pennsylvania German settlements in the neighboring province to the south.[30]

The church at Hackensack, organized in 1686, became the mother church to several new congregations organized in that area, including Schraalenburgh (1724); Paramus, now Ridgewood (1725); and English Neighborhood, now Ridgefield (1770). Similarly, Acquackanonck, later called Passaic, where a church was organized in 1693, helped organize several churches in the Passaic Valley, including Fairfield (1720); Pompton Plains (1736); Totowa, now Paterson (1755); and Montville (1756). A significant increase in the denomination was also noted in the Raritan Valley. In addition to the three churches existing there before 1714, new congregations were organized at New Brunswick (1717); North Branch, now Readington (1719); Harlingen (1727); Lebanon (1740); Neshanic (1752); Bedminster (1758); and Hillsborough, now Millstone (1766).

The first church buildings erected in these river valleys resembled the early houses of worship built under frontier conditions elsewhere in that they followed no particular architectural style and were constructed of whatever materials were close at hand. Thus, the Hackensack church, built in 1696, was octagonal in shape, while that at nearby Schraalenburgh, built in 1725, was square. Similarly, the Hackensack church was constructed of sandstone, but that at Ponds was made of logs. Although masons and carpenters often assisted in the construction of these churches, volunteer laborers drawn from among the congregations performed most of the work. The first churches were intended to be primarily functional, with few critical tastes to consider regarding their general appearance. The following description of the church erected at Bedminster about 1758 would no doubt apply to most other early houses of worship built in New Jersey during this period:

> When completed, a more bare or a more unimaginative structure could hardly have been conceived. Prosaic to a degree, and entirely wanting in decorative details, it was wholly without architectural results save that it enclosed space and shut off the weather; in other words, it was a meeting-house, nothing more.[31]

As was true of the newly organized churches in New York, those in the Hackensack, Passaic, and Raritan valleys of New Jersey frequently shared ministers or were for many years little more than preaching stations served by a minister from a larger congregation in the vicinity.

Thus, Totowa and Montville, organized in 1755 and 1756 respectively, shared ministers throughout the eighteenth century, and the Ponds church, organized in 1710, never had a minister of its own until 1845. Similarly, despite the prevalance of Netherlandish customs, non-Dutch elements in the population of New Jersey sometimes played an important role of the development of these churches. Thus the Hackensack congregation had a significant French Reformed element, and the churches at Lebanon and Hardwick were initially founded by Germans and Swiss and, strictly speaking, did not become Dutch Reformed until the early part of the nineteenth century.[32]

Some denominational growth can also be noted in Monmouth County during this period. Dutch settlers from Long Island began locating here during the latter part of the seventeenth century, and in 1699, a Dutch Reformed congregation was organized there for the communities of Freehold and Middletown, which were about an hour and a half's journey apart. Churches were eventually built at each of these settlements, but their members were considered as a single congregation with a common consistory until 1825. Freehold later became known as the Marlboro church, while the name Middletown was replaced by Holmdel. From an early date, the two churches were often referred to collectively as the "Church on the Navesink." The churches were served by visiting pastors from Long Island, including Lupardus, Antonides, and Freeman, until 1709, when a Presbyterian, the Reverend Joseph Morgan, who had some proficiency in Dutch, was installed as pastor. This was done with the approval of the Long Island ministers and with the understanding that Morgan would devote three-fourths of his time to looking after the Dutch churches and one fourth to a local Scottish Presbyterian church.

Despite his twenty-two years of service among the Dutch Reformed people, Morgan never mastered the Dutch language. This was a constant source of anxiety to both him and his listeners. The latter were especially concerned because the youth were not being taught "the Catechism in Dutch."[33] Therefore, when Morgan asked to be released from his agreement in order to devote more time to the Presbyterians, the request was granted. The congregation thereupon, wanting to resemble "the other Dutch Churches in this country," petitioned the mother church in Holland for a minister. The call stipulated that the candidate be "a capable person, not over thirty-five years of age, whether married or unmarried, orthodox according to the teachings of our Reformed Church, being learned and of good deportment in life, and prudent in his intercourse."[34] In response to this call, Dominie

Gerardus Haeghoort arrived in 1731 to take charge of the Monmouth churches. By 1735, when he left to become pastor at Second River, New Jersey, the congregation had expanded to one hundred nineteen members, of whom sixty-seven worshipped at Freehold and fifty-two at Middletown.[35] Although no new churches were organized here during the eighteenth century, the Monmouth congregation became the mother church to seven new congregations during the nineteenth century.

Several churches were also organized at this time in the upper Delaware Valley in what was known as the Minisink region, near the juncture of New Jersey and Pennsylvania. Dutch settlers had located there during the New Netherland period to engage in open pit copper mining and were later joined by farmers. Itinerant ministers occasionally traversed the region by horseback from an early date, but it was the Reverend George Wilhelm Mancius of Kingston who did this on a regular basis. He established four preaching stations along a fifty-mile stretch of the valley at Minisink, Mahackemack, Walpack, and Smithfield and began visiting them twice a year, usually in May and November. According to one report, he baptized five hundred ten children during his visits between 1736 and 1741.[36] In 1737, churches were organized at these four communities, and in 1741 the Reverend Johannes Casparus Fryenmoet was installed as their first pastor. During his fifteen year pastorate here, he officiated at five hundred four baptisms and received one hundred ten new members.[37] Smithfield, located on the Pennsylvania side of the Delaware, later became Presbyterian, but the other three churches remained Dutch Reformed. Mahackemack and Minisink eventually became known as the Port Jervis and Montague Reformed churches respectively. Still later, Port Jervis was called the Reformed Church of Deerpark.

A few Dutch Reformed churches were also organized in Pennsylvania during the eighteenth century. Dutchmen, mostly from Long Island and Staten Island but perhaps also from the older Dutch settlements on the Lower Delaware and from the Minisink region, began settling in Bucks County about 1690. This migration increased after 1700 and continued for about another twenty-five years. The first Dutch Reformed congregation was organized in 1710, with Paulus Van Vlecq as pastor. Because the congregation was spread over a wide expanse of territory, two houses of worship were erected, one in Southampton and the other in Northampton township. They were sometimes referred to collectively as the Neshaminy congregation because of their nearness to Neshaminy Creek.[38] Van Vlecq also looked after several other congregations, but their ecclesiastical affiliation is unclear because they were made up of Dutch Reformed, German Reformed, and Presbyterian elements.

For a time after Van Vlecq left in 1713, the Neshaminy congregation journeyed to nearby Abington to worship with the Scottish Presbyterians. In 1730, the congregation was reorganized and a new consistory was installed with the assistance of the Reverend Cornelius Van Santvoord of Staten Island. Calls sent to Holland for a pastor were unsuccessful. The congregation therefore finally sent money to the Netherlands to pay for the theological studies of a ministerial candidate, Peter Henry Dorsius, and for his passage to America. He arrived in 1737. It is interesting to note that as late as 1776, when the Reverend William Schenck, a Presbyterian, was called from Allentown, New Jersey, by the Neshaminy congregation, it was stipulated that he would be permitted to preach in English during his first year but was expected to learn Dutch so that in the second year he could preach at least half the time in that language. The call sent to the Reverend Peter Stryker in 1778 was the first to be written in English.[39]

Bucks County was not the only region in Pennsylvania that attracted Dutchmen from other parts of the American colonies. About 1765, a considerable number of Dutch families, mostly from Bergen and Somerset counties in New Jersey, began settling farther to the south in York and Adams counties. Despite the presence of Presbyterian meeting houses in this area, the newcomers were determined to have their own church. By 1768, Dutch Reformed congregations were established at Conewago in York County, and at nearby Hanover in Adams County. The combined membership of the two churches soon totaled one hundred fifty families, most of whom belonged to the Conewago congregation.[40]

The land in southern Pennsylvania was of rather poor quality for farming. Consequently, news about cheap, fertile land elsewhere caused most of them to leave the region beginning about 1781. Departures increased rapidly after 1793, with the result that the two Dutch Reformed churches were soon so depleted that it became difficult to hold services. In 1817, when only five Dutch Reformed families remained, the congregations dissolved and the members joined the Presbyterian church of nearby Hunterstown.[41]

Some of the Dutchmen from York and Adams counties left for Cayuga County in central New York where, together with Dutch settlers who arrived from New Jersey and other parts of New York, they formed the nuclei for several Dutch communities. The most important of the latter was Owasco, where a Dutch Reformed church was organized in 1796. Many of the Dutch pioneers in southern Pennsylvania, however, went to Kentucky, where most of them settled on the upper Salt River near the present town of Harrodsburg in Mercer County. A church was soon built which, because of its peculiar construction, became known as "the Mud House Church", the first Dutch Reformed church to be built west of the Allegheny Mountains. After holding Dutch Reformed services for a time with the assistance of laymen, they addressed a petition to General Synod in 1795 asking for a pastor who could preach in Dutch and English. A resident pastor did not arrive until 1804. In the meantime, some of the settlers began pushing farther, west. When the pastor left in 1816, the church struggled on its own for a time before finally merging with a local Presbyterian congregation.[42]

VII

The Ministry during the Eighteenth Century

The growth of the Dutch Reformed Church during the eighteenth century and a discussion of its problems cannot be dissociated from the role played by those persons most responsible for its proper functioning, namely, the ministers. It was they who stood before the assembled congregations every Sunday to preach the gospel message, who entreated their listeners to give generously for the financial support of the churches, who catechized the children in the fundamentals of the Reformed faith, who visited and comforted the people in times of sickness and bereavement, and who prayed over them at the time of their death. These were also the persons whose advice was sought on the organization of new congregations and who supervised and nurtured new churches, sometimes for many years and at great inconvenience to themselves, until they were ready to call and support ministers of their own.

What were the ministers of the eighteenth century like and did they differ in fundamental ways from those of the previous period? How well were they trained and what was the nature of their training? Were any ministers unworthy of the offices bestowed upon them? And what about ministerial salaries and sources of income for the churches? These are some of the questions this chapter will try to answer.

The ministers of the eighteenth century were of mixed backgrounds and training. Of the approximately seventy-five new Dutch Reformed ministers who were installed in the American colonies between 1714 and 1776, about forty-five came directly from Europe and thirty grew up in America. Of the latter, about twenty received their education in the colonies, where they also were examined and ordained. The remaining ten went to Holland for ordination, and several of them also took at least part of their theological training there.

Most of the ministers who came directly from Europe received their training in the Netherlands, usually at the universities of Leiden or Groningen, although a few studied at Utrecht and some of the German pastors studied at Heidelberg. To enter one of these schools, a student had to have the necessary preparation. This usually began by attending a vernacular school until about the age of ten or twelve, where the basic studies revolved around the three r's, liberally sprinkled with religious instruction. Following this, the student was ready for entering a classical school, so-called because most of his time was devoted to the study of Latin, with the remainder applied primarily to rhetoric, logic, penmanship, and, of course, religion. During the latter part of his stay at the classical school, the student was also given some instruction in Greek.

After leaving the Latin school at about age sixteen or slightly older, the student was ready to enroll in one of the universities for the study of theology. Here he was exposed to several specialized subjects, including textual or exegetical theology (which included the study of Greek and Hebrew), systematic or dogmatic theology, practical theology (including church polity and exercises in declamation and preaching), and church history. These studies lasted about four or five years. The student thus found himself ready at about age twenty-two to begin his ministerial career.[1]

Two examinations were required before a person became a fullfledged minister of the gospel. To be admitted to the first examination, called the preparatory examination, the candidate had to submit various testimonials regarding his character and training. If these were satisfactory, he was asked to appear before a classical committee to preach on a text that had been assigned earlier and be examined on his knowledge of theology and the ancient languages. Thus, Gualtherus Du Bois, the distinguished pastor of New York City from 1699 to 1751, after having his credentials examined by the Classis of Amsterdam on October 4, 1694, was told to appear before that body again on the first Monday in April 1695, to preach on Romans 3:25. Having delivered a satisfactory sermon on that day, he was further examined "in the principal articles of Sacred Theology" as well as in Greek and Hebrew. In all these matters according to the minutes of the Classis, he showed himself well-prepared "not only in giving an account of the sound Word, which is according to doctrine, but also in the removing and solving of the subterfuges and objections of those who are outside our circle." As a consequence, he was admitted unanimously to "public preaching," after he had signed the Formulae of Concord.[2] The latter included the Thirty-seven Articles, the Heidelberg Catechism, and the Canons of Dort. Candidates at this stage also had to agree to accept without change the forms for the sacraments of Baptism and Lord's Supper.

A candidate who was admitted to "public preaching" after passing

Gualtherus Du Bois.

the preparatory examination was referred to as a proponent and was licensed *proponere*, that is, he was permitted "to make propositions from the pulpit, or preach, but not to administer the sacraments."[3] To become ordained and thereby enjoy the full powers of a minister, the proponent had to undergo a second examination, called the peremptory examination, which took place after he had received a call from a congregation. The second examination was similar to the first, as illustrated by the minutes of the Classis of Amsterdam for May 4, 1761, describing the peremptory examination of John Martin Van Harlingen, who afterwards served as pastor at Millstone, New Jersey from 1762 to 1795:

In the presence of the High Rev. Deputatus Synodi, E. Ph. G. van Essen, minister in this city [of Amsterdam], he [i.e., Van Harlingen] preached a sermon on the assigned text 1 Cor. 2: 2, "For I determined not to know anything among you, save Jesus Christ, and him crucified." He was further examined by the Examiner, William van der Zouw, in Hebrew on Psalm 93, and in Greek, on 1 Cor. 2; and subsequently on the most important points of our Sacred Theology. In all of this he gave so much satisfaction to the Assembly, that with much satisfaction . . . and a unanimous vote he was adjudged fit for the ministry of the Gospel.[4]

The amount of time that elapsed between the two examinations varied. In the case of Du Bois, for example, there was an interval of four years between his preparatory examination on April 5, 1695, and the peremptory examination of June 2, 1699, which came immediately following his call to New York. On the other hand, Van Harlingen's examinations progressed very rapidly: the Classis of Amsterdam reviewed his testimonials on January 13, 1761; examined him preparatorily a few months later on April 6; and gave him his final examination the following month on May 4.[5]

As was noted, approximately one-third of the seventy-five new Dutch Reformed ministers who were installed between 1714 and 1776 received their theological training in the colonies, primarily through self-study and private tutoring. This procedure was not unique in the colonies, having been practiced already at an early date among the Congregationalists and a few other religious groups. Moreover, training for the two other "learned" professions in the colonies—law and medicine—was generally carried on in a similar manner, namely, in the offices of practicing lawyers and practicing physicians. The mother church in Holland itself had occasionally ordained persons who had no university training, particularly after the Reformation when there was a shortage of pastors. The Church Order drawn up by the great Synod of Dort in 1618-1619, approved the continuation of this procedure so long as certain safeguards were taken. These included requirements that a ministerial candidate follow a prescribed course of study in lieu of attending a university and that his examination and ordination take place before a committee approved by a classis.

Despite these precedents in the Netherlands, private tutoring for the ministry was never too popular in the colonies before about 1740. This came about in part because of the requirement that a ministerial candidate had to be examined by a committee approved by a classis. For the colonists, this meant the Classis of Amsterdam and only rarely did it permit such a committee to be organized in the colonies; instead, the candidates usually had to journey to Holland for examination and ordination. As will be explained in a following chapter, the mother church's adherence to this practice helped bring on a schism among the colonial churches that finally led to their ecclesiastical separation from the Netherlands. No doubt more young men would have undertaken private study for the ministry (especially in view of the chronic shortage of pastors) if they could have been spared the expense and hazards of an ocean voyage.

There was another reason, too, why private tutoring for young men for the ministry was uncommon before about 1740, namely, the strong tradition existing among Dutch Reformed circles for a learned ministry. Although it is true that numerous complaints were sent by the colonial churches to the Classis of Amsterdam concerning the latter's unwillingness to permit more examinations and ordinations in the colonies, there was always an element, even among the colonial ministers themselves, who opposed any relaxation of this regulation. The reason for this attitude is clearly evident in a letter of October 17, 1754 sent to the Classis by the consistory of New York:

Indeed, we admit that it would be desirable, if there were here as in the Fatherland, the proper means of instruction in certain branches of study. But while these facilities are still lacking, we think, to make ministers here would tend to tarnish the Gospel service: as when someone, taught for two or three years by some minister or other, and not having become very familiar with the languages and sciences, and not having gained much systematic knowledge of the true doctrines of the Faith, should, like some rustic, ascend the pulpit, boldly come forward with a borrowed sermon, deliver it all unabashed, *de verbo ad verbum*, before respectable congregations, thinking that he has performed a famous thing... and then, if he adds anything of his own, spoiling the entire effort not a little.[6]

To guard against the possibility that young men examined in America would be less qualified than those trained in Europe, the examination procedure that was followed in the colonies (when permission for such examinations was granted) was patterned after that of Holland. Thus, in discussing this procedure at a meeting of ministers in New York in September 1747, it was resolved that "no student shall undergo the preparatory examination except in a regular, systematic manner, not only upon theology, but also upon the original languages of the Bible, as is commonly done in the Rev. Classis of the Netherlands".[7] The extent to which examinations in the colonies resembled those in Holland is clearly shown in the minutes of a meeting held in New York on September 21, 1752, describing the final examination of David Marinus:

The *Examinatores*, proceeding to the examination of the candidate, David Marinus, called at Acquackanonck, first required him to ascend the pulpit and preach from 1 Cor. xii., 3. He was then examined in Hebrew and Greek and in Divinity, in which he gave so much satisfaction that the Assembly found no difficulty in admitting him to the office of the ministry, and whatever belongs thereto. Thereupon he signed the Formulas of Unity, and Dom. Goetschius was appointed to ordain him in his holy office, with Dom. Curtenius by the laying on of hands.[8]

Colonial pastors undertook the task of private tutoring on their own initiative and in the spirit of Christian service; it was not done as a means for increasing their income, although some financial remuneration was involved. Notwithstanding the small number of Dutch Reformed pastors who received their theological training in the colonies, the number of ministers who served as tutors was comparatively large. During the period 1714–1776, these included Peter Henry Dorsius, Gualtherus Du Bois, John Frelinghuysen, Theodorus Frelinghuysen, Theodorus Jacobus Frelinghuysen, Gerardus Haeghoort, Jacob Rutsen Hardenbergh, Johannes Leydt, David Marinus, Hermanus Meyer, Johannes Ritzema, Dirck Romeyn, Benjamin Vander Linde, Cornelius Van Santvoord, Samuel Verbryck, and Eilardus Westerlo. It is interesting to note that six of the above were themselves products of the tutorial system and also received their ordination in America. Some of these ministers taught only one pupil who later became ordained, although they may have had other students who never finished their course of studies. On the other hand, a few ministers gave instruction to several young men. The most popular tutor was John Henry Goetschius, who while pastor in Queens County, Long Island, and later at Hackensack and Schraalenberg, New Jersey, taught no less than fourteen students, or about half of all those who studied in the colonies during this period and were later ordained. In a number of instances, a ministerial candidate moved around, studying under several tutors.

The subject matter taught in the colonies under the tutorial system was similar to that received in the theological schools in Europe.[9] This was necessary because the goals in each situation were the same, namely, the preparation of young men for the ministerial examinations and for ministerial careers. Two letters written in 1746 to the Classis of Amsterdam by colonial pastors requesting special permission to examine and ordain candidates (without their having to go to Holland) give some indication of the training imparted by private tutors. The first letter was written by Dominie Haeghoort of Second River, New Jersey, in behalf of Benjamin Vanderlinde. It states that the candidate had studied two years under Dorsius of Bucks County, Pennsylvania and two years under Goetschius of Long Island, concentrating primarily on Latin and Greek, and for the past year had been living with Haeghoort where he had been receiving instruction in Hebrew. The letter adds that Vanderlinde, under Haeghoort's direction, had also made "very good progress in ethics and especially in theology and all that pertains to it."[10]

The other letter was written by the Reverends Du Bois and Ritzema of New York City in behalf of Johannes Leydt. According to this letter, Leydt studied for some years under John Frelinghuysen of Raritan and

Goetschius of Long Island, and then went to live in New York City to continue his studies. In describing his qualifications to the Classis, Du Bois and Ritzema wrote that Leydt

> now, for a year and a half, . . . has been instructed under our supervision, not to speak of what he has already accomplished in the original languages of Scripture, and in the systems of Prof. Vitringa and Gerdes. . . . We can say with all freedom in regard to this young man, that he is so far advanced that he can understand a Latin author, can help himself with Hebrew and Greek, and is reasonably well-versed in theology.[11]

With some reluctance, Classis granted permission for these two men to be examined and ordained in the colonies. Both of them later accepted calls to New Jersey, with Vanderlinde serving at Paramus and Ponds from 1748 to 1789 and Leydt at New Brunswick and Six Mile Run from 1748 to 1783.

Although the type of knowledge imparted by the colonial tutors was similar to that received in the theological schools, the methods of instruction obviously differed. In the tutorial system, teaching was a kind of sideline, as the minister had numerous pastoral duties to perform. There were books that candidates were expected to read, but these could not have been numerous because most ministerial libraries were limited in scope. Students were given sets of questions for which answers had to be prepared, and subjects were assigned on which dissertations had to be written. From time to time, the students were examined on these questions and on their readings, as well as on certain passages from Scripture. Very probably the study of Greek and Hebrew was slighted by most tutors.

Within this general framework of private tutoring, some diversity must have existed, depending on the personality and predilections of the tutor. Some of the latter no doubt were more formal in their approach than others, and some very likely placed more stress on one subject than another. There also must have been differences in how the applied subjects were taught, depending on whether the tutor favored a doctrinal or an evangelical approach to preaching.

There can be no doubt that private tutoring had certain disadvantages over formal training at a theological school. Because of other duties, the tutor was limited in the amount of time he could devote to his students. Moreover, the students did not have the advantage of being able to take each set of subjects under a specialist. The great John H. Livingston, for example, while a student at Utrecht from 1766 to 1769, was able to study theology under the distinguished Gisbertus Bonnet and New Testament Greek under the youthful but highly talented Rijklof Van Goens. He also had specialists as instructors in Hebrew and biblical criticism. Livingston's education was further broadened by his attending, when he had time, general lectures on chemistry and biology. Also lacking in the tutorial system was the stimulus that could be sparked by discussions carried on among a large body of students.

Library facilities were also limited in the colonies. The following excerpt from a letter of February 1, 1757, from Dominie John Henry Goetschius, the most popular colonial tutor, to the Classis of Amsterdam gives some hint concerning the status and size of his library:

Each of my children needs a big Bible with marginal references. Other Dutch books (I have a few in Latin) a minister also needs, for the better and more efficient performance of his work. This your Revs. very well know. And, in order that I may educate my six sons in the languages and in the sciences, I beg of your Revs. liberality, that you would send over the necessary school-books. I also have many poor catechumens in my churches. To these I should like to give certain question books, like S. de Molenaer's book, styled "Spiritual and Pure Milk" (*Redelyke, onvervalschte Melk*). I would also like, for some other poor or pious churchmembers, some other edifying books for their increase in truth and godliness. Together, these books would fill a box. And if sent by your Revs. to us, as objects of your Revs. liberality, as members of the household of faith, they would bring to us very much joy.[12]

Although most ministerial libraries were very small, there were exceptions. Thus the following notation is found in the diary of Ezra Stiles, president of Yale College, for September 27, 1786, following his visit with Dominie Johannes Ritzema, then at age seventy-nine: "a venerable Dutch Divine; viewed his learned Library of I judge 1000 to 1200 Volumes."[13]

Despite numerous problems, there were nevertheless some distinct advantages to private tutoring. A student receiving his theological training in this manner, for example, was probably obliged to do more independent thinking and enjoyed a closer student-teacher relationship than the university student. Undoubtedly, one of the greatest advantages enjoyed by the tutorial student was the practical experience he gained from being taught by someone having first-hand acquaintance with the unique conditions existing in the colonies, rather than by professors living three thousand miles across the ocean who had little conception of what conditions were like in America. In support of private tutoring and self-study, it should also be noted that some of the most successful Dutch Reformed pastors of the eighteenth century, including Bertholf, Freeman, and Hardenbergh, received their training in this way. Moreover, there was no guarantee that a university-trained minister from Europe was going to be a successful preacher—as the colonial churches occasionally learned to their sorrow.

As was true during the previous century, most calls sent to Europe were "blank" or "open" calls, with no specific minister being asked for by name but generally empowering the party to whom they were addressed to make the selection. Not all calls were sent directly to the Classis of Amsterdam, some being addressed to ministers who were acquaintances of colonial pastors and who passed the calls on to the Classis with recommendations. Occasionally, a call was directed to a layperson whose concern for the colonial churches was well known and whose assistance was asked in locating a suitable minister. Some calls were brief, while others were several pages in length.[14]

The expenses that a church had to pay in calling and bringing in a new minister frequently added up to a significant sum of money, particularly if he came directly from Europe. For example, when Dominie Cornelius Van Schie came from Holland to Poughkeepsie and Fishkill in 1731, the expenses totalled more than seventy-six pounds, which was slightly more than his annual salary. One-half these expenses were entailed before he left Holland, and included twenty pounds simply for getting himself and his wife ready for the voyage and for waiting in Amsterdam for a ship.[15] Layovers enroute and calms at sea sometimes meant, as in Van Schie's case, an ocean voyage of eleven or twelve weeks. Since a minister's salary commenced upon leaving his former pastorate, this could mean that a colonial congregation might owe a newly arrived pastor several months' salary even before having heard him preach.

Because of the extensive costs often associated with bringing in a new minister, a congregation naturally hoped that a newly arrived pastor would remain with them for a long period of time. When this did not happen and he was called by another church, the latter was expected to reimburse the minister's former congregation for some of the expenses it had incurred in obtaining him. Thus, when Dominie Barent Vrooman, pastor at New Paltz and two small neighboring villages, accepted a call to Schenectady in 1754, the latter paid more than a hundred pounds to his former churches for expenses they had incurred for sending Vrooman to Holland a few years earlier to complete his theological education and to receive ordination. Because Vrooman had served the New Paltz area for only two years after his return from

Holland, it seemed only right that Schenectady should now reimburse them for most of these expenses.

Even the expense of calling and transporting a minister who already was in the colonies was no small sum. Thus, the costs of merely seeking the dismissal of Vrooman from New Paltz, drafting his call, sending consistory members to various places to make the necessary arrangements, and transporting the dominie's goods to Schenectady totalled about fifty pounds. Another fifty pounds were appropriated for the purchase of a horse for the dominie. These costs, when added to the reimbursements made to New Paltz for having sent Vrooman to the Netherlands, meant that Schenectady had to pay a total of about two hundred twenty-five pounds to obtain a new preacher, not counting his salary.[16]

The shortage of pastors and the smallness of most congregations frequently caused two or more churches to join in calling a minister. The call sent in 1756 to the Reverend Johannes Casparus Freyenmoet to serve as pastor of the churches of Kinderhook, Claverack, and Livingston Manor was typical of many because of the manner in which it parcelled out the minister's duties:

His Reverence shall serve the three congregations by turns in succession, so that each one shall have an equal amount of service. He shall preach twice on every Lord's Day (excepting in winter, only once these days); before noon a selected text from God's holy word, and in the afternoon according to the teachings of the Heidelberg Catechism, and catechise therefrom after the sermon, unless the overseers consider something else more edifying. Catechism shall also be held on Mondays in the place where the service has been held the day before. And lastly, his Reverence shall not go outside of the congregation to preach on a Sunday or at any other time allotted for preaching, without the consent of the consistory; whereupon the congregation consenting thereto shall then lose their turn.[17]

Churches that joined together in calling a minister did not always share his services equally. Thus, the call sent in 1732 by the churches of Old Catskill (later called Leeds) and Coxsackie to the Reverend Weiss of Schoharie required "preaching of God's word purely in the Low Dutch language, twice daily on every Lord's Day ... thirty Sundays during the year at Katskill and twenty-two in Kockshackie." Similarly, the call extended by several New Jersey churches to the Reverend David Marinus in 1756 stipulated that Acquackanonck (Passaic) would enjoy one-half of Marinus' pastoral services and Pompton Plains and Totowa (Paterson) one-quarter each. Sometimes this sharing of ministers lasted for a significant period of time. Thus, Poughkeepsie and Fishkill shared a common pastor from 1731 to 1772, and Old Catskill and Coxsackie did the same from 1732 until 1794.[18]

In shared pastorates, the percentage that each congregation contributed to the salary of a minister generally determined the amount of service each congregation received. In 1753, for example, the churches of Marbletown, Rochester, and Wawarsing promised the Reverend Henricus Frelinghuysen a salary of one hundred five pounds if he would become their pastor, with Marbletown and Rochester each contributing forty-five pounds, while Wawarsing was obligated for only fifteen pounds. This distribution of salary commitments was in accordance with the call which stated that "Marbletown and Rochester shall each, in turn, have three times as many services as Wawarsing, so that Wawarsing will have but one seventh part of the services."[19]

What happened if one congregation did not honor its salary obligations? The agreement of 1756 between the churches of Acquackanonck, Pompton Plains, and Totowa and the Reverend David Marinus provides the following answer: "In case any of the congregations [shall] fail to contribute its rightful share in the salary, the other churches [are] to pay the share of the delinquent church, but [have] also a right upon his services in proportion to their increased contribution".[20] And what if a church missed its turn for Sunday preaching for some other reason? Again, for an answer, one can turn to the procedure followed by the churches of Acquackanonck, Pompton Plains, and Totowa. An entry in the consistory book of April 9, 1765, states that "any of the three congregations neglecting to send for the domine in time shall lose its turn, whether on account of thunder storm or negligence. The turns shall revolve at the fixed time, whether the domine comes or not."[21]

Responsibility for the maintenance of the parsonage generally rested with the community in which the parsonage was located. This was done on the basis that persons living closest to the parsonage had greater access to the services of the minister and therefore should have this added obligation. For the same reason, the congregation having greatest access to the minister was usually responsible for supplying firewood for the parsonage as well as special "fodder" for the minister's horse. However, when a minister was visiting another community in the discharge of his responsibilities, that community had to provide him with meals and suitable lodging during such a visit.

How adequate were the salaries of the ministers? An historian writing about the middle of the eighteenth century reported that "the clergy of this province [of New York] are, in general, but indifferently supported: it is true they live easily, but few of them leave any thing to their children."[22] Actually, salaries varied greatly as to time and place. New York, as might be expected, paid the highest salaries, and these increased during the century. Thus, Dominie Gualtherus Du Bois accepted a call there in 1699 for a salary of one hundred twenty-five pounds. Henry Boel came there in 1713 for that same amount, as did Johannes Ritzema in 1744. But by 1754, salaries for New York ministers had increased to two hundred pounds, and Archibald Laidlie was called there in 1763 at a salary of three hundred pounds. With reference to Laidlie, his call stated that such a sum, "together with the perquisites of marriages and burials," would be "sufficient to support a family in a genteel manner, and yearly to lay up something for posterity."[23]

Ministerial salaries elsewhere were considerably lower, as shown by the following statistics dating from about the mid-eighteenth century: Old Catskill and Coxsackie, £ 80; Marbletown, Rochester, and Wawarsing £ 105; Kings County, Long Island £107; and Poughkeepsie and Fishkill, £ 130.[24] It should be noted, however, that agreements of the eighteenth century between ministers and their congregations also included a rent-free house and free firewood. Most ministers also received free use of some land for keeping a few cows and a horse, as well as a garden and an orchard. In New York, salaries were paid quarterly, while at most other places they were paid semi-annually. In view of the long wait between salary payments, ministers and their families were undoubtedly often hard-pressed for funds. In this respect, it was fortunate that they were provided with such "fringe benefits" as a parsonage, firewood, and free pasturage. Ministers were able to supplement their salaries somewhat by officiating at marriages and funerals, and in some instances even by baptisms. A pastor could also add to his income by preaching occasionally in churches that had no minister.

As in the past, some salaries continued to be paid partially in kind. Thus, the agreement made with the Reverend George Michael Weiss at Schoharie on November 12, 1731 stated that in addition to the cash salary and parsonage, every family "that is able" was duty bound to give him a "*schepel* of corn." A *schepel* was about one bushel. Twenty-six years later, in 1757, this same congregation at Schoharie promised its preacher, John Mauritius Goetschius, "forty *schepels* of wheat or peas" to help defray his costs of ordination. As late as 1795, the churches of Pompton Plains and Boonton agreed that for the partial support of their minister, the Pompton Plains consistory would supply him with a hundred loads of firewood annually, while the Boonton consistory promised "to furnish 50 bushels of grain per annum."[25]

In a few instances, a minister supplemented his pastoral salary by engaging in farming. Thus, in a call of 1730 sent to the Netherlands by the churches of Freehold and Middletown in New Jersey, the pastor was promised seventy pounds salary, a suitable parsonage, a good riding horse, and the use of a hundred acre farm. According to the call, the previous minister had worked the farm himself, realizing therefrom about thirty pounds annually "besides his own bread wheat." The call further stated that if the new pastor were unacquainted with farming he could rent it in return for one-third of its yield, but added that "by the aid and instructions of the well disposed—of whom, we believe, there will be no lack—there can be but little doubt that in a few years he could manage the farm himself."[26]

Salaries of Dutch Reformed ministers in the colonies during the eighteenth century were about the equivalent of what was being received by pastors in the Netherlands, and probably were even slightly higher. The cost of living, however, was higher in the colonies, as is clear in the following communication of 1732 sent by a newly arrived pastor to friends in the Netherlands:

I only want to say, that it is not Holland by any means. And although a pound here is equivalent to eight Holland guilders, these eight guilders equal no more than six guilders in Holland. For money is very scarce here, and therefore worth much more than in Holland. Excepting food and drink, everything here is almost as dear again as in Holland, and some things actually twice as dear.[27]

In meeting expenses such as ministerial salaries, church maintenance, care of the poor, and the like, churches drew their revenues from a variety of sources. From an early date, subscriptions were common. They were used already during the New Netherland period by those churches not supported by the West India Company, and this method was continued after the colony fell to the English in 1664. A notation of 1673 regarding the Harlem church, for example, informs us that one Vander Vin was re-engaged as parish clerk and *voorlezer* at his former salary, "to wit: 400 guilders, dwelling house and fuel," with the salary paid in grain at market value every six months "according to the old list of free-will contributions." This subscription list contained twenty-five names, and the amount pledged varied from four to thirty guilders. Of course, the entire salary was not raised by contributions, but a notation of 1675 indicates that 272 of the needed 400 guilders were raised by voluntary subscriptions. Most of the rest was no doubt acquired from the rental of the glebe land, since from the beginning when the town was laid out, some land was set aside for the support of the church.[28]

Subscriptions continued to be a popular way of raising money during the eighteenth century. Thus, about 1715, some fifty churchgoers in Bucks County, Pennsylvania, subscribed 124 pounds, 10 shillings, and 4 pence for the construction of a church there. Similarly, a subscription list that was circulated at Schenectady in 1752 to help pay the minister's salary, carried the names of one hundred sixty-eight persons who subscribed a total of sixty-six pounds two shillings in amounts varying from one to thirty-six shillings. In that same year, the consistory of New York after discussing "means to call another minister from Holland" resolved that it should be done by a subscription list, "under which each voluntary subscriber should state the sum he promises for the yearly support of another minister." Once drawn up, attempts were sometimes made to increase the amounts of the subscriptions promised. Thus, about 1750, the consistories of Acquackanonck, Pompton Plains, and Totowa agreed to canvas the church members to determine if they could give a little more to the minister's salary.[29]

Churches also gave one another financial aid from time to time. The amounts were usually small by today's standards of giving but were undoubtedly considered important at the time. Thus, the Long Island churches contributed "generously," as they expressed it, four pounds and ten shillings to help in the construction of the church in Bucks County. Later, the Bucks County congregation sent a contribution to the Minisink churches which had suffered severely in the Revolution. The larger and more established churches could, of course, contribute significantly more. For example, as early as about 1702, the New York church sent more than fifty-seven pounds to Schenectady to assist it in building a church. Similarly, "the Albany people" gave significant aid to Poughkeepsie and Fishkill in 1731 to help meet the extraordinary expenses involved in bringing over a minister from the Netherlands.[30]

For some churches during the eighteenth century, income from real estate and other property became an important source of revenue. Church-owned real estate was usually the result of gifts bequeathed on condition that the church maintain the donor in his or her old age, but real estate was sometimes purchased as an investment. Several transactions concerning the Schenectady church can illustrate this method of raising revenue. In 1675, Hans Janse Eenkluys, a former soldier, bequeathed thirty-six acres for the use of the poor on condition that the church maintain him in his old age. This land became known as the "Poor Pasture," and was not sold until 1863. Income from such land was substantial. Thus, an entry dated May 18, 1809 in the Church

Minute Book states that "the price of pasturage for the ensuing season shall be $5.50 a head for horses, and $4.00 for cows. And that the number of horses admitted to the pasture of the church shall not exceed thirty-one and of cows, thirty-two." Proceeds from the Poor Pasture was only one of several sources of income enjoyed by the Schenectady church. For example, an entry in the Minute Book for March 16, 1802, gives the annual income as totalling about 552 pounds, of which 319 came from annual quit rents on land or leases, 58 from the church pasture, 50 from the church grist mill, 35 from pew rentals, and 90 from interest on bonds, notes, and the like. The mill was the result of a gift bequeathed in 1696. [31]

The Schenectady church was not unique in owning real estate and other property as sources of income. According to one account, income from real estate owned by the church at Kingston was so substantial that at one time it formed the major part of the revenues needed for the maintenance of the church. The church at Tappan, New York too was able to support itself in part from real estate given by generous donors. Several churches in the Mohawk Valley also derived some of their income from land. In 1813, for example, the German Flats (Fort Herkimer) church owned 1,377 acres of land, the rent of which was $235 annually. The New York City churches also owned a considerable amount of real estate in the form of farm lands and building lots. Property on Manhattan Island bequeathed by John Harpending, who died about 1724, became one of the principal sources of wealth of the Collegiate Church, and in 1749, it turned down an offer of three thousand pounds for its claims to Fordham Manor, an estate of about five square miles in the Bronx. [32]

The sale or rental of seats in the churches also became an important source of revenue. [33] In cases in which seats were sold, the selling price during the colonial period was generally about thirty shillings. Usually, however, seats were rented at prices varying from two to six shillings with men paying slightly more than women. Each sitting was generally marked with a number or with the name of the person or family for whom it was reserved. Whether purchased or rented, the seat was held for life and could be forfeited only upon a member's leaving the congregation. On the death of the holder, the seat passed to the closest heir upon payment of a nominal fee. This meant that sometimes a certain seat was retained by the same family for several generations. If the "inheritance fee" were not paid within a specified time, the seat reverted back to the church and could be re-sold or re-rented.

The construction of a new church or the remodeling of an old one was frequently financed in part by the selling or renting of pews. For example, when chairs in the central part of the Flatbush Church (built about 1700) were removed in 1775 and replaced by sixty-four pews containing six seats each, about two-thirds of the cost for the remodeling was paid by the new pew holders. This method of raising money was continued long after the close of the colonial period. Thus, in 1813, following the decision to build a new church at Owasco, New York, pew sales brought in $3,772, which was more than half the cost of the new edifice. Following the dedication of the new church at Preakness, New Jersey in 1853, the rights to fifty-four pews were sold to the highest bidders at prices varying from eleven to ninety-five dollars and brought in a total of $3,071.59. At Schenectady, the levying of pew rentals continued until 1916.[34]

Disputes among pew holders were not uncommon, and when they occurred, the task of solving them fell upon the consistory. These problems included questions concerning the proper heir to a seat following the death of its former holder as well as complaints about persons occupying seats that properly belonged to others. There were also complaints about overcrowding. As a means of raising money, it was of course advantageous to squeeze as many persons as possible on each bench or pew. It is therefore not surprising that the following petition was presented to the consistory of the Collegiate Church of New York in 1731:

Since many in the Old Church, both men and women, complain that they are compelled to sit too close to each other; therefore, whenever a place in any bench or pew comes back to the Church, either by death or removal of the owner . . . then at the request of those who belong to that bench or pew, the vacant seat shall not be sold to any one else; yet not more than one such seat shall be done away with, in such bench or pew.[35]

A noticeable change among the eighteenth century ministers was their great interest in writing and publishing. Other than a catechetical instruction book for the youth and a treatise on the Mohawk Indians, both written by Dominie Johannes Megapolensis and published in Holland, and the poetry composed by Dominie Henricus Selyns, the colonial ministers of the seventeenth century did very little serious writing. Eighteenth century ministers, on the other hand, wrote a number of books, nearly all in Dutch and most of them published in the colonies.[36]

Catechetical instruction books were particularly popular, and at least six such works were published in the colonies during the first half of the century. The authors, with the dates when their studies were first published, include Johannes Lydius (1700), Gualtherus Du Bois (1706), Peter Van Driessen (1730), Peter Vas (1730), Gerardus Haeghoort (1738), and Theodorus Frelinghuysen (1749). Du Bois' work was reprinted in an enlarged edition in 1712, and a third edition was published at Amsterdam in 1725. Most of these works, which varied from about forty to one hundred fifty pages in length, were in the form of questions and answers and were based on the Heidelberg Catechism. They were intended primarily to instruct the youth in the fundamentals of Reformed doctrine as preparation for their becoming communicant members of the Church. The more comprehensive studies, such as the one by Frelinghuysen, were also designed as study guides for young men who were being tutored privately for the ministry. All of the above were in Dutch, but in 1763, Dominie Lambertus De Ronde of New York wrote a study in English on the Heidelberg Catechism. It was one hundred eighty-five pages in length and was the first book written in English by a Dutch Reformed pastor that was published in America.

In addition to the appearance of catechetical instruction books, a number of sermons were also published. Particularly popular were sermons by the evangelistic preacher from the Raritan, Theodorus Jacobus Frelinghuysen, who had three sermons published in the colonies in 1721, two in 1729, and four in 1747. A few sermons by colonial pastors also appeared in Holland. Bernardus Freeman, for example, had a collection of sermons published there in 1721, as did Frelinghuysen in 1736 and in 1738. In some instances, English translations of Dutch sermons also appeared. Thus, English translations of three sermons of Dominie Peter Van Driessen were published in the same year (1726) that the Dutch edition was printed. English translations of several of Frelinghuysen's sermons also appeared.

As might be expected, controversies within the Church resulted in the publication of a number of polemical works. A few such studies discussed the pros and cons of Frelinghuysen's approach to religion. Arguments between the Coetus and Conferentie factions during the 1740's and 1750's also led to the appearance of several partisan works. Sometimes when a polemical work appeared, it led to an immediate published reply from the opposing group, which in turn would bring on a counter-reply. Thus the reverends Johannes Leydt, who was pro-Coetus, and Johannes Ritzema, who was pro-Conferentie, took up the pen several times to defend their respective causes and to answer charges being brought up by the opposition.

There were occasional instances when a minister was unable to serve out his full, normal life because of misconduct. Paulus Van Vlecq, for example, was obliged to leave his parish in Bucks County, Pennsylvania in 1713 because of bigamy.[37] Similarly, on at least two occasions, ministers had to leave their pastorates because of having presented forged credentials at their examinations. These were Johannes Van Driessen who served for a time at Kinderhook and later at Acquackanonck, and Peter De Wint who officiated briefly at Staten Island.[38]

A few ministers were also obliged to leave the ministry because of inability to get along with their parishioners or colleagues. Thus, Benjamin Meinema, pastor at Poughkeepsie and Fishkill from 1745 to 1756, was forced to resign his pastorate because of unpleasant relations between him and his congregations. In the case of Johannes Arondeus of Kings County, Long Island, more serious steps were taken— because of the dislike that developed between him and some of his parishioners and his inability to get along with his colleague, Ulpianus Van Sinderen, he was suspended from the ministry in 1750 and deposed in 1752. This action was taken by a committee of colonial ministers but with the full approval of the Classis of Amsterdam.

Addiction to strong drink also was a cause for occasional suspension from the ministry. Many pastors labored under stressful conditions and liquor no doubt became a means for some of them to escape from their daily cares. It must also be remembered that the Church itself did not frown upon the use of liquor in moderation; indeed, it was frequently served at some church functions. Even respected ministers became victims. Peter Henry Dorsius, about whom the great Theodorus Jacobus Frelinghuysen spoke as being "a learned, gifted, graciously-endowed and fruitful minister," became so addicted to strong drink that he even sold his household furniture to pay for it. In 1748, he was suspended from the ministry on account of continued drunkenness and offensive conduct, including the abandonment of his wife and three children. David Marinus, pastor of several New Jersey churches from 1752 to 1773 and "a man of unusual talent as a preacher and a writer," was also suspended because of his too free use of intoxicating drink. Conscious of his problem, he is reported to have admonished his parishioners from time to time with the following dictum: "Do as I tell you, but not as I do." The reverends Joseph Morgan and Reinhardt Erickzon, who served as ministers of Freehold and Middletown, New Jersey from 1709 to 1731 and 1736 to 1764 respectively, were also removed from the ministry because of intemperance.[39]

Fortunately, the ministers who were dismissed because of misconduct were few in number. Most others were capable and dedicated men, and if their health permitted it, they generally remained active in the ministry until their death. For example, the churches in Kings County, Long Island reported to the Classis of Amsterdam in 1740 that their present pastors, Vincentius Antonides and Bernardus Freeman, were still officiating at ages seventy-three and seventy-eight. Gualtherus Du Bois of New York City was planning a visit to pastorless Bergen, New Jersey to preach and administer the sacraments at the time of his death in 1751 at age eighty, while Johannes Ritzema baptized a child at Kinderhook in 1792 at about age eighty-four. Benjamin Du Bois of Freehold and Middletown, New Jersey remained active until he was eighty-eight. But the record was no doubt set by the Reverend Peter Vas of Kingston, who lived to be ninety-six and performed occasional duties until within a short time of his death in 1752. [40]

VIII

Church Life during the Eighteenth Century

As has been noted, the number of Dutch Reformed churches increased threefold between 1714 and 1776, and the number of ministers doubled. Many congregations also increased significantly in size, and steps were taken to train ministers in America. As will be explained in later chapters, the eighteenth century also saw the beginnings of change in matters of polity and language as the colonial churches gradually became independent of the mother church in Holland and as English began replacing Dutch in the worship services.

In many respects, however, church life during the eighteenth century did not change significantly. Although the standard of living was gradually improving in the colonies, the way of life of the people remained basically unchanged. If one discounts exceptions like New York City, most areas in which Dutch Reformed churches were located continued to be primarily rural and sparsely settled, with the vast majority of inhabitants engaged in agriculture. In 1700, New York colony had a population of about 19,000 and New Jersey had 14,000, which by 1770 had increased to only 163,000 and 117,000 respectively. Even the largest communities were small when compared to the European cities where most clergymen had received their training. New York City had only about 5,000 people in 1700, and at the outbreak of the Revolution, not more than 21,000. A census taken in 1697 shows that there were only 1,452 people living in Albany, and a visitor there in 1744 reported that it had "about 4,000 inhabitants, mostly Dutch or of Dutch extract."[1] The historian William Smith writing about the middle of the eighteenth century stated that there were perhaps about 150 houses in Kingston, and according to one report, Kinderhook as late as 1763 contained only about "fifteen houses and a Dutch Reformed Church."[2]

Not only were most settlements small, but they were generally isolated and widely scattered. Farms were also widely dispersed. Despite some progress in transportation, there were few roads, with most travel being done along bridle paths and Indian trails or by boats. Streams without bridges made land journeys in some regions almost impossible in times of high water, and heavy snows made travel even for short distances difficult during the winter months. The latter problem explains why most churches held only one service per Sunday from about the first of November until the first of March. In some instances, a new minister arriving in New York from Europe during the winter months had to wait until spring before proceeding to his new pastorate.

Conditions such as the above increased the problems that churches had in keeping in touch with one another and made it virtually impossible for close personal contacts among the widely scattered ministers. This is clearly illustrated in a letter of 1750 sent by a group of colonial pastors to the Classis of Amsterdam. The purpose of the letter was to calm the fears of the Classis that assemblies of the colonial ministers might occur too frequently and thereby lead to their becoming independent of the mother church in Holland. The letter reads in part as follows: "The Rev. Classis need not be anxious lest our meetings . . . should be frequent; rather is there need to exhort the members not to neglect the yearly gatherings, since our distance from each other is great, and the pains and expense of traveling are considerable, and the desire of being absent so long from one's family is small."[3] In May 1760, the Reverend Abraham Rosenkrantz of the Mohawk Valley declared it would be impossible to attend a meeting of ministers in New York because of the six-day journey that was involved.[4]

Except in the older and more settled communities, agreements between ministers and their congregations during the eighteenth century continued to reflect the rural atmosphere that had prevailed in the colonies since the beginning. The agreement of 1714, for example, between the congregation of Schenectady and the Reverend Thomas Brouwer of the Netherlands promised the pastor a salary of ninety pounds plus "a dwelling free of rent, firewood at the door, a large garden, and free pasturage for two cows and a horse." Similarly, the joint call of 1757 from Claverack, Kinderhook, and Livingston Manor to Dominie Johannes Fryenmoet specified that in addition to the usual provisions of a salary and parsonage, he would be provided with a "stable, etc., together with several acres of land for a garden, pasture, mowground, orchard, etc." Nor had the rural surroundings of most churches changed much by the close of the eighteenth century. Dominie Dirck Romeyn's call of 1784 to Schenectady, for example, promising him the use of a "pasture for two cows and a horse and seventy cords of firewood delivered on his premises," reads almost like the call sent by that same church seventy years earlier to Dominie Brouwer.[5]

Ministers who came from Europe to accept rural pastorates in America were frequently amazed at the new surroundings in which they found themselves. This is clearly brought out in a letter written by Dominie Cornelius Van Schie of Poughkeepsie and Fishkill to several ministers in Amsterdam soon after his arrival from Holland in 1731:

Many people here were born, and grew up, in the woods, and know little of anything else except what belongs to farming. Indeed it can hardly be believed what trouble and toil a minister has, to introduce any civility into these places where there never has been a minister before. For many people here are like the wild horses of the woods which have never yet been broken, and which will not allow the bit to be placed in their mouth till after some time.[6]

Van Schie reported that his two churches were "three good hours from each other; and every other Sunday I must ride that distance, thither and back, through the woods and along steep paths." In view of this, and his having to visit widely scattered parishioners and preach occasionally at neighboring villages, it is no wonder that he added that, "A preacher here . . . by much horseback riding, and otherwise wears out more clothes and other articles, than in Holland."[7]

Although education in the isolated communities was often a function of the home and many Dutch Reformed church-goers therefore remained illiterate or nearly so, such conditions apparently did not diminish an interest in spiritual matters so long as church services were held at least somewhat regularly. Thus Dominie Van Schie, in writing his friends in Amsterdam about the boorish behavior of his parishioners and their being unlettered, nevertheless reported that they continued to have respect for spiritual affairs. To again quote from his letter: "We ought to thank God," he wrote, "that although most of these people can neither read nor write, yet most of them have so much respect for God and His Word, that when one smites them with the sword of God's Word, they willingly submit."[8]

It is interesting to note in this respect, too, the observation made in 1802 by the Reverend John Taylor of Massachusetts who undertook a missionary journey of about three months through the Mohawk Valley and surrounding region. During that visit, he spent some time among settlements that were heavily Dutch Reformed. With respect to the Dutch, his *Journal* tells us that he found them to be seriously lacking in matters of book learning, referring to them as being "extremely ignorant" and noting that a considerable proportion of them could "neither read nor write." However, to their credit and in contrast to some groups he visited who had "no sense of religion," Taylor had nothing but praise for the interest the Dutch showed in spiritual matters, describing them on various occasions as being "very fond of hearing preaching," of being "thankful for religious instruction," and as having "great respect for pious clergymen." Following his visit to Fonda, he wrote that the minister there, the Reverend Abram Van Horne, was a man of "excellent character" and in charge of "a respectable congregation."[9]

Most churches held two services every Lord's Day except during the winter months, when there would be only one. Occasionally, however, a call stated that the minister would preach but once per Sunday throughout the year, while a few churches, including Schenectady and New York held two services every Sunday, in addition to special services on certain "Festival Days" such as Ascension Day, Christmas, and New Year's. When a pastor served more than one church, it was sometimes specified that preaching on those days, together with Easter and Pentecost, would be equally shared by the churches.[10]

The people were usually summoned to church on Sundays by the ringing of a bell, which was tolled at various intervals to let them know how much time remained before services commenced. But because bells were costly and not readily available, it was not uncommon for churches that were poor or had only recently been organized to use other means for summoning the worshippers. Thus, for twenty-three years the church at Flatlands on Long Island announced the approach of church services by the beating of a drum, while churches in the Minisink Valley of the upper Delaware resorted to sounding a tin horn. When bells were used, they were not always of the monstrous size that one ordinarily associates with church bells. For example, the bell imported from Holland by the Flatlands church in 1686 weighed only twenty-two pounds and was used for more than a century, being replaced in 1794 by one weighing nearly four hundred sixty pounds.[11]

In some of the larger communities, such as New York and Kingston, some church goers who were of a high social standing and of moderate means were informed of the approach of "church time" in a special way. Dr. Alexander Hamilton, a physician from Annapolis who dined at the home of Stephen Bayard of New York on a Sunday in 1744, made the following notation in his diary, explaining this unique custom:

Just as we had done dinner, we heard two raps at the door solemnly laid on with a knocker. A gentleman in the company was going to see who it was, but Mr. Bayard desired him not to trouble himself, for it was only the *domper*. I asked who that was. He told me it was a fellow who made a course thro' one quarter of the town, giving two raps at each door as he passed to let the people in the houses know that the second bell had rung out. This man has a gratutity from each family for so doing every new year.[12]

The order of worship in the Sunday services generally conformed to that of the mother church in the Netherlands, particularly as it was drawn up at the great Synod of Dort of 1618–1619.[13] This was done to secure a degree of conformity in public worship throughout the denomination, rather than leave such matters to caprice. But there were variations among the churches because of differences in the size and sophistication of congregations and because of the personal preferences of some ministers. Pastors influenced by the pietist movement, for example, were less prone than others to follow a written liturgy. This was especially true with respect to liturgical prayers versus "free" or extemporaneous prayers, with the more evangelical ministers preferring the latter. Most reports relate that the morning service lasted at least two hours and that of the afternoon, nearly as long. Moreover, before the Revolution, most services, including the singing, were conducted entirely in the Dutch language, although in some areas German was popular and in a few instances services were conducted in French. English services, however, were very rare among the Dutch Reformed churches during the colonial period.

In many churches, the services were opened by the *voorlezer*, who usually occupied a seat in the front of the church beneath the pulpit. The *voorlezer* took over most of the duties once exercised by the *ziekentrooster*, or "comforter of the sick," and he also frequently served as schoolmaster. His varied duties are clearly shown in Gerrit Van Wagenen's letter of appointment to this office for the Garden Street Church in New York City in 1733. The appointment stated that he was to serve as "Clerk and Foresinger . . . and also to be the Visitor of the Sick for the whole congregation, and to keep school in the Low Dutch language, and finally to keep the books of the Elders, Deacons and Church Masters."[14] Similarly, when Anthony Welp was appointed schoolmaster in 1773 by the Dutch Reformed citizens of Flatbush, Long Island, he was expected to devote one afternoon each week to catechizing the children as well as "attend to the church services, such as reading and singing," and assist at burials.[15]

Before the appearance of the minister in the sanctuary, the *voorlezer* read a passage from Scripture and perhaps sang a few verses from a favorite Psalm. This was followed by reading the Ten Commandments at the morning service and the Apostles' Creed at the afternoon service. It was from this activity that he derived the title of *voorlezer*, meaning "forereader." According to one authority, the custom of

*Gerrit Van Wagenen, appointed Comforter of the Sick in New York in 1733.
(Portrait from Henry Dunshee,* History of the School of the Collegiate Reformed Dutch Church)

scriptural reading before the appearance of the minister, came "into being as a substitute for the organ prelude at a time when organs were not permitted."[16] The practice was no doubt continued because of the shortage of organs, especially among poorer congregations.

The reading by the *voorlezer* was followed by the singing of a Psalm by the congregation. The numbers of the Psalms to be sung during each service were posted on "Psalm boards" suspended in the front of the church to the right and left of the pulpit. The singing was led by the *voorzanger*, who more than likely was the same person as the *voorlezer*, since a frequent prerequisite for the latter office was an ability "to tune the Psalms." The *voorzanger* had an important role to fill because, as was noted, few churches in the eighteenth century had an organ to accompany the singing. The church in New York, for example, did not obtain an organ until 1727. In some instances, the *voorzanger* tried to get the congregation in harmony before each singing by the use of a pitch pipe or flute. He also frequently sang a few of the first lines by himself.

The minister entered the sanctuary during the singing of the first Psalm. As he walked down the aisle, he would perhaps bow here and there to important personages in the congregation and shake hands with the members of the consistory. On reaching the pulpit, he reverently paused a moment in silent prayer before ascending the pulpit steps. Upon reaching his elevated place before the congregation, the minister pronounced the *votum*, or invocation, and the salutation. The *exordium remotum* which followed was a general introduction to the sermon that was about to be preached. It included an outline of the main points that the minister intended to cover and an explanation of their relation to the scriptural text that had been read earlier. The *exordium remotum* was prolonged for several minutes by some ministers, and according to some critics it lasted too long. It was followed by a prayer, which might be extemporaneous, but more than likely was taken, at least in part, from the written liturgy. Another Psalm might also be sung at this point.

Then came the focal point of the service, namely, the sermon. It was usually an hour in length, but it might be longer and even stretch on for two hours. It was timed by the hour-glass placed on the right side of the pulpit. When its sands ran out, the hour-glass was turned over by the *voorlezer*, who in some churches was obligated to give a slight rap with a rod or cane on the side of the pulpit to inform the minister that one hour had elapsed. Some ministers, however, seemed to have unlimited staying power when it came to preaching. The consistory of the New York Collegiate Church on January 29, 1747, recommended that the ministers limit themselves to not more than one hour "so as to remove the complaints about the long sermon, to increase the audiences and hold the people together, and so enlarge the alms and other revenues of the Church."[17] The dominies expressed agreement with the proposal, but it was not well observed. When the Swedish traveler, Peter Kalm, attended two Dutch services in a single Sunday in New York in 1749, he reported that the morning sermon lasted two hours, and that of the afternoon two and a half hours. He added that it was impossible to remember a sermon lasting that long, and began the entry in his diary for that date, November 9, as follows: "*Hunc diem perdidi*" (This day I have spent uselessly).[18] The story is told that when James Schureman, one of the Reverend William Jackson's parishioners, held up his watch as a hint that the sermon was lasting too long, the dominie, eyeing him keenly, declared: "Schureman, Schureman, put up your watch; Paul preached till midnight."[19]

Because some of the listeners might become drowsy during the lengthy pontifications by the ministers, sermons were sometimes temporarily interrupted at about mid-point and a diversion introduced, after which preaching would be resumed. Kalm, for example, reported that halfway through the sermons that he heard at New York, the minister took time "to read a lot of prayers."[20] It is difficult to perceive how this would leave one refreshed to listen to the remainder of the sermon. More helpful no doubt was the practice of reading some special announcements or having the congregation join in singing a Psalm. According to some reports, it was not considered an affront for a listener to stand for a while during the sermon in order to refresh himself. Other reports tell of *voorlezers* awakening those who had fallen asleep. In some instances, the offering was collected during a pause in the sermon.[21]

The sermon was followed by prayer, usually termed the great or long prayer because of its length. According to one writer, "for some divines a prayer [of this sort] lasting half an hour was only a warm-up!"[22] The long prayer was usually concluded with the Lord's Prayer recited by the minister without the congregation joining in audibly. The long prayer included special supplications for certain members of the congregation who were experiencing misfortune and were seeking divine help or who had been delivered from adversity and were now wishing to express their thanks to God in a special way. These requests were written down and given to the *voorlezer* before the service. At the appropriate time, he handed them up to the minister by placing them on a cane or slender rod having a cleft at one end. Announcements presented to the minister in this manner and read to the congregation were not always of a religious nature. Because of the absence of newspapers, they were frequently used to inform the people about approaching neighborhood events such as an auction or marriage.

If the offering had not been collected at some other point in the worship service, it occurred at the close of the long prayer. It was preceded by a few appropriate remarks by the minister admonishing the congregation to remember the expenses of the church and the needs of the poor. On a few occasions, special offerings were collected for needy churches. The deacons were responsible for collecting the offering, which was frequently done by passing small cloth bags attached to short handles down the pews or rows of chairs, or by the deacons deftly manipulating long poles that had small sacks attached to one end. Small bells were sometimes fastened to the bags for the two-fold purpose of announcing the approach of the deacons and to awaken sleepers.

The service was finally brought to a close by the singing of another Psalm and by the minister's pronouncing the benediction. The consistory members then stood at the foot of the pulpit to receive the minister who offered his hand to each in turn. According to some accounts, a consistory member could indicate his dissatisfaction with a sermon by refusing to shake the minister's hand.

Persons living some distance from church brought their lunches which they ate during the interval between the first and second services. It was impractical for them to return home between services because of poor transportation facilities, since most church members arrived by foot or horseback or on uncomfortable, springless farm wagons. Moreover, in the rural areas, the intermission between services was frequently too brief to do otherwise. The lunches were eaten in the church in the event of inclement weather and outside on other occasions. In the latter event, the affair took on the appearance of a picnic. For example, according to one report, at Bedminister, New Jersey, during Reverend Hardenbergh's ministry, "some of the neighborhood slaves, of good repute, were given the privilege of having stands on the church-green for the sale of root and malt beer, thick slices of buttered rye bread, sugared olekokes, Dutch crullers, and gingerbread."[23]

All members of the family undoubtedly looked forward to this weekly affair, as daily life, especially in the more isolated areas, was rather dull and uneventful. It gave the people an opportunity to discuss recent happenings and engage in neighborly gossip. No doubt, many marriage matches were made among the young people during these sabbath noon-hour breaks. Very probably, too, because formal consistory meetings were rare during the eighteenth century, the minister took advantage of this opportunity to confer, if need be, with his elders and deacons.

It was customary to administer the Lord's Supper four times a year, but this varied in cases where several churches shared a common pastor. For example, Freehold and Middletown in New Jersey in 1730 celebrated it by turns, one quarter in the one church, and the next quarter in the other. The same was true of Bergen and Staten Island during the latter half of the eighteenth century. Acquackanonck, Pompton Plains, and Totowa, on the other hand, according to a report of 1756, administered it four times per year in *each* church, while a call of 1753 for a minister to Marbletown, Rochester, and Wawarsing stipulated that the first two places would each have the Lord's Supper twice annually but Wawarsing would have it only once. This was done in proportion to the financial support each congregation gave to the minister.

The times for the celebration of the Lord's Supper also varied. At Tappan, New York, in the early eighteenth century, for example, it was observed in the months of January, April, July, and October. Some

Church at Bergen, New Jersey, erected 1773. (Courtesy of Sage Library, New Brunswick Seminary)

churches followed the procedure of Catskill and Coxsackie, where it was observed once on Christmas Sunday (or the Sunday after when Christmas did not fall on a Sunday) and again on Easter Sunday, with the other occasions being arranged with reference to these two. Preparatory sermons, known as *voorbereydingen*, were usually delivered on the Thursday or Friday preceding the celebration of the Lord's Supper.[24]

The elements were customarily served at tables placed in the front of the church below the pulpit, and in larger congregations tables might also be placed in the aisles. The *voorlezer* or the minister himself often read an appropriate passage from Scripture while the communicants took their seats at the communion tables. The minister, facing the congregation, read the appropriate liturgical form and, with the help of the consistory, saw to the proper distribution of the bread and the wine. For the latter, a common cup was used. In larger congregations, the shortage of space meant that the communicants came to the tables in groups until all had been served. Indeed, at New York as early as

1712, to avoid the "unpleasant encounters" and "unseemly pressure" that occurred at communion time because of overcrowding, the minister had to announce from the pulpit special directions for the flow of traffic.. In the words of the announcement, this would help "to preserve suitable order in such a holy service. In acting thus no unpleasant crowding will disturb our pious thoughts, but these will rather be aided by a seemly approach and an undisturbed departure."[25]

Preaching once or twice on Sundays was the minister's primary obligation, but he had other duties as well. These included, among other things, serving as chairman of the consistory, visiting the sick, occasionally serving as a scribe for church members who were illiterate, officiating at baptisms, marriages, and funerals, catechizing the youth, and performing the required house visitations. The last two duties were usually specified in ministerial contracts and demand fuller treatment because of their importance.

Although Sunday School as an institution did not develop until the nineteenth century, the colonial pastors were expected to instruct the youth in the principles of the Heidelberg Catechism. This document, completed in 1563 by two theological professors at the University of Heidelberg, Germany, became one of the basic doctrinal standards of the Reformed Church in the Netherlands as well as of several other denominations. The great Synod of Dort of 1618–1619 stated that one service per Sunday should be devoted at least partially to explaining a segment of the Catechism in such a way as to cover it from beginning to end within a year's time. Most pastoral calls to the colonial churches specified that this regulation had to be carefully observed.[26] Before a person became a confessing member of the Church, he was usually examined by the minister and his consistory concerning his or her knowledge of the Catechism.

In view of the importance of the Heidelberg Catechism, it is not surprising that each minister was expected to devote part of his time to catechising the youth. Usually this was done once per week. As a typical requirement, one can note the stipulation found in the call sent by the churches of Freehold and Middletown, New Jersey to the Netherlands in 1730: "In that part of the congregations where he preaches on Sunday, he [i.e., the minister] shall hold catechical classes during the week, if the weather permits, at such time and place as best suits the community." Although in some instances the minister did not have to hold regular catechism classes during the winter months, in larger congregations, more than one class was held per week throughout the year. Thus, when Dominie Barent Vrooman came to Schenectady in 1754, it was specified that he would catechize twice a week at a time convenient to the pastor. According to a letter of May 4, 1698, the church in New York was already at that early date holding catechism classes as often as four times a week.[27]

A primary means for keeping a minister in touch with the members of his congregation was through house visitation, which usually took place once annually, but in some cases occurred twice a year. Thus, the call sent to Holland in 1730 by the consistories of Poughkeepsie and Fishkill stated that "house to house pastoral visitation shall be performed at least twice a year, in each village, at the time most convenient, according to the resolution of the Consistory." At Schenectady in 1754, the newly arrived pastor was told he would be expected to visit the parishioners living in Schenectady "twice a year and the people living out of town once a year." Sometimes when a pastor served more than one congregation, the number of house visitations varied with the percentage that each paid to the minister's salary. Thus David Marinus' call of 1756 stated: "Twice per year your honor shall visit every family in the church of Acquackanonck; once per year in the church of Totowa, and once per year in the church of Pompton as long as your honor's physical condition permits." The minister was usually accompanied by a member of his consistory during these pastoral visits.[28]

Because the minister was a man of considerable importance in the community, these visits were looked forward to with anticipation but also with some trembling. The following describes very well the family preparations that went into a visit from the dominie:

At such times, great preparations were made for receiving the man of God, who was looked upon with peculiar awe and veneration. The good-man of the house put on his Sunday clothes, the good-wife spread her most attractive board; the children's brown feet were encased in shoes, and, dressed in their best, with their faces polished, they waited with great fear and trepidation.[29]

The trepidation was the result of the very personal and terse questions that the minister directed to all members of the family, young and old. They were questioned on such matters as irregularities in church attendance, failure to give adequate financial support to the church, and any personal behavior that might be considered sinful. Inquiry was also made into whether everyone was engaging in daily Bible reading and daily prayers and, with special reference to the young, the study of catechism lessons.

Until the latter part of the eighteenth century, men and women were often separated in the churches, with the men seated on long benches or on chairs, sometimes raised, running parallel along the walls, while the women were seated in the center of the sanctuary.[30] According to some reports, this arrangement gave the men the advantage because they had a better view of what was going on throughout the church, while the women, if they wanted to observe the proper rules of etiquette, could only note what was taking place to the front of them! Children apparently sat with their mothers rather than their fathers, as is evident in the distribution of the seats. Only in this way, for example, can one explain why the list of pew holders for the Rhinebeck church in 1741 recorded sixteen benches for women and only eight for men, or why there were 328 women's seats as compared to 104 men's seats in the Schenectady church in 1754.

Separation of the sexes was only one of several ways in which the seating arrangements in the sanctuary indicate that the churches were

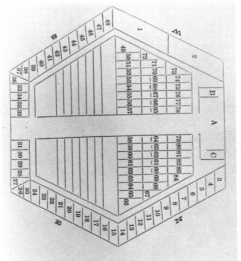

Platform van den Christelyk Needer duytsche Kerk op Staten Eiland, den 30en 7ber Anno Dom: 1751.

DANL. CORSEN FECIT.

Diagram of 1751 for the church at Port Richmond, Staten Island. Key to the diagram: A—pulpit; B—bench for the elders; C—bench for the deacons; 1 & 2—benches for civil officials; chairs 76, 77, and 78 were reserved in the name of the minister; most of 3–48 were for males, while 49–84 were for females. (From J. J. Clute, Annals of Staten Island) "respecters of persons" during the eighteenth century. Blacks were often segregated by seating them in the rear of the church or in the gallery if there was one. At the Flatbush church on Long Island at the time of the Revolution, for example, one of the two galleries was set aside for blacks.[31] Similarly, when the Tappan church was enlarged in 1716, "the gallery on the right of the pulpit was appropriated to the young men, and that on the left was for use of the negro slaves."[32] Such segregation was sometimes continued even after slavery was abolished in the northern states. In 1853, for example, when a new Reformed church was built at Preakness, New Jersey, "the last seat in the gallery was appropriated to the colored people."[33]

Needless to say, most churches had special benches for official dignitaries such as mayors and judges as well as for the local landed magnates. As late as 1790, when the church was rebuilt at Hackensack, the plans stated that the magistrates' pew "shall be particularly constructed, and have a canopy over it."[34] Consistory members, too, had special seats in the front of the church, usually just to the right and left of the pulpit. There was also the *juffrouw bank*, or special bench for the minister's wife and her children. To the credit of the churches, it must be noted that special seats were also provided for the infirm and hard-of-hearing.

It is obvious from the above that wealth frequently counted in determining where one sat in the church sanctuary. Persons who contributed the most toward the construction of a new church were often given the first choice of seats. In some instances, a more comfortable seat could be obtained for a higher fee. A set of rules adopted April 23, 1753 for the church at Pompton Plains, for example, distinguished between "finished" and "unfinished" seats, with the former costing fourteen shillings and the latter ten shillings. In the churches at New York, according to consistory minutes of 1730, a seat could be remodeled "for convenience" at the owner's expense and with the approval of the church authorities.[35] Persons sitting in the front of the church were generally charged more than those sitting farther back. This practice was continued in some churches even during the nineteenth century, as is revealed in the following entry in the Minute Book of the Schenectady church: "Dec. 30, 1848. Resolved that on and after the first of January 1849 the rent of the front tier of pews shall be at the rate of $6.00 per year; the second tier $5.00 and the fourth tier $3.00."[36] Seating in the far back of the church was sometimes set aside for the indigent and was free. In some cases, too, people brought their own chairs and placed them wherever there was room.

In the same way that the church was a respecter of wealth in the matter of seating for the living, so, too, the dead were given special consideration in return for a fee. For some, this special attention involved burial within the church, which was looked upon as a great honor and was commonly practiced during the eighteenth century. Arrangements of this kind and their cost can be clearly seen in an extract from the "Articles, Laws and Ordinances" adopted by the Flatbush church in 1701:

Those who are inclined to be interred within the church, are required to pay for an adult corps of sixteen years and upwards, £ 4; for a corps under sixteen years, to six years of age, £ 3; and for a child of six years and under, £ 2... for the profit of the church.[37]

There were also small additional expenses at Flatbush for the different categories of corpses noted above. These fees had to be paid to the schoolmaster who at this time was responsible for the manual labor associated with burials, whether they occurred in the church or in the churchyard. The schoolmaster's instructions for burials in the church

Gravestone in Sleepy Hollow cemetery.

were carefully spelled out. Among other things, he was "required to see that the graves are to be dug so deep that two coffins can be placed therein, one above the other, and that the grave for the coffin is seven feet deep, and that he shall remove all dirt out of the church."[38]

As might be expected, ministers were customarily interred in the church, generally in the front, near or under the pulpit. When possible, others who were interred in the church were often buried under the pew where they had customarily sat when attending church. The practice of interring the dead beneath the church ended at about the time of the Revolution, although ministers were occasionally accorded this honor for a time longer. Thus, Abraham Rosencrantz was buried beneath the church at Fort Herkimer in 1796, as was Christian Bork at the Franklin Street Church in New York in 1823, and Benjamin Westfall at Stone Arabia in 1844.

For those who could afford it, the *voorlezer* was frequently given the special function of acting as *aanspreker*, or "funeral-inviter." Properly attired, he made the rounds calling on relatives and friends of the deceased to inform them of the date and hour of the funeral and requesting their presence. Despite the important role played by the churches in the lives of the people at this time, funeral services usually took place in the home of the deceased; services in the churches did not become commonplace until the nineteenth century. While the body lay in state in the best room of the house, the *doodkleed*, a pall of fringed black cloth or velvet, was spread over the coffin. The pall was the property of the church and its use was often free to families who had contributed toward its purchase, but it had to be rented by others. In 1728 in the New York Collegiate Church, for example, the rental fee was eight shillings for use of the "old" black cloth pall, twelve shillings for the "new" black cloth pall, and eighteen shillings for the velvet pall.[39]

The discomfort that church-goers frequently experienced from having to sit on uncomfortable benches for two or more hours was compounded during the winter because of the absence of heating facilities. This resulted from lack of funds and because many church members looked upon the purchase of stoves and fuel as extravagant luxuries. The women tried to deal with this problem by using *stoofjes*, which were portable, perforated boxes made of wood with metal liners in which live coals were placed. These resembled footstools and were almost a fetish with the women. As explained by one diaryist, the boxes were placed on the floor below their skirts so that the heat "therefrom might go up to the *regiones superiores* and to all parts of the body which the skirts covered."[40] The extent to which these "foot stoves" were popular can be judged from a report concerning the Albany church:

It was not an uncommon occurrance to see, on a Sunday, from fifty to seventy-five colored servants or slaves, at the church door, awaiting the arrival of master or mistress, with two or more foot stoves in hand, filled with live hickory coals taken from an old Dutch fireplace . . . in those days it was no laughable matter to sit in a cold church for three long hours to listen to the preaching of the gospel, when the thermometer was below zero.[41]

Among families in which there was a shortage of foot warmers, the latter were slid along the floor and passed back and forth from mother to daughters. Not wanting to be accused of being effeminate, the male church-goers had to keep themselves warm by wearing sufficient clothing. Even the ministers in times of extreme cold did not hesitate to preach while clad in woolen caps and mittens, although one early account states that at Pompton Plains "the Dominie would keep warm by the extreme of gesture."[42]

Stoves did not make a common appearance in the churches until the Revolution or later, and then only in the face of much opposition. Wood-burning stoves were not introduced at Bedminister, New Jersey, for example until 1818, and the Flatlands church was without heating facilities until 1825, when thirty persons subscribed $69.00 for the purchase of a wood-stove. When stoves were first introduced, they were often placed on high pedestals and could be reached only by a ladder or by a short catwalk leading from the gallery. As suggested by one writer, this practice probably pleased only the sexton because it gave him an opportunity to acquaint the congregation with the importance of his office by making an unnecessary amount of noise while he replenished the stoves.[43] Only after trial and error, was it discovered that this was not the most advantageous way to heat the sanctuary. After installing two stoves in the Schenectady church in 1792 at gallery level, it is interesting to note the consistory minutes of December 25, 1798: "Finding that the stoves are not placed to the best advantage of scattering warmth to the audience, be it resolved that the Consistory will meet in the church tomorrow to endeavor to place them to more advantage."[44]

In common with church leaders of other denominations, ministers of the Dutch Reformed churches and their consistories grappled from time to time with what they considered to be the increasing worldliness of their day. Dominie Theodorus Frelinghuysen, minister at Albany

Interior of Albany Church showing position of the stoves. (From Joel Munsell,
Collections on the History of Albany, *I)*

from 1745 to 1759, for example, by his preaching from the pulpit on
Sundays and by his daily exhortations denounced the growing popular-
ity of worldly amusements. He no doubt was serious about the changes
taking place, especially when a theatrical company was organized in
the community, but his criticism seems to have been in part a reaction
to the gradual assimilation of English manners by a people that had
been very Dutch in the past. The Reverend Archibald Laidlie, the first
minister of the Dutch Reformed Church to be called specifically for
preaching in English, also quickly gained a reputation by denouncing
excessive gaiety and pleasure-seeking as sinful. From the moment he
arrived in New York in 1764, he preached long and earnestly against
dancing, shooting matches, and other amusements.

One cannot leave the story of ministerial concern about worldly
pleasures without recounting an amusing yet tragic incident perpe-
trated at Albany by the detractors of the Reverend Theodorus Frelinghuysen. It occurred on a Monday morning in the spring of 1759, and
was in response to the sermons of the previous day in which the

dominie had been, according to one observer, "peculiarly eloquent on the subject of theatrical amusements and pernicious innovations."[45] On stepping outside from his parsonage on the following morning, he found on his doorstep a staff, a pair of old shoes, a loaf of black bread, and a coin—all items that a person could use if he were leaving on a journey. It was an "emblematic message" signifying a desire on the part of some of his parishioners to see the dominie leave the community. Greatly offended by the prank, the highly sensitive Freling-huysen soon left Albany and sailed for Holland on a trip that he had been contemplating for some time. He never returned, but disap-peared mysteriously at sea during the return voyage.

As the right hand of the ministers, the consistories joined in the denunciation of worldly amusements. For example, the Great Consis-tory of several churches in central New Jersey, including Raritan, Bedminster, Readington, and Harlingen, condemned dancing as "wan-tonness [that was] unbecoming of Christians, and [was] a temptation to fleshly lusts, and besides an offense to the pious." In reference to shooting matches, it described them as an "inducement for the assem-bling of many idle and fickle persons, where nothing is ever transacted except that which is utterly worthless, and usually ungodly." When a member of the Readington church persisted in attending such events, he was declared "an unworthy partaker of the Holy Sacrament" and forbidden "the use thereof... until he shall manifest sorrow and re-pentance."[46]

Some of the decisions of the consistories seem archaic by today's standards, as the following examples illustrate. On August 7, 1707, the consistory of the New York church resolved that "to obviate scandal," no children born out of wedlock should be baptized until the parents, or at least the mother, have appeared before the consistory and ac-knowledged "the greatness of their sin, and been warned of repentance and conversion, and have also made declaration of the same." The declaration was usually performed in the presence of the entire con-gregation.[47] The Church during the eighteenth century also opposed marriages within certain degrees. Thus, on August 25, 1766, the con-sistory at New York declared that the marriage of one Jacob Le Roy with his deceased wife's sister was "inconsistent with laws human and divine" and that he should therefore "be denied the Lord's Supper so long as he continues in this relation."[48]

If special problems arose for which the consistories had no ready answer, they did not hesitate to consult their immediate superior, the Classis of Amsterdam. Thus, on April 9, 1739, the consistory of Kings-ton asked advice on whether a husband and his second wife, both of whom were members of the local Dutch Reformed church, should be permitted to take communion because there was a question as to whether the man had been legally separated from his first wife. Classis sent word back on July 20, 1739 (on some matters Classis acted promptly!) that "these people must be requested, and if need be, commanded, to refrain from the enjoyment of the Lord's Supper, so long as the case has not been settled by the [civil] court."[49]

Although the Dutch Reformed Church played a significant role in the daily life of the people and her ministers and consistories kept a watchful eye for wrongdoers and signs of impiety, Dutch Reformed church-goers were not ascetics and certainly were less puritanical than some of their Calvinist brethren to the northeast in New England. As was true during the New Netherland period, even Sunday observance was sometimes lax. A New England physician during a visit to New York City in 1697 remarked that "the Dutch seem not very strict in Keepeing the Sabbath, you should see some shelling peas at theyr doors children playing at theyr usuall games in the streetes & and ye taverns filled."[50] Similarly, a visitor to New York in 1704 noted that the people there were not as "strict in keeping the Sabbath as in Boston and other places where I have been."[51] Church records seem to indicate that the women were more regular in their attendance than the men.

It was particularly in the matter of using intoxicating drinks that the Dutch Reformed church-goers demonstrated that their daily lives were not always of the austere and strict type traditionally associated with the followers of Calvinism. Far from being prohibitionists, liquor flowed freely at such communal events as barn and house raisings, sheep shearing, harvesting and haying, and cutting and stacking the minister's supply of firewood. Church leaders not only condoned drinking but often became active participants. When Rip Van Dam of New York, acting as advocate for the Dutch Reformed inhabitants of Kingston, succeeded in thwarting Governor Cornbury's attempt to foist an Anglican clergyman on them, the Kingston consistory rewarded Van Dam with a "valued keg of rum."[52] Church account books contain entries for the purchase of liquor for the "entertainment" of visiting ministers. And during house visitation, as one writer has stated, "it was a sad breach of politeness" not to offer the pastor some choice brew.[53] The churches, moreover, saw nothing amiss with serving liquor at such functions as baptisms, marriages, the ordination of elders and deacons, and funerals.

Funerals during the eighteenth century especially tended to take on the appearance of a public feast and by today's standards would be considered in poor taste by most segments of society. The expenses for "entertaining" those who attended often exceeded the actual costs of the burial, a custom that apparently was sanctioned by the Church. When Claes Janse, who was of the "poorer sort," died in 1695, the church at Albany paid the funeral expense of one hundred fifty-nine guilders, about two-thirds of which were payment for two half vats of beer, six bottles of rum, and five gallons of Madeira wine. As a consequence, as described by one writer, although Claes Janse was of the "church poor," he was able to end his days "with a good dry coffin, a good dry grave, and a far from dry funeral."[54] Similarly, when Marritje Lievertse, a pauper, died in Albany in 1700, the church saw to her proper burial. Over half the expense was for beer, wine, and rum. When Pieter Jacob Marius, a wealthy New Yorker and member of the consistory, died in 1703, twenty-nine gallons of wine and a half vat of beer were consumed at his burial. It is also worth noting that the funeral costs in 1751 for the wife of the Reverend Johannes Van Driessen, which were paid by the church at Pompton Plains, included "15 shillings for her burial; 2 pounds and fifteen shillings for sugar, rum and butter; 8 shillings for baking; and 10 shillings for a barrel of beer.[55] Tobacco and pipes were also supplied to the mourners, as well as fancy cakes and cookies—800 cookies were eaten at Marius' funeral! Special mementoes of scarves, handkerchiefs, gloves, rings, and silverware were sometimes presented to the pallbearers and close relatives and friends of the deceased. As might be expected, complaints about the extravagance of funerals arose occasionally during the eighteenth century. Sometimes this criticism came from laymen, as is revealed in the increasing number of persons who "requested in their wills that they be buried very simply." Others, however, continued to leave instructions that they be buried in "the old Dutch fashion" rather than the simpler modern mode.[56]

Although their drinking habits might belie their otherwise austere religious upbringing, in one respect particularly the Dutch Reformed during the eighteenth century lived up to a trait commonly associated with the Calvinists, namely, their work ethic. Numerous accounts written by travelers and other observers of this period relate how the Dutch Reformed were hard workers and were thrifty to the point of being parsimonious. To again quote the New England physician who visited New York in 1697: "I cannot say I saw any of ye Dutch that were tollerably well drest, though rich enough to weare what they pleased, they are a parcimonious people, & expend Little on theyr livelyhood, which makes them usually well moneyed, & good paymasters."[57] Similarly, an English traveler reported about the middle of the eighteenth century that the Dutch of New York were "habitually frugal, industrious, and parsimonious."[58] These observations applied equally to rural church-goers. The Frenchman Hector St. John de Crèvecoeur, who settled in New York in 1756 and wrote about American agriculture, described a typical Dutchman as "one who implicitly believes the rules laid down by the synod of Dort" but at the same time as one who, to "judge by his waggon and fat horses . . . thinks more of the affairs of this world than those of the next. He is sober and laborious, therefore he is all he ought to be as to the affairs of this life; as for those of the next, he must trust to the great Creator."[59]

IX

Relations with the Indians and the Blacks

The primary motive for founding New Netherland in the early seventeenth century was a desire for financial gain. It is therefore not surprising that the Dutch from the beginning established close relations with the Indians whose assistance was indispensable for the fur trade. Similarly, it is not surprising that black slaves were introduced at an early date as a means for furthering the economic exploitation of the colony. In considering these matters, the student of church history must ask himself how the Dutch Reformed Church felt about the Indians and the blacks. Did it condone the treatment they received at the hands of the white men? What attempts did the colonial pastors make to Christianize them and how successful were these efforts? Were the opinions of the colonial pastors about missions a reflection of views held by the mother church in Holland? Did the fall of New Netherland to England in 1664 bring about any changes between the Dutch Reformed Church and the Indians and the blacks? These are some of the questions this chapter will attempt to answer. Because the experiences of the two groups differed somewhat in their relations with the Church, they will be treated separately.

Although most Protestant denominations were not too active in overseas missions until the nineteenth century, a missionary spirit was not lacking in seventeenth century Holland when New Netherland was founded. The noted geographer and theologian Petrus Plancius (1552–1622), for example, labored diligently at efforts to have preachers and qualified laymen accompany Dutch explorers and colonists as missionaries. Similarly, professors Antonius Walaeus (1573–1639) and Johannes Hoornbeek (1617–1664) of Leiden and Gisbertus Voetius (1589–1676) at Utrecht were strong proponents of missions. Ecclesiastical bodies in the Netherlands also issued pronouncements from time to time encouraging missionary endeavors. Thus, as early as November 1599, the Classis of Amsterdam recommended that a minister accompany the Dutch fleet to the East Indies so that "the people living there in darkness might be drawn to the true Christian religion."[1] Similarly, the Classis of Delft in April 1614 requested that ministers going overseas learn the native languages and study the local religions in order to facilitate the conversion of non-Christians.[2]

In light of the above observations, it is not surprising that an interest was shown at an early date in converting the Indians of New Netherland. The West India Company itself, usually under prodding by the ecclesiastical authorities in Holland, occasionally issued proclamations bearing on missions. Article Two of the "Provisional Regulations" of March 28, 1624, outlining the terms by which the Company would send colonists to New Netherland, stipulated that the settlers shall "by their Christian life and conduct seek to draw the Indians and other blind people to the Knowledge of God and His Word."[3] A similar enjoinder was included in the mandate given several months later to William Verhulst at the time of his appointment as New Netherland's governor.[4]

It is very possible that Bastiaen Jansz Krol, who was sent to New Netherland in 1624 as the colony's first comforter of the sick, carried on missionary work among the Indians. If true, it would mean that his efforts in this regard preceded those of the highly-acclaimed John Eliot of Massachusetts by about two decades. Although the instructions given Krol at the time of his appointment make no mention of missionary work, Governor Verhulst's mandate of about January 1625, stipulated that he was to encourage Krol in instructing "the Indians in the Christian religion out of God's Holy Word."[5] Moreover, the orders given to comforters of the sick soon after Krol's appointment specified that they were to carry on missionary work along with their regular duties.[6]

As additional evidence that Krol probably carried on missionary work among the Indians, there is the statement of September 23, 1626 by Isaac de Rasière, a leading Dutch official in New Netherland, explaining why Krol was appointed commissary or agent of the West India Company at Fort Orange to replace David Van Krieckenbeeck, who had been killed by the Indians. According to De Rasière, Krol was given the appointment "because he is well acquainted with the language."[7] If the reference here is to the Indian language, it definitely means that Krol as Comforter of the Sick had extensive dealings with the Indians. Their language was extremely difficult to learn, and only through close contact could Krol have become "well acquainted" with it.

The records of Dominie Jonas Michaelius, who arrived in New Netherland in 1628 as the colony's first ordained minister, are somewhat more enlightening than those of Krol on the matter of missionary work among the Indians. Unfortunately, Michaelius looked upon the latter with contempt, declaring that considerable false information had been circulated in Holland concerning their "docility" and "good nature." He described them as "entirely savage and wild, strangers to all decency, yea, uncivil and stupid as garden stakes, proficient in all wickedness and ungodliness."[8] In light of these views, it is not surprising that he considered it impossible to convert the adult Indians to Christianity until they had become more civilized. He therefore advocated that the Dutch Reformed Church, for the present, concentrate on winning over the children.

Michaelius' plans for working with the Indian children called for separating them from their parents. "For without this," he declared, "they would forthwith be as much accustomed as their elders to the heathenish tricks and devilries, which of itself are kneaded in their heart by nature by a just judgment of God, so that having once, by habit, obtained deep root, they would with great difficulty be brought away from it." After separation, the children could then be placed "under the instruction of some experienced and godly schoolmaster . . . [to be] instructed not only to speak, read, and write our language, but especially in the fundamentals of our Christian religion, and where, besides, they will see nothing but good examples of virtuous living." Michaelius believed that the Indian children could later become "a principle means of spreading the knowledge of religion through [their] whole nation," and he therefore recommended that, while at school, they occasionally "speak their native tongue among themselves in order not to forget it."[9]

Michaelius' plans for separating the Indian children from their parents were fraught with two major difficulties. First, as the dominie himself acknowledged, the Indian parents had a strong affection for their children, and would be unwilling to part with them. Secondly, the profit-conscious West India Company would oppose separating the children against parental wishes out of fear that antagonizing the Indians would jeapordize the fur trade. In view of these considerations, and bearing in mind that Michaelius remained in New Netherland less than four years, it is not likely that his missionary "program" was even attempted.

Of the various ministers who served in New Netherland, none showed a greater interest in the spiritual welfare of the Indians than Johannes Megapolensis, who served at Rensselaerswyck from 1642 to 1649 and at New Amsterdam from 1649 to 1670. His efforts in this respect were in accord with the wishes of the Classis of Amsterdam, which in its call of March 22, 1642, urged him "to proclaim Christ to

[both] christians and heathens."[10] His contract with the patroon, Kiliaen Van Rensselaer, also specifically stated that his duties at Rensselaerswyck would include "the edification of the inhabitants and Indians."[11] In 1643, Van Rensselaer, a religious man himself, wrote Megapolensis that it was his daily prayer that through the dominie's labors among the Indians,

their stony hearts may be softened, their blind eyes opened and their deaf ears unstopped by the power of the Holy Ghost, in order that they may see and understand the wonders of His law, recognize their sins and His grace and that they may be brought to the fold of Jesus Christ and go among other heathen bringing forth righteous fruits of confession and gratitude.[12]

Megapolensis' interest in the Indians is clearly shown in the lengthy description he wrote about them in 1644, which he apparently enclosed in a letter to a friend in Holland. It was soon published at Alkmaar as a pamphlet entitled *Een Kort Ontwerp vande Mahakvase Indianen, Haer Landt, Tale, Statuere, Dracht, Godes-Dienst ende Magistrature*. In addition to describing the physical features of the Indians and their dress, the study includes considerable information about their customs regarding marriage, childrearing, burials, government, and, of course, religion. Particularly informative are Megapolensis' comments on the Indian language because they illustrate the problems the Dutch ministers faced in trying to preach in the native tongue.[13]

As was true of Michaelius, Megapolensis found little to admire among the Indians' customs, but these feelings, rather than dissuading him, seemed to make him more determined to convert the Indians. He visited them in the woods and frequently traveled with them "ten, twelve, and fourteen persons" at a time in their hollowed log canoes. He also opened his house to the Indians and once remarked that he sometimes had up to "eight at once lying and sleeping upon the floor near my bed." Occasionally the Indians, as many as ten or twelve at a time, would attend Megapolensis' church services.[14]

Despite the fact that Megapolensis made a careful study of the Mohawk people and became somewhat acquainted with their language, the number of converts that he won during his six year stay at Rensselaerswyck was small. Indeed, one authority has recently stated that by the time Megapolensis left Rensselaerswyck for New Amsterdam in 1649, he "had almost certainly failed to convert a single Indian."[15] It must not be overlooked, however, that he did make the Indians of the upper Hudson more aware of the white man's religion and thereby helped lay the groundwork for some of the ministers who followed him.

Megapolensis' missionary endeavors during his long pastorate of twenty years at New Amsterdam also had only limited success. The Indians around Manhattan Island had been mistreated several times by the Dutch and were definitely more hostile than the Mohawks. The Classis of Amsterdam, however, had been led to believe that Megapolensis and his colleague Drisius had won a signifcant number of converts. To set the record straight, the two dominies wrote the Classis on July 15, 1654, that although they wished it were otherwise, little progress had been made, and their one major success proved to be only temporary:

It is true that a sachem of the Indians has sojourned for a length of time among us at the Manhattans, who was diligent in learning to read and write, which he learned to do tolerably well. He was also instructed in the principal grounds of the Christian faith, and publicly joined in recitations on the catechism by Christian children. We gave him a Bible that he might peruse it and teach his own countrymen from it. We hoped that in due time he might be the instrument of accomplishing considerable good among the Indians. But we acknowledge that he has only the bare knowledge of the truth, without the practice of godliness. He is greatly inclined to drunkenness, and indeed, is not better than the other Indians.[16]

Megapolensis and Drisius later reported that their efforts, after two years of working with this Indian, "resulted in nothing. He took to drinking brandy, he pawned the Bible, and turned into a regular beast, doing more harm than good among the Indians."[17]

The knowledge that Megapolensis developed regarding the customs and language of the Indians and the confidence they showed in him enabled the dominie to play an important role in obtaining the release of, or aiding in the escape of, white people held prisoner by the Indians. The most celebrated of these instances was that involving Father Isaac Jogues, a French Jesuit missionary, who was captured on August 3, 1642 by some Mohawk Indians. For thirteen cruel months he was held prisoner at the Indian village of Osseruenon (near the present Auriesville, New York), about forty miles above Fort Orange. Upon learning that Jogues might soon be burned by the Indians, Megapolensis and some friends arranged for his escape in late August 1643. After being hidden for about seven weeks, he was finally put aboard a ship headed for France.[18]

Jogues returned to America in the following year to renew his missionary labors. Once again he was taken captive by the Mohawks but this time he was quickly executed. The Indians presented Megapolensis with Jogues' missal and breviary along with various clothes of the martyred man. The Dutch minister rebuked the Indians for their wretched deed, but the Indians responded with the explanation that "the Father had left the devil among some clothes which he had stored in their custody, [and these] had caused their Indian corn, or maize, to be devoured by worms." They also expressed surprise over the dominie's concern about Jogues' death, considering the longstanding enmity that existed between the French and the Dutch.[19]

In view of the frequent directives that came from Holland in support of Indian missions and the efforts put forth by men like Dominie Megapolensis, one must perforce ask why greater success was not achieved during the period of Dutch rule. Several explanations can be given, but perhaps chief among them were the differences between the two cultures. From the beginning of the New Netherland period, the opinion was expressed by various Dutch leaders that only after the white man's civilization had been introduced in a marked degree among the Indians could any measure of success be achieved in Christianizing them. As was mentioned, this was the reasoning behind Dominie Michaelius' plan for converting the Indian children by separating them from the parents.

Some of the white man's religious customs were particularly incomprehensible to the Indians and to become accustomed to them would take time. Megapolensis, for example, reported that the Indians were especially astonished at the Christian manner of prayer, which often made them laugh. They likewise found it difficult to understand the Dutch dominie's manner of preaching, particularly how he could "stand there alone and make so many words, while none of the rest may speak."[20] At a time when Catholics were competing with Protestants for the souls of the Indians, the latter also expressed difficulty in comprehending how Christians using the same "book of truth" could hold diametrically opposing views on such matters as the Virgin Mary and the use of Crucifixes.[21]

A fundamental problem in bridging the gap between the two cultures was the language barrier. All the ministers who worked among the Indians exclaimed about the tremendous difficulties they had in learning their language. These difficulties were clearly brought out in the tract that Megapolensis wrote about the Indians in 1644:

This nation has a very difficult language, and it costs me great pains to learn it, so as to be able to speak and preach in it fluently. There is no Chrisitan here who understands the language thoroughly; those who have lived here long can use a kind of jargon just sufficient to carry on trade with it, but they do not understand the fundamentals of the language. I am making a vocabularly of the Mahakuaas' language, and when I am among them I ask them how things are called; but as they are very stupid, I sometimes cannot make them understand what I want. Moreover when they tell me, one tells me the word in the infinitive mood, another in the indicative; one in the first, another in the second person; one in the present, another in the preterit. So I stand oftentimes and look, but do not know how to put it down. And as they have declensions and conjugations also, and have their augments like the Greeks, I am like one distracted, and frequently cannot tell what to do, and there is no one to set me right. I shall have to speculate in this alone, in order to become in time an Indian grammarian. When I first observed that they pronounce their words so differently, I asked the commissary of the company what it meant... and, although he has been connected with them here these twenty years, he can afford me no assistance.[22]

The bad example set by many of the whites in such matters as excessive drinking, disorderly conduct, and cheating was also a deterrent to spreading the gospel. When Dominie Megapolensis, in answer to a question from a group of Indians, informed them that his sermons were designed to admonish the Christians not to "steal, nor commit lewdness, nor get drunk, nor commit murder," the Indians replied with keep perception that he did well to teach such things, but they found it difficult to understand why so many Christians continued to do them.[23] In some instances, the behavior of the Dutch toward the Indians during the New Netherland period was anything but Christian, as, for example, during Kieft's Indian War of 1641–1643, when innocent Indian women and children were wantonly slain and a scorched-earth policy was followed. Moreover, on at least two occasions under Dutch rule, Indian captives were sent to the Caribbean Islands as slaves.

The number of Indian converts won by the Dutch Reformed Church was particularly small when compared to the success enjoyed by the Roman Catholic Church. In explaining this, it must be remembered that the Dutch Reformed pastors were only part-time missionaries; they did not live for long periods among the Indians as did the Jesuits, but made only sporadic visits to their villages or preached to them when they visited a white settlement served by a Dutch Reformed minister. In contrasting their work with that of the Jesuits, one must also take note of another special problem faced by the Dutch Reformed missionary-pastors. As described by one authority:

That the Dutch made such a poor showing compared with the French [missionaries]... was largely owing to differences between their respective faiths, Roman Catholicism, with its ritual, ceremony, and visible symbols of faith, had a stronger appeal for a people whose religion and very ways of thought were expressed in terms symbolic of the physical universe and their forest environment. How many Indians penetrated beyond the outer symbolism of the Catholic faith is another matter, but certainly very few of them at this point were ready to appreciate the introspective and unadorned Calvinism offered them by the Dutch Reformed Church. The two churches also differed in the standards required for baptism. The Jesuit fathers labored throughout Canada and Iroquoia baptizing those who requested it—and many who did not—with little regard to age or previous instruction. In accordance with general Protestant practice, however, the classis of Amsterdam ruled in 1661 that baptism should be administered only to adult Indians who had confessed their faith and to their children.[24]

The ruling of 1661 mentioned above is worth quoting because of its far-reaching implications not only for the conversion of the Indians but also the blacks. It declared that

no one, who is an adult, is [to be] admitted to baptism without previous confession of his faith. Accordingly the adult Negroes and Indians must also be previously instructed and make confession of their faith before Holy Baptism may be administered to them. As to their children, the Classis answers, that as long as the parents are actually heathen . . . the children may not be baptized, unless the parents pass over to Christianity, and abandon heathenism.[25]

With the exception of the Albany-Schenectady area, Dutch Reformed missionary work tended to lag after the fall of New Netherland in 1664. This came about in part because of the shortage of ministers. In 1676, for example, there were only two Dutch ministers in the colonies to look after a dozen churches and preaching stations. Perhaps, too, because civic responsibilities henceforth rested with the English, the Dutch Reformed leaders felt that their religious obligations toward the Indians were also correspondingly lessened. Even some of the great names among the ministry during the period of English rule were surprisingly inactive in the matter of Indian missions. There is no record, for example, that the distinguished Henry Selyns, minister at New York from 1682 to 1701, carried on any personal missionary work among the Indians. He did, however, make a few passing references to Indian converts in some of his poetry, and in 1689 he sent a copy of John Eliot's Indian Bible to the Classis of Amsterdam so that their reverences could "see how God teaches in a savage tongue for the conversion of the Indians, and in order to bring

Japheth into the tents of Shem."[26] Similarly, the great Theodorus Jacobus Frelinghuysen, despite his deep concern over winning souls among the colonists of the Raritan Valley, showed virtually no outward interest in Christianizing the Indians.[27]

That the Albany-Schenectady area became an important center for Dutch Reformed missionary activity was due to several factors: its being located on the frontier, its relatively easy access to the interior via the Hudson and Mohawk rivers, its continued importance in the fur trade, and the fact that the Dutch Reformed Church was for several decades the strongest religious body in the area. It must also be noted that because the English government for a time had difficulty in attracting Anglican missionaries to this region, it was willing to pay an annual stipend (usually 60 to 75 pounds) to any Dutch dominies who would carry on some missionary work along with their regular pastoral duties. The government was motivated in this as much by political considerations as by concern about the spiritual welfare of the Indians. The Dutch preachers, it was thought, could help counteract the influence of the Jesuits, who the English claimed were advancing the political interests of the French among the Iroquois nations. In the minds of many Indians, according to one writer, becoming a Protestant Christian was associated with loyalty to the British crown, and therefore for the English "to contribute to their conversion was as truly politic as it was nobly Christian."[28]

Beginning at the close of the seventeenth century, a succession of Dutch Reformed ministers undertook serious missionary work in the Albany-Schenectady area. These men included Godfriedus Dellius at Albany, 1683–1699; Johannes Lydius, also at Albany, 1700–1709; Bernardus Freeman at Schenectady, 1700–1705; and Peter Van Driessen at Albany, 1712–1738.[29]

Dellius, a graduate of the University of Leiden, was thirty years of age when he arrived at Albany in 1683 to assist the aging Gideon Schaats. He began his missionary endeavors in a modest way by brief visits to the Indian villages, doing some preaching and distributing small gifts. With the assistance of an interpreter of mixed blood, Dellius later translated the Ten Commandments and the Apostles' Creed, as well as several prayers, for the use of the Indians, using the Roman alphabet in approximating Mohawk phonetics. Several Psalms were also translated and set to music, which, according to Dellius, the Indians sang "with sweet melody."[30] The high respect in which he was held by the Indians is shown by the success he enjoyed in occasionally ameliorating the sufferings of Catholic missionaries held captive by the Indians, just as Megapolensis did about a half century earlier. In 1698,

Page from a polyglot Indian Bible, Mohawk and English. (From H. A. Hill, The Gospel according to Saint Luke Translated into the Mohawk Tongue)

following the end of King William's War, Dellius was chosen as one of two special agents to go to Canada to explain the peace terms to the French and their Indian allies and to arrange an exchange of prisoners.

The records of the Albany church covering the years of Dellius' ministry indicate that about one hundred twenty-five Indians were baptized, ranging in age from four weeks to eighty years.[31] About 85 per cent of these were baptized before 1696 and were mostly older children and adults; those who were baptized later were nearly all infant children of proselytes, indicating a slackening of missionary interest during Dominie Dellius' last years as minister at Albany. The first recorded baptism is for December 27, 1689 and its description is typical of many that followed:

Paulus. After a previous public confession [there] was baptized a certain heathen who had become blind a number of years ago, and whose name among his nation had been Ock-Kweese. He is about 40 years old, and the name Paulus was given to him. The interpreters of the confession were Aarnout Cornelisz Vile and Hilletje Cornelisz.[32]

It was customary at this time to give a Christian name to an Indian following his or her conversion. Thus, after their baptism on December 26, 1694, Kanarongwe, meaning "Drawer out of arrows," was renamed Pieter; Thowariage, i.e., "One whose fence has broken down," became Brant; and Sakkoherriho, i.e., "One who re-enters the bushes," was henceforth called Dorcas.[33] A predilection was shown for Biblical names, especially during the early period. For example, the new names given to twelve converts following their baptism on July 11, 1690, included Seth, Rachel, Adam, Sara, Jacob, Lidia, Isac, Rebecca, and David.[34] The baptism of several Indians on the same date was not unusual and no doubt occurred because of the stipulation of 1661 by the Classis of Amsterdam declaring that the baptism of adult "heathens" could not be disassociated from confession of faith. It is likely therefore that Indians were sometimes instructed in the Reformed faith as a group, following which they were then also baptized as a group.

Dellius' work among the Indians came to a sudden end in 1699 as a result of partisan politics. Like other Dutch Reformed ministers of his day, he became an outspoken critic of Jacob Leisler, the would-be governor of New York during the late 1680's, and the pro-Leisler faction never forgave him for this.[35] Later, when Dellius became involved in several questionable land deals involving many hundred square miles above Albany and in the Mohawk Valley, the pro-Leisler element in the colonial assembly got its revenge. Following an investigation, the land grants were annulled and Dellius was suspended from his ministerial duties until his name could be cleared. Discouraged, Dellius returned to Holland and later accepted a call to a church in Antwerp, despite pleas from the SPG to return to Albany and resume his work among the Indians.[36]

Even more popular than Dellius, was Bernardus Freeman. Born in Westphalia and a tailor by trade, the Classis of Amsterdam had refused to license him as a preacher on the grounds that his education was insufficient. Undaunted, Freeman persuaded the Classis of Lingen to ordain him, after which he left for America to become pastor at Schenectady. He proved to have a natural talent for preaching and was an indefatigable worker. According to a contemporary, he acquired greater skill in the Indian language than any Dutch Reformed minister before him, being able to write it as well as speak it.[37] He, too, trans-

Bernardus Freeman.

lated several prayers and creeds as well as parts of the Old and New Testaments. In 1710, five years after he left Schenectady, to take charge of the collegiate churches on Long Island, a group of Indians petitioned Governor Hunter for Freeman's return, asking that this time he live not at Schenectady but directly among them. Freeman did not accept, perhaps because of his wife's aversion to living among the Indians.

When Dellius left Albany in 1699, several Indian sachems requested the English governor to appoint another missionary in his place. Dominie Johannes Lydius of the Netherlands was that man. He was looked upon as a person of exemplary piety and virtue, especially by the Indians. In 1702, for example, a group of "praying Indians," as the converts were frequently called, made a public testimony in his behalf, declaring that because of his efforts, they no longer lived "in envy and malice, which are the works of Satan, . . . but in Peace and concord."[38] When Lydius died in 1709, his Indian followers presented the local Indian agent with four beaver skins as a memorial to him.

The reverend Peter Van Driessen, during his long pastorate of twenty-six years at Albany, labored diligently to carry on the work of his predecessors. In a letter of 1731 to the Classis of Amsterdam he reported that one of the tribes near Albany had been "altogether Christianized" and that about two-thirds of another tribe living a few days journey farther on had also "enlisted under the banner of Christianity."[39] In a letter to some friends in Holland, written in the following year, he suggested that because of the increasing number of Indian converts, a chain of native churches should be established so that they can "be gathered . . . for morning and evening worship on the Lord's days" and that "catechetical exercises [can be] conducted by the most expert among them." Van Driessen pointed out that since the Jesuits were successful in using such methods to "propagate their religious harlotry," those persons who preach "the pure doctrine of the Gospel" should be even more successful.[40] Nothing apparently came of Van Driessen's plan, but the Indians did give him a liberal gift of land in appreciation for his missionary efforts.

In discussing the work of these missionary-pastors, the historian must be careful not to exaggerate their success. Reports to the Classis of Amsterdam concerning the number of converts does not mean that these Indians remained Christianized or that all who were baptized (at least among the children) became full-fledged church members. For example, although Dellius in a letter of 1693 reported that he could count two hundred Indian converts at Albany, his report of the following year speaks of only sixteen communicant members. Sixteen years later, at the time of Lydius' death, there were still only about thirty Indians who were communicant members of the Albany church. At Schenectady, Dominie Freeman baptized one hundred one Indians during his five year stay there, but only fourteen of them joined as communicant members.[41]

Progress among the Indians continued to be relatively slow because many of the problems that confronted the ministers during the New Netherland period were still present. One of these was the language problem. Even the great Dellius had to rely on the assistance of an interpreter, as did Freeman to some degree. The shortage of ministers also continued to create difficulties. Thus, from 1705 to 1715, when Schenectady was without a resident Dutch Reformed pastor, only nineteen Indians were baptized there and, at most, only one communicant member was received.[42]

The behavior of the white men at times continued to be a problem just as it did in the New Netherland period, and the Indians were quick to note the gap existing between what the preachers proclaimed from the pulpit and the actual behavior of the Christians. About 1705, the Reverend Thoroughgood Moor, an Anglican, remarked after spending about a year at Albany that it was "preposterous" to begin missionary work among the Indians, without first getting the white inhabitants to mend their ways. According to Moor, "it is from the behaviour of the Christians here, that [the Indians] have had, and still have, their notions of Christianity, which God knows, hath been generally such that it hath made the Indians to hate our religion."[43] Other missionaries, as well as Indian tribal sachems themselves, made similar remarks from time to time.[44] Although the enslavement of Indians was not nearly as commonplace as Negro slavery and was more popular in the New England colonies, its practice was not unknown in New York and New Jersey where most of the Dutch Reformed churches were located.[45] Even its limited practice could not help cause some Indians to question the Christian precept of brotherly love.

The hypocrisy that the Indians observed in the white man's behavior is well-illustrated in a comment by Mrs. Grant. In recalling her experiences at Albany about 1750, she remarked that the following question was frequently asked by the Indians: "How can people, who believe that God and good spirits view and take an interest in all their actions, [continue to] cheat and dissemble, drink and fight, quarrel and backbite, if they believe the great fire burns for those who do such things?"[46] Of course, Christianized Indians were themselves guilty at times of "backsliding." Thus, a report of 1710 mentions a group of Indian converts at Albany as leading such scandalous lives "that they can scarce be reputed Christians."[47]

In view of these continuing problems, it is not surprising that progress was relatively slow for many years. Nevertheless, solid foundations were being laid. By the middle of the eighteenth century, interest in missions at Albany had reached the point in which a few "Dutch" lay persons, mostly women, were carrying on missionary work among detached Indian families who came to live on the outskirts of Albany during the summer months. Converts who were won in this way occasionally did some proselyting of their own when they returned to their tribes for the winter months. Indeed, the burial records of the Albany Church indicate that perhaps beginning already early in the eighteenth century some Christianized Indians remained closely attached to the Dutch Reformed congregation throughout the entire year. It is even possible that in 1769 an Indian was serving as a member of the church consistory.[48]

In addition to the Albany-Schenectady region, a limited amount of missionary work was carried on farther up the Mohawk Valley and in the Schoharie area by the middle of the eighteenth century. George Michael Weiss, for example, minister in the upper Mohawk Valley from 1736 to 1742, wrote the Classis of Amsterdam in 1741 that he had preached to the Indians on several occasions through an interpreter and had baptized some of them at their request.[49] At Schoharie, a number of Indians were accepted into the church. Thus, as early as

April 28, 1731, its records mention the baptism of two children of converted Indians. From that date until May 10, 1778, about one hundred Indians, adults and children, were brought into the church. The records also indicate that several Indians were married according to the rites of the church, including one instance of an Indian man marrying a white woman and another of a white man taking an Indian wife.[50]

A discussion of the relations of the Dutch Reformed Church and the blacks, like that of the Indians, must also begin with developments in New Netherland. The first slaves arrived at New Amsterdam about 1626, and additional ones were brought in as they were needed. They were utilized in a variety of ways: for the construction and upkeep of public buildings and military fortifications, for work on the farms of the West India Company, and as laborers serving the free white farmers. After New Netherland fell to the English in 1664, slavery continued to be practiced as before, but on an increasing scale. New York and New Jersey, where most of the Dutch Reformed churches were located, eventually had the largest number of slaves of any of the northern colonies. Even more significant is the fact that persons of Dutch and German descent living in these colonies were among the most active users of slave labor. In Bergen County, New Jersey, for example, which was heavily Dutch, slaves made up twenty per cent of the population in 1738. Similar situations existed among predominantly Dutch areas in New York. Thus, according to the federal census of 1790, sixteen per cent of the population of Kinderhook township was slave, and in Albany, only 238 out of 1,146 heads of families reported that they owned no slaves.[51]

In order to understand the attitude of the Dutch Reformed Church in the American colonies toward slavery, it is necessary first to examine the attitude of the people in the Netherlands, especially the religious leaders, toward this nefarious institution. In brief, the Netherlands was deeply involved in the slave trade throughout the western hemisphere and the country's ministers and theologians voiced little opposition to it. Even those few religious leaders who did criticize slavery were generally mild in their reproach. Rather than urge its abolition, the critics tended to emphasize the need for kind treatment of the slaves and the need to Christianize them.

The views held in the Netherlands concerning slavery were clearly delineated in a Latin work published in 1742, entitled *Dissertatio Politico-Theologica de Servitute, Libertati Christianae non Contraria*. Written by the Reverend Jacobus Elisa Joannes Capitein (1717–1747), the *Dissertatio* was based on a lengthy oration the author had given, also in Latin, while a student at the University of Leiden.[52] Capitein argued that although masters had to treat their slaves kindly, slavery, as an institution, was justified. In vindicating slavery, he quoted extensively from such classical writers as Aristotle and Seneca, but he relied especially on the Bible. Capitein declared there were no specific biblical injunctions against it and, furthermore, it was frequently condoned in both the Old and New Testaments. He also quoted from John Calvin's *Institutes* to demonstrate that spiritual freedom can exist in conjunction with bodily servitude. Dominie Capitein further justified slavery on the basis that it could be a blessed means to civilize the black people.

Several observations indicate that Capitein's views on slavery were shared by most of Holland's religious leaders. For example, it is significant to note that he was permitted to deliver an oration defending slavery on biblical grounds while he was enrolled as a student of theology at one of the Netherlands' most distinguished schools. Furthermore, one of the country's noted theologians of that time, Professor Joan Van Den Honert, directed Capitein in the preparation of the *Dissertatio*. The fact that Capitein was ordained into the ministry shortly after he delivered his oration also demonstrates that the Dutch Reformed Church had virtually no compunction against slavery. Not only was the *Dissertatio* soon translated into Dutch, but the Dutch translation went through four editions within a year.

Inasmuch as the Dutch Reformed ministers in the American colonies looked to Holland for spiritual and theological leadership, and many of them received their training there, it is not surprising that they accepted the views of the mother country toward slavery. Some of the ministers of New Netherland were slaveowners themselves. It is very possible that the Reverend Johannes Megapolensis had one or two slaves as domestic servants. Dominie Johannes Polhemus, before coming to New Netherland in 1654, engaged in the sale of slaves on at least one occasion while serving in the Dutch colony of Brazil. Later, while serving as minister of several congregations on Long Island, he purchased in May 1664 a slave at a public auction on Manhattan Island for 440 guilders. Similarly, Dominie Gideon Schaats, while serving the church at Fort Orange owned a slave named Black Barent.[53]

This attitude toward slavery did not change appreciably during the eighteenth century. Indeed, a number of distinguished lay members of the Church were still buying and selling slaves at the very close of the century. For example, on February 6, 1792, Albert Hoogland, a trustee of the church at Jamaica, Long Island, placed the following advertisement in the newspaper: "For sale cheap, for no fault but only for want of employ, a negro wench, aged thirty, who understands all kinds of country house work with her two children, a girl aged eighteen and a boy aged six."[54] General Peter Gansevoort, of Revolutionary War fame and a member of the consistory of the church of Albany, purchased three slaves and sold another during the years 1795 to 1808. As late as 1770, the consistory of the church in New York accepted a young slave valued at forty-five pounds sterling, as payment for back-rent that a John Van Zandt owed the church for using some of its land. Even some of the ministers still continued to own slaves. The Reverend Simeon Van Arsdale, for example, who served the church at Readington, New Jersey, from 1783 to 1786, possessed a slave, as did his successor, the Reverend Peter Studdiford.[55]

It is thus obvious that the Dutch Reformed churches and their ministers concerned themselves very little with the question of whether slavery was an evil system. This does not mean, however, that the leaders of the Church were also unconcerned about their salvation. On the contrary, from an early date various religious leaders and ecclesiastical bodies showed an interest in this matter. The Reverend Jonas Michaelius, for example, while serving on the coast of Guinea in Africa before going to America in 1628, suggested that two young mulattoes be sent to the Netherlands for Christian training in order that they might be used later as missionaries in their native land.[56] In 1644, the Classis of Brazil declared that slaveowners were "responsible for instructing their Negroes in the Christian Religion and that time should be provided for all Negroes to assemble in a suitable place in order to receive instruction from a catechist."[57] Similarly, in October 1648, the Classis of Amsterdam drafted a memorial requesting the directors of the West India Company to establish regulations for the religious instruction of the blacks.[58]

In light of these developments, it is not surprising that an interest was also shown in the spiritual welfare of the slaves of New Netherland. As early as 1638, Dominie Everardus Bogardus of New Amsterdam requested the authorities in Holland to send a schoolmaster in order "to teach and train the youth of both Dutch and blacks in the knowledge of Jesus Christ."[59] In 1641, the Classis of Amsterdam took notice of a communication from the consistory of New Amsterdam that some progress was being made in bringing the slaves to "the right knowledge of God."[60] According to the records of the church at New Amsterdam, from one to three black children were baptized annually from 1639 to 1655. This church was also the scene of occasional marriages between slaves, probably the first such marriages to be performed in a Protestant church in the Thirteen Colonies.[61]

Dominie Henricus Selyns, while serving congregations on Long Island and at Stuyvesant's bowery from 1660 to 1664, made a conscientious effort to instruct blacks in the Christian faith. Although he did not expect much success from his work among the adults, he did anticipate some worthwhile results from teaching the children. On June 9, 1664, he wrote to the Classis of Amsterdam that

when it was seemly to do so, we have to the best of our ability, taken much trouble in private and public catechizing [of the slaves]. This has borne but little fruit among the elder people who have no faculty of comprehension; but there is some hope for the youth who have improved reasonably well.[62]

According to Dominie Samuel Drisius of New Amsterdam, Selyns, by his "diligence and success in preaching and catechizing, and his humble and edifying life," attracted some slaves to his church services.[63]

The Dutch Reformed Church showed a lessening interest in the spiritual welfare of the slaves after New Netherland fell to the English in 1664, just as it seemed to do in the case of the Indians. As evidence of this, one can cite the communications of Dominie Selyns during his second tour of service in America. His published correspondence makes no mention of slaves during that time, which is surprising when one recalls the favorable impression he made earlier in his attempts to catechize them. It is even more surprising when one notes that his second stay in America involved almost twenty years of service, 1682–1701, in New York, which had a large slave population.[64]

Published church records of the English period make only scattered references to slaves. For example, the burial records of the First Reformed Church of Albany contain only four entries from the eighteenth century in which the deceased are listed as "servants" or as children of "servants." There may have been others, of course, who were not so designated by the church clerks, but it is significant that these four entries were recorded by the same clerk, Barent Bradt, who served in that capacity for twenty-five years (1722–1757) and recorded more than fifteen hundred burials. The Albany records are strangely silent about the possible burial of blacks thereafter until the nineteenth century, when between 1858 and 1879, eight persons are listed as "colored."[65]

The records are even more discouraging when one examines the situation in New York. Out of a total of about six thousand baptisms listed in the published records of the Collegiate Church of New York for the last half century of the colonial period, 1726–1776, only nineteen children are listed whose parents had a servile status.[66] This small number becomes even more significant when one considers that eleven of the nineteen notations are for children of the same parents, Frans Franse and Elisabet Bickers. (Frans is variously referred to as *neger* or *knecht*, meaning respectively "negro" and "servant," and as belonging to Hermanus Van Gelder, while, Elisabet is variously listed as *negerin* or *meyd*, meaning respectively "negress" and "maid," and as being the property of Guiliaam Ver Plank.) Even allowing for occasional failures on the part of the church clerk to make special notations for baptisms involving black parents, the record indicates that the number of blacks who were members of the Collegiate Church was very small.[67]

In comparison to the efforts put forth by some religious groups, such as the Anglicans (working through the SPG), Moravians, and Quakers, the Dutch Reformed Church did not make an *organized* effort to win converts among the slaves during the English period. Slaves who became members of the Dutch Church after 1664 did so primarily as a result of the close personal relations that often existed between slaveowners and their slaves. To understand this, it must be noted that although slavery was common in New York and New Jersey, the number of slaves owned by individual families in these colonies was small. In Kinderhook township in New York in 1790, for example, the largest slaveowner, Philip Van Alstine, had only sixteen slaves and the average number of slaves per slaveholding household was less than four.[68] This situation can be attributed to there being no plantation-type agriculture comparable to that of the South, where large crews of slaves were not unusual.

When relations between master and slave were close, a slaveowner who had deep religious convictions tended to take a personal interest in the spiritual welfare of his slaves. The latter oftentimes participated in the family worship of the whites, and their children were likely to share in the same religious instruction received by the children of their masters. Such instruction was usually given by the mistress or one of her older daughters. On Sundays, such slaves sometimes accompanied their masters and mistresses to church.

It is impossible to judge how many Dutch Reformed slaveowners took such an interest in the spiritual welfare of their slaves. Nor can one determine how many of the latter actually became communicant members or were even baptized. It does not necessarily follow that because slaves accompanied their white owners to services on Sundays and that because churches had segregated areas for seating blacks, that a significant number of them became church members. Reliable histories written in commemoration of anniversaries of churches dating back to the colonial period generally mention slaves only occasionally.[69]

In addition to the absence of an organized attempt by the Dutch Reformed Church to convert the blacks, several enervative factors made proselyting difficult. In common with other religious groups, the Church was initially hindered in this because of the presumption held by some individuals that a Christian could not be kept in slavery nor could children who were born to a Christian. Dominie Godefridus Udemans (ca. 1580–1649), for example, a minister in Holland and one of the few Dutch critics of slavery, declared that once a slave was converted he should be emancipated. In *'t Geestelyk Roer Van 't Coopmanschip*, first published in 1638, he stated that if the slaves "want to submit themselves to the lovely yoke of our Lord Jesus Christ, Christian love requires that they be discharged from the yoke of human slavery."[70] If this reasoning were valid, it would mean that a slaveowner could be deprived of his property if he permitted the proselytism of his slaves.

By the close of the New Netherland period, some of the Dutch Reformed pastors were taking seriously the idea that being a Christian and a slave were incompatible. Even Dominie Selyns, in June 1664, wrote the Classis of Amsterdam that he sometimes refrained from baptizing slave children because the parents "wanted nothing else than to deliver their children from bodily slavery, without striving for piety and Christian virtues." He added that his colleagues in New Netherland also were hesitant to baptize slave children for the same reason.[71]

Despite the views of Udemans, Selyns, and others, the opinion that conversion altered the legal status of a slave or his children was not universally accepted in Dutch Reformed circles during the seventeenth century. Nor was the question immediately resolved after the fall of New Netherland. The courts of England generally followed the rule that a person could be held as a slave until he became a Christian, at which time he was to be freed. There were some judicial decisions handed down in England, however, which refuted this rule, thus leaving the matter in some doubt. Furthermore, the rules which applied in English courts were not necessarily applicable in the colonies.[72]

The lack of clarification of the laws regarding the effect of baptism on slavery impeded the conversion of slaves. As long as the possibility existed that the conversion of slaves would prove to be a financial risk for the slaveowners, the latter were prone to discourage missionary work among them. Some of the slaveowners also were worried that the preaching of too equalitarian a gospel would endanger the conventions between master and slave because it would give the slave ideas about liberty and equality.[73]

The question of equating Christianity with freedom was eventually clarified. Between 1664 and 1706, six of the colonial legislatures, including those of New York and New Jersey, passed acts declaring it was legal for a Christian to be held as a slave. The provincial government of New York, for example, decreed in 1706 that "the Baptizing of any . . . Slave shall not be any cause or reason for the setting them or any of them at Liberty."[74] Pronouncements by religious leaders and organizations in Europe also indicated that from an ecclesiastical point of view, conversion to Christianity would no longer be a cause for manumission. In 1727, the Bishop of London declared that conversion to Christianity did not make "the least Alteration in Civil Property; that the Freedom which Christianity gives is a Freedom from the bondage of Sin and Satan . . . but as to their outward condition [slaves] remained as before even after baptism."[75] In 1747 the Classis of Amsterdam declared that "the acceptance of Christianity . . . does not make servants, male and female slaves, free persons."[76]

Although these decrees and pronouncements facilitated the proselyting of slaves, the Dutch Reformed Church when compared to the evangelical churches, still labored under several handicaps—just as it did in its attempts to convert the Indians. As was noted, the decree issued by the Classis of Amsterdam in 1661 prohibiting the baptizing of adults without previous confession of faith, and the baptizing of children until the parents had first passed over to Christianity, applied equally to Indians and blacks. Similarly, as was the case in dealing with the Indians, the emphasis that the Church placed upon doctrine, together with the unemotional and sophisticated sermons of the Dutch Reformed pastors, could not have held much attraction for most blacks.[77]

Prejudicial views about the black people also severely handicapped attempts to carry on meaningful missionary work among them. Dutch Reformed religious leaders were themselves inclined to cast the blacks as an irresponsible and inferior race. For example, on August 11, 1628, Dominie Jonas Michaelius wrote from New Amsterdam to a friend in Holland that "the Angola slave women are thievish, lazy, and useless trash."[78] Similarly, on May 7, 1695, a committee of the Dutch Reformed churches on Long Island asked the Classis of Amsterdam to send someone to replace the Reverend Rudolphus Varick, who had just died. Classis was informed that if a replacement did not arrive soon, the people, in the absence of preaching of the Gospel, "may be turned into negroes, and become black and polluted."[79] The Reverend Ulpianus Van Sinderen, pastor of several congregations on Long Island, in an effort in 1749 to discredit his colleague, the Reverend Johannes Arondeus, claimed that the latter was unlawfully ordained and "therefore, all his baptizings and marryings had no more legalization than if a negro had done them."[80] This condescending attitude was also shown in the instructions given in 1767 to John Montanye on his appointment as sexton for the Garden Street Church in New York. Instruction Number V read as follows: "You are to prevent any disorders in the church by children, negroes, or dogs, either before, during and after service-time."[81]

Bigoted opinions such as the above reflected the treatment the blacks sometimes received at the hands of the whites. As was true in the case of the Indians, this treatment pointed out the gap that often existed between what the Christians preached and what they practiced and thereby further impaired missionary efforts. How, for example, could a slave believe in the sanctity of marriage or in the brotherhood of man knowing that at a public auction a slave family could be broken up at the whim of a seller or buyer? As one Reformed Church writer has recently pointed out, slaves, in the minds of many persons, "were considered as 'things,' not as human beings for whom Christ also died. They were chattels to be bought, sold, and used to the advantage of the owner."[82]

The black people also found it difficult to understand the Christian concept of love and justice in view of the kind of punishment sometimes meted out. Surprisingly enough, despite the generally close relations often existing between slaves and their owners in New York and New Jersey, these two colonies developed the most severe Black Codes of any of the northern colonies. Examples of brutal punishment can readily be cited to illustrate this problem. Near Somerville, New Jersey, in 1734, an alleged slave uprising was prevented by hanging one slave, cutting off the ears of several others, and whipping the remainder. Following the so-called slave insurrection in New York on February 28, 1741, one hundred thirty-four black people were brought to trial, of whom thirteen were burned alive, eighteen were hanged, seventy were transported to the West Indies, and thirty-three were acquitted. Also in 1741, two slaves, one belonging to Albert Van Vooreze and the other to Demeck Van Horn, were executed by burning near Hackensack, New Jersey, for having set fire to several barns. When punishments were inflicted, the slaves from the surrounding area were frequently summoned to witness the event as a warning of what lay in store for anyone who broke the law. The effect such shameful treatment had on efforts to convert the black people is obvious. As one authority has stated, their "contempt for hypocrisy caused [them] to reject religious formulas which could not be put into actual practice. ...The truth is they understood only too well the impossibility of reconciling preachment with reality."[83]

In fairness to the Dutch Reformed Church, it must be noted that its attitude toward slavery during the colonial period was not greatly at variance with that of other religious groups. Generally speaking, churches at both ends of the religious spectrum were apathetic toward slavery as an evil institution. Although the Puritans had a few abolitionists in their midst, such as Samuel Sewall, the Puritans as a group did not speak out boldly against slavery or question its morality. Even among the Quakers there was no widespread anti-slavery movement until about the middle of the eighteenth century, and it was not until just before the American Revolution that strong measures were taken against those Quakers who refused to dispose of their slaves. At the other end of the religious spectrum, it can be noted that the Church of England did not question the right of its members to hold slaves. In fact, Anglican clergymen themselves frequently owned slaves and the Anglican Church accepted them as a form of endowment.[84]

Similarly, although some denominations worked more diligently at missions than did the Dutch Reformed Church and some were less doctrinaire in their approach to religion, this did not necessarily result in their being more successful in winning converts. Other denominations, too, faced difficulties relative to hostility of slaveowners toward proselyting their slaves, and also had the problem of trying to reconcile, in the minds of the black people, the harshness that was inherent in slavery with Christ's teachings about brotherly love. Although the SPG made a strenuous effort in behalf of the Anglican Church to win converts among the slaves, their work was not too successful. Even the more evangelical churches, such as the Methodists and the Baptists, did not enjoy a great deal of success from their missionary work until the time of the American Revolution. A careful study of missionary activity among the blacks of colonial New England has disclosed that by the end of the colonial period possibly the majority of the slaves in that region were still "heathen"; and of those who were listed as converted, many were only nominal Christians. One authority, after surveying the total missionary effort during the colonial period, has stated that "most of the slaves lived and died strangers to Christianity."[85]

X

Internal Discord and Controversy

The Leisler Troubles, described earlier,[1] was only one of many controversies that disturbed the tranquility of the churches during the colonial period. The causes for dissension varied from mundane and trivial matters to such fundamental issues as the irregular ordination of ministers and controversial methods of preaching. Sometimes the problems were local in nature and remained confined to a small area, while at other times they affected a large segment of the Church, with ministers pitted against ministers and congregations against congregations. Many problems were compounded because of the need to refer them to the Classis of Amsterdam for solutions.

In view of the fact that the colonial churches were unable to exercise independent action in solving ecclesiastical disputes or in ordaining men for the ministry, it is important to reconstruct the story of how the Classis of Amsterdam came to exercise its authority in the American colonies. Such a review is necessary in order to better comprehend the problems that arose from this subordination. The recapitulation of this development is also helpful for understanding the steps that were taken during the 1750's and 1760's leading to the eventual ecclesiastical independence of the colonial churches.

The claims of the Classis of Amsterdam to exercise ecclesiastical jurisdiction over the colonial churches date from the New Netherland period. As early as 1624, the Synod of North Holland decreed that the direction and supervision of the churches in the East Indies "shall remain with the churches and Classis within whose bounds are located the East India (Company's) Chambers."[2] The supervision of the churches in the territories of the West India Company was conducted on the same basis. This left the situation somewhat confusing because not all Company chambers or offices were located within the boundaries of the same classis. As a consequence, for a time during the early 1600's the Classes of Amsterdam, Hoorn, and Enkhuysen supervised the churches overseas. For example, in the case of New Netherland, it was the Classis of Enkhuizen that in 1628 sent over the first ordained minister, the Reverend Jonas Michaelius. Adding to the confusion was the fact that the Consistory of Amsterdam also for a time played a role in supervising the overseas churches. Thus, New Netherland's first comforter of the sick, Bastiaen Jansz Krol, was sent there in 1624 by the Consistory of Amsterdam.

The confusion subsided as the supervision of ecclesiastical affairs outside the Netherlands gradually devolved on the Classis of Amsterdam, particularly with respect to New Netherland. This transmission was natural as more and more business of the West India Company gravitated toward Amsterdam from the northern ports. Although some of the inland classes, such as Utrecht, at first complained about Amsterdam's special role, they too finally acquiesced. By 1636, when the Consistory of Amsterdam transferred its foreign responsibilities to the Classis of Amsterdam, the latter was virtually supreme in directing the ecclesiastical affairs of the Dutch Reformed Church in America.[3]

The fall of New Netherland to the English in 1664 did little to alter the old ties between the Classis of Amsterdam and the American churches. For its part, the Classis was determined that the offspring it had nurtured for about a half century would not lose its unique identity and be absorbed into English ways. Thus as early as 1665, it instructed the reverends Megapolensis and Drisius of New York "to oppose the introduction of the English Liturgy into our church as much as possible."[4] Similarly, in 1683, the church at New Castle, Delaware, was told to "not undertake, in ecclesiastical matters, anything of importance which savors of change without first communication with the Classis of Amsterdam."[5]

Considering the important role it played throughout the colonial period in examining young men for the ministry, solving internal disputes, and dealing with disciplinary problems, it is not surprising that one writer has referred to the Classis of Amsterdam as "the Metropolitan for the [Dutch] church in North America."[6] Unfortunately, it was three thousand miles across the Atlantic and this caused numerous problems as the colonial churches grew in size and numbers.

Questions about the qualifications of ministers were one of the most frequent issues that disturbed the tranquility of the churches and were brought to the attention of the Classis. These questions might concern a minister's orthodoxy, or his manner of preaching, or doubts about his ordination. Some controversies involved all three factors. As early as 1685, Dominie Selyns complained to the Classis of Amsterdam about tailors, cobblers, and others who were coming from Holland and endeavoring to be lay preachers and schoolmasters. "They speak against the church, public prayers and the liturgy of the church. . . .True believers are grieved at these things and look forward to very great troubles therefrom to the church of God."[7]

Selyn's colleagues joined him in his concern about allowing unfit persons to preach. This is clearly shown in their attitude toward Guiliam Bertholf, who, as described earlier, was extremely successful as a lay preacher in northern New Jersey. In June 1693, Dominie Rudolphus Varick of Long Island warned the Classis of Amsterdam to keep a careful eye out for Bertholf as he was contemplating going to Holland to check into several classes to determine "where he might most readily be examined and qualified as a minister." Varick characterized him as a schismatic, and urged Classis to oppose his ordination because not to do so would cause others to follow his example, to the great detriment of the churches and the colonial ministers.[8] Similarly, when Bertholf bypassed the Classis of Amsterdam, which together with the Synod of North Holland had made some critical remarks about him, and received ordination from the Classis of Walcheren, the Reverend Godfriedus Dellius of Albany wrote the divines in Amsterdam on October 7, 1694, that if such practice were allowed to continue, then "soon some marvelous kind of theology will develop here; ministers will be self-created, and the last will be first and the first shall be last. Rev. Gentlemen it grieves us much that on account of this man, our church and its ordinations have become a matter of ridicule."[9]

The manner in which the Reverend Bernardus Freeman received ordination also provoked controversy. In 1699, the Classis of Amsterdam rejected his candidacy to the ministry, stating that he had no ability for his craft of tailoring and "less for that demanded of a pastor," adding that he could not even pass with them the examination for a *ziekentrooster*.[10] Undaunted, Freeman went to the Classis of Lingen in Germany, a short distance from the Dutch border, and secured ordination.[11] He then left for America in the hope of being installed in the church at Albany which was vacant at the time. The Classis of Amsterdam hastily sent letters to America warning the ministers there about Freeman. It also dispatched Johannes Lydius to assume the pastorate at Albany. Lydius arrived first and was duly installed. Freeman therefore went to Schenectady, which had been without a settled pastor since 1690. Freeman was gladly received by Schenectady, but he and the congregation were shunned as outcasts for a time. Only after the exchange of numerous letters did the Classis of Amsterdam finally approve Freeman's call.

In looking back upon these developments, the historian of today can see them as part of a gradually developing dichotomy between two groups of churchmen: those wanting to maintain the old, orthodox approach to the ministry, and those favoring a more evangelical type of preaching. This is not surprising, because the churches in Holland, too, at this time were frequently embroiled in controversies, with heated exchanges taking place among Cocceians, Voetians, Cartesians, Labadists, and others, all of whom drew their inspiration from their favorite theologians and academicians. Factions increased in number as main parties were broken up into splinter groups reflecting different theological views. The Voetians, for example, became divided into "old" and "new" Voetians, and into "Marckians" and "Brakelians," depending on whether they followed the theological system of Johannes à Marck or Willem à Brakel. This partisanship was manifested not only among the clergy but also among the people as a whole.

The Voetians wore their hair short; the Cocceians wore it long. . . . The Voetians called Sunday "the day of rest;" the Cocceians called it "the Lord's day." The former kept the day strictly, refraining even from eating warm dinners; the latter allowed considerable freedom, and taught that after morning service, the people might indulge in recreation and even do some work. The Cocceian ladies were in the habit of spiting the ladies of the opposite party by seating themselves on Sunday at their parlor windows engaged in embroidering. The Voetians dressed plainly and lived moderately; the Cocceians dressed fashionably and lived luxuriously. The common people followed the former; the aristocracy the latter.[12]

It is therefore not surprising that the pastors on arrival in the colonies often reflected particular theological views being voiced in the Netherlands.[13] This was especially true in the case of Bertholf. Bertholf was born in the small town of Sluis near Middelburg, in the southern part of the Netherlands, which was "the heartland of the earliest Dutch Reformed pietism."[14] Among the pietist preachers in this area was Jacobus Koelman, pastor at Sluis from 1662–1674. Koelman was "a declared enemy of rules that forced ministers to abide by Formulas, and he therefore refused to submit to Church Orders, especially those regarding the observance of feastdays and the use of liturgical regulations."[15] His pastorate at Sluis occurred when Bertholf was between the ages of six and eighteen—an impressionable period in the life of a person—and his influence on young Bertholf was extensive. According to one authority, he became a "fiery supporter" of Koelman's ideas.[16]

The bifurcation that had been gradually developing among the colonial ministers between a kind of nonconformist, evangelical approach to religion and the traditional, orthodox method, reached a climax in the ministry of the Reverend Theodorus Jacobus Frelinghuysen, who in 1720 accepted a call to serve several villages in the Raritan Valley of New Jersey, including New Brunswick, Six Mile Run, Three Mile

Run, and North Branch. Frelinghuysen was born in 1692 in East Fries-land, Germany, adjoining the Dutch border, and received his ad-vanced education at the University of Lingen, also in Germany. Al-though of German birth, Frelinghuysen's religious upbringing was Dutch Reformed. Politically and economically, East Friesland and Lingen had long been closely tied to the Netherlands. Indeed, the district of Lingen had been a personal possession of the Dutch House of Orange since the time of William the Silent, and not until 1702, with the death of William III of Orange, did it revert to the German state of Prussia. Religiously, too, the Reformed element in these regions had been more closely tied to the Dutch than the German Reformed Church, the churches being often served by Dutch ministers or by German pastors who had studied at universities in the Netherlands. Both Johannes Wilehelmius and Otto Verbrugge, who occupied the chairs in theology at Lingen when Frelinghuysen enrolled there in 1711, were born in Holland and had studied at Leiden University.[17]

Frelinghuysen's theological views were a reflection of his training and experiences in Europe. Professor Wilhelmius at Lingen was an outspoken pietist, and had considerable influence on him. So, too, did the writings of the pietists Herman Witsius and Johannes à Marck. Later, the pietistic atmosphere of Frelinghuysen's first parish near Emden in East Friesland further crystallized his evangelistic approach to preaching. It is therefore not surprising that by the time of his arrival in America in 1720, Frelinghuysen, according to one of his recent biographers, had become "attached to a very narrow variety of puritan Calvinistic pietism."[18] Nor is it surprising, in view of his background, that Frelinghuysen quickly made common cause with the evangelical preachers, Bertholf and Freeman, as well as with the Reverend Cor-nelius Van Santvoord, pastor at Staten Island from 1718 to 1742 and at Schenectady from 1742 to 1752. Van Santvoord was a former student of Johannes à Marck of Leiden, who considered him one of his most brilliant pupils.

Frelinghuysen's manner of preaching became suspect in the minds of some churchmen immediately after his arrival in the colonies. Upon disembarking at New York, he was invited to be a guest minister at the local Dutch Reformed Church on the following Sunday. The two ser-mons he delivered on that day were thought by many of his listeners to be at variance with tradition, both as to their style of delivery and their content. Many, including the city's two Dutch Reformed ministers, Gualtherus Du Bois and Henricus Boel, were particularly annoyed because he omitted the Lord's Prayer from the prescribed order of church service.

On arrival in the Raritan Valley in late January 1720, Frelinghuysen plunged immediately into his work. The task confronting him was not easy. His parish covered an area of about two hundred fifty square miles which could be traversed only with great difficulty. The parishioners were mostly farmers with little education and were woefully ignorant of the gospel; they had never had a settled ministry, but were visited only on rare occasions by itinerant pastors.

As was foreshadowed by the sermons he had delivered in New York City, Frelinghuysen's preaching in New Jersey was of an emotional type as were also his prayers, which his opponents soon termed "howling prayers." In his sermons, he charged his hearers with being too concerned with tradition and formalism, and of taking their religion too much for granted by observing only the outward forms of Christianity. Above all else, he stressed the need to experience an inner conversion. The essence of his views on the need for spiritual regeneration is clearly manifested in an excerpt from a communion sermon he preached soon after his arrival in the Raritan Valley:

Much-loved hearers, who have so often been at the Lord's table, do you know that the unconverted may not approach? Have you then, with the utmost care examined, whether you be born again? . . . Or did you go blindly forward, . . . not examining whether you were of the number of those who are invited? . . . Let us then here be careful . . . here, by a morsel and swallow, can the covenant of God be desecrated; his wrath brought upon the whole congregation; and ourselves made liable to temporal and eternal punishment. Reflect, therefore, upon, and bear in mind this truth; and remember, that though moral and outwardly religious, if still you be un-regenerate and destitute of spiritual life, you have no warrant for an approach to the table of grace.[19]

Many of Frelinghuysen's parishioners were offended by his rigid standards for admission to the Lord's Supper and his direct and outspoken manner of preaching. His strict ecclesiastical discipline, which even included excommunicating members of the consistory, and his procedure for electing new consistory members were not always administered according to official church order. He also provoked criticism in other ways: by training young men without authorization as lay pastors or "under-shepherds" to assist him in looking after his widely dispersed flock; by associating familiarly with Dissenters, even to the point of asking the evangelistic Presbyterian minister of New Brunswick, the Reverend Gilbert Tennent, to share the pulpit with him; and by preaching without invitation in other Dutch Reformed parishes, such as in Monmouth County, New Jersey. In time, he advocated greater independence for the American churches and the establishment of a seminary for training ministers.

Frelinghuysen's preaching and actions divided not only his own parishioners in the Raritan Valley, but also Dutch Reformed congregations elsewhere as news of his style of preaching and his theological views were circulated. His colleagues in the Dutch Reformed ministry were also divided in their attitudes. As was noted, Bertholf of northern New Jersey, Freeman of Long Island, and Van Santvoord of Staten Island strongly praised Frelinghuysen and his work. When three of his sermons were published in 1721, Bertholf and Freeman described them as "three learned, well-digested, and thrilling sermons" that were "highly sound and scriptural, and agreeing in the smallest particulars not only with the written Word of God, but also with the teachings of our Heidelberg Catechism, adopted as a rule of doctrine, as well as with the forms employed in our Dutch churches."[20]

Other preachers opposed him. His chief detractor was the Reverend Henricus Boel of New York, but his critics also included the reverends Vincentius Antonides of Long Island, Peter Vas of Kingston, and for a time, Gualtherus Du Bois, the senior minister of New York. In 1725, an anti-Frelinghuysen publication, the *Klagte* (meaning "Complaint"), appeared in print. It probably was drafted by Tobias Boel, a lawyer brother of Dominie Boel, although the latter supplied most of the content and it carried the signatures of sixty-four heads of families from the Raritan region. Totalling no less than one hundred forty-six pages, the *Klagte* levelled several accusations against the fiery Raritan preacher: withholding communion from some of his parishioners without due cause; refusing to baptize certain children; departing from the Church Order in the election of consistory members; denouncing parts of the liturgy as dead formalism; refusing to listen to counsel when it was offered to him; and making disparaging remarks about other Dutch Reformed pastors.[21]

The controversy surrounding Frelinghuysen dragged on for almost fifteen years, and became increasingly public with the printing of the *Klagte* and of pamphlets written in answer to it by Freeman and Van Santvoord. The publication in Dutch of more than twenty of Frelinghuysen's sermons (some of which were translated and printed in English) also helped spread discussion among other churches. Both sides in the controversy presented their cases to the Classis of Amsterdam through a steady flow of correspondence. The Classis at first followed a rather neutral policy and even slightly berated the opponents of Frelinghuysen for trying too hard in preventing the circulation of his message, which Classis did not consider unorthodox. Gradually, however, the attitude of the Amsterdam divines shifted, and they sided more with the opposition.

In particular, Classis criticized Frelinghuysen for his stern disciplinary measures and for his non-observance of the rules of Church Order. As one writer has carefully pointed out, he "did by himself what should have been done by the Consistory... and did in Consistory what should have been done by Classis."[22] The language used by Frelinghuysen in his letters to the Classis in which he defended his behavior and his views made that body more angry. On January 28, 1728, the divines at Amsterdam wrote Frelinghuysen:

We cannot conceal the fact that we are grieved that the faithful counsels of peace given to you [earlier]... have been so lightly regarded by you. Yes, indeed, we are very sorry at the ungentle and bitter, the common and exasperating expressions which you use in your reply, and which are certainly very much out of place....We cannot understand how such cutting and immoderate expressions can be reconciled with the spirit of gentleness and humility, which is becoming to a minister above all things else. On the other hand, we consider that by such a style of speech the accusers will be more embittered, and alienations intensified, and the schism made worse.[23]

The reverends Freeman and Van Santvoord were also rebuked by Classis for their support of Frelinghuysen. Freeman was informed by letter of December 1, 1726, that his publication, *Defence against the Church of Raritan, 1726*, was read "with very little satisfaction, because so little appears therein to the point....We think that by this publication, you have only further fomented the quarrel, instead of doing something to extinguish it."[24] A similar letter was sent to Van Santvoord for his having also published a defense of Frelinghuysen. Although the critics of Frelinghuysen were also reprimanded occasionally by the Classis, the letters sent to them were milder in tone. Not until about 1738, was the dispute resolved, partly through pressure from Classis but also due to compromises reached independently in the colonies.

What was the final impact of Frelinghuysen's career on the Dutch Reformed Church? Opinions differ, but the following summarizes the views of most writers:

His congregations throve; revivals and "ingatherings" followed in his wake; his labors were commended by George Whitefield, Gilbert Tennent, and Jonathan Edwards. He did as much as any one to invoke the

Great Awakening in the Middle Colonies, and the region where he wrought remains a stronghold of his denomination.[25]

Eventually, many of his critics saw the worth of his evangelistic manner of preaching. Thus, in 1740, Dominie Du Bois of New York sat side by side on the same platform with Frelinghuysen to hear an open air sermon delivered by the impassioned English revivalist, George Whitefield. Despite his accomplishments as a preacher, however, there can be no doubt that Frelinghuysen was frequently in error in matters of church order and government. Moreover, in dealing with his critics, he was often tactless to the point of being arrogant. It is a blight on what was otherwise a distinguished preaching career, that in trying to bring about a spiritual awakening, Frelinghuysen himself did not practice the humility he demanded in others. He could have accomplished the same thing and perhaps even more without creating so much disaffection.[26]

Factional strife was also prevalent on Long Island, where in 1702, following the death of the Reverend William Lupardus, two candidates were called to replace him: the controversial Bernardus Freeman of Schenectady and Vincentius Antonides of the Netherlands. Freeman had the support of the evangelical wing of the Long Island churches as well as the old pro-Leislerian faction. He also eventually received the recommendation of Governor Cornbury. Some Long Islanders were unhappy with this choice. They did not care for Freeman's style of preaching and his having bypassed normal channels in seeking ordination. Moreover, they resented the governor's role in the matter, looking upon it as a usurpation of power over ecclesiastical affairs. In answer to an appeal from the anti-Freeman group, the Classis of Amsterdam sent the Reverend Antonides to serve the Long Island congregations.

Both men arrived at about the same time to assume their duties, and because each had a personal following among the congregations, factional strife developed. The Classis of Amsterdam supported Antonides and condemned Freeman for his actions. Some of the colonial ministers, such as Gualtherus Du Bois of New York, finally succeeded in getting each side to yield on certain points. In the end, both ministers were retained, preaching alternately in the various churches, but bitter feelings lingered for many years.[27]

In 1741, Freeman was declared emeritus and was soon replaced by Johannes Arondeus, and in 1746 Antonides was replaced by Ulpianus Van Sinderen. Quarrels between the two new ministers, both of whom came from the Netherlands, broke out quickly and soon became as rife as those between their predecessors. Because Van Sinderen, on arrival, had officiated at a marriage without first informing Arondeus, the latter refused to introduce him to his congregations. When the consistory tried to reconcile the two men at a private gathering, Van Sinderen refused, insisting on a public reconciliation. For this, the consistory for a time refused to attend Van Sinderen's services. Dissension also developed over the attitude taken toward the recently created Coetus, a quasi-classical organization of the colonial churches.[28] Arondeus was a bitter foe of it from the beginning, while Van Sinderen supported it at first. Arondeus was also more conservative in his manner of preaching and strongly opposed all evangelistic methods. In 1750, he was suspended from the ministry and shortly after deposed, but he continued to preach from time to time until his return to Holland in 1754.

In addition to questionable ordinations that took place in Holland, such as those of Bertholf and Freeman, several irregular ordinations occurred in the colonies that also caused problems. The circumstances surrounding the ordination of Paulus Van Vlecq can be cited as an example. Van Vlecq was an immigrant from Holland who about 1702 became a schoolmaster at Kinderhook, New York. He also did some lay preaching. In 1709, he was asked to serve as chaplain to a contingent of Dutch-speaking colonial troops accompanying a British army that was about to depart for Canada. The governor of New York therefore requested the reverends Du Bois of New York City and Antonides and Freeman of Long Island to ordain Van Vlecq. Du Bois and Antonides refused on the grounds that it was contrary to their Church Order. Freeman, however, was strongly in favor of complying with the request, and even seriously considered doing it on his own. In fact, the Classis of Amsterdam thought he had actually examined and ordained Van Vlecq and severely reprimanded him.

Van Vlecq was finally ordained by the Presbyterians and, as described in a preceding chapter, later served Dutch Reformed congregations in Bucks County, Pennsylvania. He also acted as an itinerant preacher at several out-stations, some of which were German Reformed or Presbyterian. All seemed to go well until it was discovered that he was a bigamist. In 1711, not long after his arrival in Bucks County, he married a local girl, although at the time he already had a wife in Holland. When news of this came out, Van Vlecq "fled the country" in 1715 and was not heard of again.[29]

The manner of Johannes Van Driessen's ordination created an even greater stir. When he appeared before the Classis of Amsterdam in September 1719 to seek ordination, he failed the examination so badly that a careful scrutiny was made of the documents submitted in support of his candidacy. This revealed that a certificate purportedly signed by two professors at the University of Groningen had been forged. Van Driessen was thereupon severely reprimanded and told to give up any further thoughts about entering the ministry. Later, however, he went to America, where on April 13, 1727, again with forged testimonials, he was licensed and ordained by the Congregationalists at Yale College. This was done with the assistance of his brother, Peter, the Dutch Reformed minister at Albany, who soon after, without proper authorization, installed Johannes as pastor at Kinderhook and Claverack, New York.

These highly irregular procedures evoked considerable criticism, first from the ministers at New York and Kingston, and later from the Classis of Amsterdam. The latter declared that the Congregationalists had no authority to commission persons for the Dutch Reformed ministry. Classis also censured the Reverend Peter Van Driessen for his role in the proceedings, while at the same time commending those colonial ministers who had denounced the procedure.

While serving the churches at Kinderhook and Claverack, Johannes Van Driessen made several visits to neighboring Kingston to win support from the Dutch Reformed congregation there and to counteract efforts being made to have his credentials invalidated. On February 9, 1732, the Kingston consistory held a hearing on the matter, which was also attended by the Van Driessens and some of their adherents. The meeting displayed little evidence of Christian forbearance. As reported by the Reverend Peter Vas of Kingston and his consistory, when discussion occurred that was detrimental to Johannes Van Driessen's case,

some of his ringleaders immediately arose to their feet and made a great tumult. The one called out one thing, and another an other thing. Indeed, they even threatened to drag certain members of the Consistory through the church by the hair. This they would have easily done, if they had not been afraid of the law. While this was going on, Peter Van Driessen and his brother went out, after which the meeting was adjourned. But along the street they belched forth much indecent slander and vituperation against Rev. Vas and his Consistory.[30]

Other ministers shared Vas' concern about Van Driessen's ordination. Dominie Reinhart Erickzon of Schenectady, for example, joined Vas in asking the Classis to send a letter "written in such Dutch that plain men can understand that [Van Driessen has]... no lawful right to occupy the minister's office in our church."[31]

It is interesting to note that although most colonial ministers, as well as the Classis of Amsterdam, were greatly concerned about irregular ordinations, many of the laymen gave little heed to them. Thus, as was noted, the Reverends Bertholf and Freeman had long and eminently successful ministries. Van Vlecq's brief ministry was also marked by success. "In three years he had organized three congregations, supplied ten preaching points, married thirteen couples, received into church membership 88 persons, and baptized 94 children."[32] Johannes Van Driessen, despite his checkered past, served various Dutch Reformed congregations for twenty-one years. He officiated at Kinderhook and some nearby preaching stations until 1735, after which until 1748 he served several churches in New Jersey, including Acquackanonck, Pompton Plains, and Paramus.

The irregular ordination of John Henery Goetschius also disturbed the peace of the Church for a time. Goetschius had received some theological training in Switzerland before coming to Pennsylvania in 1735 at the age of seventeen. After serving as a lay preacher among German congregations in the Philadelphia area, he began studying theology under the direction of Peter Henry Dorsius, a Dutch Reformed pastor in Bucks County, Pennsylvania. On April 7, 1741 he was ordained, without prior approval from the Netherlands, by Dorsius, Theodorus Jacobus Frelinghuysen, and Gilbert Tennent. The latter was a Presbyterian minister at New Brunswick and a close friend of Frelinghuysen. Goetschius was shortly after installed as minister of the four Dutch Reformed churches in Queens County Long Island—Jamaica, Newtown, Success, and Oyster Bay.

From the beginning, the Classis of Amsterdam criticized the ordination of Goetschius because it had taken place without its prior approval. The problem quickly became enmeshed in two other controversies: the longstanding factional strife on Long Island between Antonides and Freeman (whom Goetschius supported) and the troubles that still occasionally reappeared concerning Frelinghuysen's preaching in the Raritan Valley. To add to Goetschius' problems, some of the more conservative colonial ministers were also upset at his irregular ordination. Dominie Boel of New York City, for example, made periodic visits to Long Island to preach to the disaffected elements among Goetschius' churches, and even encouraged parents to bring any children who had been baptized by Goetschius, to him for rebaptism, declaring that those performed by Goetschius were invalid. The question about Goetschius' ordination was not settled until 1748, when he consented to being reexamined and reordained, this time with the approval of the Classis of Amsterdam, by a delegation of ministers meeting in New York City.

If the examination and ordination of ministers had been permitted to take place in the colonies on some kind of a regular basis, some of the difficulties described above could have been averted. Unfortunately, only on rare occasions did the Classis of Amsterdam permit this. The first person to be ordained on this side of the Atlantic was Peter Tesschenmaeker, who arrived in the colonies about 1673, after studying for a brief period at the University of Utrecht. In 1675, he began serving as "theological licentiate" or "proponent" at Kingston, New York. The following year, a petition signed by forty-nine Dutch and English inhabitants of Kingston was presented to Governor Edmund Andros, requesting that some means be found for ordaining Tesschenmaeker, "hee being a man of a sobar life and conversacon having Deportted himselfe to sattisfaction of ye Inhabitantce."[33]

There was no response to this petition, but in 1679, when Tesschenmaeker was serving at New Castle (formerly New Amstel) on the Delaware, a similar request was made by its congregation. On this occasion, Andros approved the request and, "by virtue of his Majesty's letters patent" and the authority entrusted in him by the crown, authorized Dominie Wilhelmus Van Nieuwenhuysen of New York to proceed with an examination and to ordain him if he were found "capable."[34] On October 9, 1679, the four Dutch Reformed pastors who were then serving in the colonies proceeded with the examination. The ministers, in addition to Van Nieuwenhuysen, included Gideon Schaats of Albany, Laurentius Van Gassbeeck of Kingston, and Casparus Van Zuuren of Long Island. The examination was satisfactory, and was therefore followed by ordination.

The ministers who conducted the examination, realizing that their action was unprecedented and "fraught with weighty consequences," sent a lengthy letter of explanation to the Classis of Amsterdam. They asked the Classis, in evaluating what they had done, to bear the following matters in mind: that Tesschenmaeker had studied for a time at the University of Utrecht; that he had served several congregations "to the general gratification of everybody," as shown by excellent testimonials; that the ministers were "legally compelled" by the governor to proceed with the examination; and that the examination had been conducted in accordance with "the laudable customs and orders of the churches in our Fatherland." Classis was also reminded of "the inconvenience of the winter season here; the dangers of the voyage, if the candidate should seek to obtain his advancement from your Reverences; [and] the embarrassments of the congregation by the long delay."[35]

The Classis of Amsterdam made no criticism of what had taken place, which is surprising in light of its later actions. Indeed, the Classis praised the ministers for their action, stating in a letter of April 2, 1680, "we cannot judge otherwise than that your Reverences have acted legally, wisely and well in that matter, even as present need and service of the church demanded. We cordially and fully assent to all that was done, and gratefully acknowledge that the same has been communicated to us so circumstantially, clearly and with so well-cut a quill."[36]

Fifty years later, in 1729, the Classis of Amsterdam took a similar step by granting permission to a committee of colonial pastors to examine and ordain John Philip Boehme to serve several German Reformed churches in Pennsylvania. The committee consisted of the reverends Du Bois and Boel of New York City, and Antonides of Long Island. Boehme had been a schoolteacher in Germany for twelve years before coming to Pennsylvania in 1720, where he immediately began work as a lay preacher among German Reformed immigrants. The interest of the Classis of Amsterdam in the Germans in Pennsylvania came about in 1728 when, because of war and poverty in the Palatinate, the Consistory of the Palatinate—the head of the Reformed Church there—appealed to the Reformed Church in the Netherlands to look after the German immigrants in Pennsylvania. Thereafter, for more than sixty years, the Reformed Church in Holland served as the ecclesiastical overseer of the German Reformed churches in Pennsylvania. It carried on a regular correspondence with them and also provided money as well as Bibles and religious tracts. Upon the recommendation of the Consistory of the Palatinate, it also supervised the dispatch of numerous German Reformed pastors.[37]

Although the ordination of Boehm was allowed, the Classis was determined that it would not set a precedent for similar procedures in the future, declaring that it had permitted a committee of colonial clergymen to ordain him only because "of the lack of the usual means of obtaining an ordination at the new planting of a church in such a distant region; and also because the ministry of the Word was so necessary there." It was made clear to Boehme's three consistories in Pennsylvania that if a new minister were ever needed, they would have to send to the Classis "for one that is competent and duly qualified." The New York ministers and their consistory also agreed "that nothing of the kind should be undertaken or performed hereafter, without an express order of the Classis."[38]

Despite its misgivings about ordinations taking place in the colonies, the Classis of Amsterdam, a few years after the Boehme case, gave permission to several ministers in New Jersey to examine and ordain Johannes Schuyler. Schuyler had received some theological training in Holland, and had continued his theological studies privately after his arrival in the colonies. In 1736, he began serving the church at Schoharie, New York, as a ministerial candidate. His examination and ordination as a full-fledged minister occurred on April 18, 1738, in the presence of the Reverends Reinhardt Erickzon of Freehold and Middletown, Gerardus Haeghoort of Belleville, and Antonius Curtenius of Hackensack and Schraalenburgh. As in the Boehme case, the letter granting this permission clearly stated that it "must never be taken as a precedent by any others in any place whatsoever; any attempt in this direction being in danger of immediate rejection."[39]

The dependence of the colonial churches on far-off Holland for their ministers obviously made it difficult to fill vacancies promptly. Consequently, during most of the colonial period there were about three times as many Dutch Reformed churches as there were ministers. As was true during the seventeenth century, the shortage of pastors during the eighteenth century meant that most ministers had to serve more than one church, and some of them were in charge of several congregations. Sometimes the churches had to rely for long periods of time on *ziekentroosters* or *voorlezers*, with an occasional visit from an ordained clergyman to administer the sacraments. Bergen, New Jersey, for example, had no resident pastor from 1662 to 1749. In a few instances, as in the case of the churches of Monmouth County, New Jersey, from 1709 to 1731, the churches had to rely on a minister from another denomination.

The problems that resulted from the refusal of the mother church to permit ordinations in the colonies on a regular basis were pointed out in a letter of April 23, 1741 from Dominie Freeman to the Classis of Amsterdam. Freeman, writing in his eightieth year, reminded Classis that several congregations had made calls through the Classis to fill vacancies but with little success: Jamaica at the time being without a pastor for nine years, Schenectady for almost as long, and Fishkill, Raritan, and Flatbush having also sent out calls. Moreover, several congregations were too poor to afford bringing out a pastor from Holland. All of this, wrote Freeman, was occurring at a time when there "are here pious and godly persons, and youth fitted for the service, who are called by the church, [but] who by reason of classical authority and order must be refused."[40] Dominie Du Bois made similar observations in a letter of May 14, 1741, to the Classis, adding that when a vacant church continues to fail in its efforts to find a "Dutchman to preach to them, some will assuredly go over to the Independents, and others to the Episcopalians. This some have already done."[41]

In addition to the problems resulting from limitations placed upon ordination in the colonies, the requirement that disputes among the churches and the ministers be submitted to the Classis of Amsterdam for adjudication meant that ecclesiastical disagreements were often unnecessarily prolonged. Several examples can be cited to illustrate how this hurt the growth of the church. Thus, in a communication of February 4, 1711, concerning the effect of the long-standing quarrel on Long Island between the reverends Freeman and Antonides, the following communication was sent by an Anglican lay leader to the London office of the Society for the Propagation of the Christian Gospel:

I am informed . . . that the [Episcopal] Church at Jamaica [in Queens County] is of late very much strengthened by a violent division which hath for a considerable time been raging among the Dutch in some of the neighboring towns concerning their minister of whom they have two and their heats being grown to that degree that there is now no hope of a reconciliation many of those people have joined Mr. Poyer's [Episcopal] Church.[42]

As another example of how a prolonged dispute hindered the growth of the church, one can cite the dissension that centered around the activities of the Reverends Johannes and Peter Van Driessen. In a letter of 1732, Dominie Vas and the Kingston consistory wrote the Classis of Amsterdam:

The conduct of these two brothers here, has caused such an alienation of feeling, that some hold themselves aloof from the church, not caring to come to the preaching at all. The services of the pastor are held by them in contempt, and they do not come to the Holy Supper of the Lord. The Rev. Consistory is also despised; all of its enterprises are thwarted; and some are even unwilling to pay their promised salary, as we have discovered. Hence the ultimate ruin of the church is threatened, unless speedy efforts are made to save her.[43]

In making decisions bearing on the colonial churches, the Classis had to rely on written reports that were often tardily received and frequently biased and incomplete. For example, when the Classis asked Dominie Frelinghuysen for answers to a number of specific questions about the situation in the Raritan Valley, the New Jersey pastor sent back a reply of twenty folio pages. According to Classis, his answer, despite its length, "completely passed by" some of the things Classis had referred to him for explanation, and contained instead a considerable amount of extraneous information.[44] It goes without saying that procrastination and biased reports made it difficult to solve problems quickly.

Poor communications across the Atlantic resulting in the delay of letters reaching their destinations also caused problems. In the case of Johannes Schuyler, for example, the request by his consistory at Schoharie, New York for permission to take steps to proceed with his examination in the colonies had been made May 12, 1736. Not until October 1, five and one-half months later did the Classis answer in the affirmative. For some unexplained reason, the reply from Amsterdam did not reach Schoharie until March 3, 1738, seventeen months after it had been sent! Actually, it was lucky that it reached its destination at all; as reported by the committee of ministers that examined Schuyler, "the envelope was almost worn away [and] the seals were broken."[45]

In informing the Classis of what happened, the committee that examined Schuyler sent some good advice to the mother church in Holland. Noting that the long delays in hearing from the Classis were trying the patience of many, the suggestion was made that the Classis consider the "advisability" of creating some kind of an ecclesiastical organization in the colonies "in order to prevent future inconveniences and disorders" and to examine and ordain "when a worthy individual comes before us." The committee added that they would be highly obliged "if your Reverences would please to communicate to us and send over your thoughts and advices concerning this matter."[46]

The suggestion that a special ecclesiastical organization be established in the colonies was not a new one, having been proposed several times in the past. As early as 1662, for example, the Reverend Johannes Theodorus Polhemus, pastor of several churches on Long Island, proposed to the Classis of Amsterdam that an association of Dutch Reformed ministers and churches be formed in New Netherland because "we stand in need of communication with one another in the form of a Classis, after the manner of the Fatherland." Similarly, in 1706, the reverends Gualtherus Du Bois of New York, Henricus Beys of Kingston, and Vincentius Antonides of Long Island, along with several elders and deacons recommended to the Classis that "the ministers of the Dutch churches here, together with their Consistories, [be permitted to] select delegates to meet once or oftener, each year, for the welfare of their churches, and for the maintenance of their discipline . . . but remaining always dependent upon. . . the Rev. Classis of Amsterdam." Shortly after his arrival from Holland at Poughkeepsie, New York, the Reverend Cornelius Van Schie in 1732, also wrote the Classis of Amsterdam about the need to organize "some sort of a Classis" in the colonies.[47]

The Classis of Amsterdam, tenacious of her authority, opposed such plans for many years. In 1709, the Classis replied to the request of 1706 as follows: "The formation of a Classis among you to correspond to ours at home, is yet far in the future, and we hardly dare to think of it." In the following year, Classis added that "such a Classis would be the ruin of the churches of New York. This is so obvious that it needs no proof."[48] Fortunately, about a generation later the Classis of Amsterdam began viewing the situation somewhat differently.

XI

The Americanization of the Church:
Separation from Holland

After opposing for many years the idea of an ecclesiastical organization for the American churches, the Classis of Amsterdam began relenting somewhat about the middle of the eighteenth century. For example, when the controversy over the Frelinghuysen affair in the Raritan Valley began subsiding, the Classis, in a letter dated January 11, 1735 to the clergy of New York City, expressed relief that the contesting parties were finally "disposed to make peace" and then added a surprising suggestion:

> We should be especially pleased if we could receive from you some Plan, which would tend to promote the union of the Dutch churches in your portion of the world, in doctrine and ecclesiastical business, according to the Church-Order, and the resolution of Synod—but without impairing our Correspondence—either by holding a yearly Convention, or in such other way as you may think best.[1]

The Classis made a similar recommendation at this time to the Reverend Gerardus Haeghoort, pastor at Second River, New Jersey. Although Haeghoort in the past had generally followed a neutral policy on controversial issues, such as the Frelinghuysen matter, he quickly followed up this suggestion by drafting a "statement of Reasons for the Necessity of a Coetus." He forwarded this, in the name of his consistory, to the Collegiate Church at New York.

In view of the importance of the Coetus in the history of the colonial churches, a brief description of this term is necessary. Pronounced "see-tus," it is derived from Latin and was used to designate a convention or assembly of churches that lacked full classical authority. It was not an unfamiliar institution in the Dutch Reformed Church, having been established among Dutch colonial churches in the East Indies, South Africa, and Surinam, and also for a time among the churches in Brazil when it was a Dutch colony. Similarly, for many years, the relations between the churches in East Friesland, Germany and those in the Netherlands were carried on by means of a Coetus.

Upon receipt of the suggestions from the Classis and from Dominie Haeghoort, the consistory in New York began discussing the matter, and finally on May 24, 1737, it sent a circular letter to all Dutch Reformed churches in New York and New Jersey, together with Haeghoort's "Statement of Reasons," urging the formation of a Coetus. The letter stated that

a Coetus, established on a proper basis, would be highly useful; that not only the Classis, but others who are interested in our Welfare, would thus obtain a true view of the condition of our churches, which is now not well known to them. Conflicting accounts are now sent to them, and they declare that they hear of nothing but complaints and defences; of false doctrines and private feuds; so that ministers and candidates are deterred from coming over; that dissensions are not healed, but are daily becoming worse....Now a Coetus would be useful to guard against prevailing errors, to provide wisely against offenses, and more quickly to restore peace to the churches.[2]

Congregations receiving the circular were urged to discuss its contents among themselves. Those agreeing that such an organization "would be useful and salutary" were asked to send delegates to New York in order that "a friendly conference may be held to consult on what should constitute the Fundamental Articles of such an annual Assembly or Coetus of Ministers and Elders."[3]

The conference met September 7 through 12, 1737. Letters were received beforehand from eight consistories stating they would send delegates. After considerable discussion about the duties and limitations of the proposed assembly, several propositions were drafted and referred back to the churches with the request that they be carefully considered "in the fear of the Lord, and with a spirit of impartiality, and a sincere desire for the welfare of God's Church."[4] Each church was asked to send its minister and an elder to meet again at a later date for further discussion of the proposals and to give them their final approval.

Another conference was therefore held in New York on April 24 and 25, 1738. On this occasion, a constitution was drafted that was signed by nine ministers and eleven elders. It provided for annual meetings to take place on the first Monday in September. Each church could send a minister and an elder, but churches which had two ministers could send both pastors and two elders; churches without a pastor could send a *voorlezer*. The Coetus was empowered to "consider, determine, give sentence upon, and settle all matters and dissensions that occur, or which are brought before us for action; for being on the ground, we are in the best possible position to judge of them and to check and smother them in their very beginnings." Assurances were sent to the Classis of Amsterdam that the new assembly would conform "to the Churches of the Fatherland" and would continue to correspond with the Classis regularly. Anyone who felt himself aggrieved by the decisions of the Coetus could appeal to the Classis.[5]

Classical approval of these proceedings was not immediately forthcoming, primarily because it had learned in the meantime that not all the colonial ministers were in favor of a Coetus. A letter received by Classis from four pastors—Henricus Boel of New York, Vincentius Antonides of Long Island, George Wilhelmus Mancius of Kingston, and Frederick Muzelius of Tappan—accused the pro-Coetus group of misrepresenting past communications from the Classis regarding the establishment of an American assembly and that its members did not really intend to remain subordinate to the Classis. The opponents of the Coetus, on the other hand, portrayed themselves as having nothing but "intense solicitude" and "high Regard" for "Classical rights," and beseeched the Classis not to take any action on matters sent to Amsterdam by the pro-Coetus ministers until it had heard more from the opposition group.[6]

By letters of June 9, 1738, the Classis of Amsterdam asked the pro-and anti-Coetus ministers for more information regarding the bases for their respective views, adding that until these were received it would keep an open mind on the matter, but that its final decision would be impartial and would be binding on everyone. There was no question, however, that Classis would look upon the Coetus as a subordinate body. Thus, in its letter to the anti-Coetus faction, it wrote, "A Coetus in your region, co-ordinate and not subordinate to the Rev. Classis of Amsterdam, would militate against church regulations. Such a Coetus must not be thought of." The letter also commended Dominie Boel, the junior pastor of New York, and the chief spokesman of the anti-Coetus group, for his having "ever been very careful to advocate the rights of our Classis and to maintain the subordination."[7]

Not until August 20, 1739, did the Classis finally give its approval, but with qualifications. It reminded the Coetus ministers once again, for example, that they would have to consider themselves subordinate to the Classis. The letter also clearly stated that the Coetus must be careful not to express opinions concerning doctrine and that no examinations of ministerial candidates, not even examinations of a preliminary kind, could be conducted for the licensing and ordaining of ministers, because "these things were reserved, by the Synod of Dort to the respective Classes."[8] Within these limits, Classis not only approved the formation of the Coetus but in November 1739 requested Boel and his party to support it.

The Coetus met only a few times during the decade following its formation and accomplished virtually nothing. Several reasons can be cited for this failure. Some of the colonial ministers remained bitterly opposed to the idea of an American assembly. In their frequent letters to the Classis, they continued to denounce the Coetus ministers for falsely representing themselves as willing to remain subordinate to the Classis and for not keeping the opposition party fully informed of their plans, despite occasional orders from Classis to do this. The anti-Coetus group also expressed apprehension that the Coetus might undercut the role of the consistories, making the latter superfluous, and that its actions might even be declared illegal with respect to those churches which had no charters from the English government.[9]

The Coetus was also hampered during these years because of the limitations placed upon it by the Classis of Amsterdam. A particular handicap was its not having the right to examine and ordain ministers, a function that should have been its main *raison d'être*. Despite pleas from Coetus members that the restriction be rescinded, Classis remained adamant on this issue.

Finally, the Coetus was kept from accomplishing much because of its small size. In 1738, when it was organized, there were only fourteen Dutch Reformed ministers in New York and New Jersey. If one excluded Dominie Boel and the opposition group, this left only ten pastors. Because of poor communications and other reasons, attendance was low. Thus, at a meeting in April 1741, only three pastors were present: Du Bois, Freeman, and Frelinghuysen. Haeghoort was ill and Van Santvoord's wife had just died. Erickzon, because of contrary winds, did not arrive until after the conference had ended. Schuyler and Curtenius probably were absent also because of inclement weather.[10] At meetings so poorly attended, one obviously could not expect that much serious business would be accomplished.

In 1747, an attempt was made to revitalize the Coetus. Inspiration for this came in part from the decision by the Classis to grant permission at this time to the German Reformed churches in Pennsylvania to create a Coetus of their own. Another incentive was added when the Reverend Ulpianus Van Sinderen arrived from Holland in 1746 as a replacement for Antonides on Long Island, and brought with him a letter from the Classis urging the rehabilitation of the Coetus.[11] The Collegiate ministers of New York, Du Bois and Ritzema, with their consistory, thereupon invited all the churches to send delegates to a meeting to take place in the consistory room of the Garden Street

Church on the second Tuesday of September 1747, with a view to reorganizing the Coetus.

The meeting took place as scheduled on September 8 through 10, with the following ministers present: Antonius Curtenius of Hackensack and Schraalenburgh, New Jersey; Gualtherus Du Bois of New York; Reinhardt Erickzon of Freehold and Middletown, New Jersey; Gerardus Haeghoort of Second River, New Jersey; Benjamin Meinema of Poughkeepsie and Fishkill, New York; Johannes Ritzema of New York; and Ulpianus Van Sinderen of Kings County, Long Island. Each minister was accompanied by one of his elders. Cornelius Van Santvoord of Schenectady could not attend because of illness. Theodorus Frelinghuysen of Albany would have been present but was prevented by the anti-Coetus views of his consistory. Similarly, John Henry Goetschius of Queens County, Long Island, would have liked to attend but refrained from doing so because of questions about the validity of his ordination. Absent because of their anti-Coetus views were the following ministers: Johannes Arondeus of Kings County, Long Island; Henricus Boel of New York; Johannes Casparus Fryenmoet of the Minisink Valley in New Jersey; George Wilhelmus Mancius of Kingston, New York; and Frederick Muzelius of Tappan, New York.

The decisions made at this session reaffirmed those made about a decade earlier, except that the manner of organization was more clearly stated. For administrative purposes and for consideration of problems that could not be solved at the local congregational level, three "Circles" were extablished: the New York Circle, embracing the churches of New York City, Long Island, and Poughkeepsie; the Jersey Circle, embracing the churches of Navesink, Second River, and Hackensack; and the Albany Circle, embracing the churches of Schenectady and Schoharie. Problems that the Circles could not solve, were to be taken under advisement by the Coetus. All of this, however, was to be performed in a spirit of subservience to the Classis of Amsterdam.[12]

Between 1748 and 1754, the Coetus met at least annually and usually twice a year. The meetings were held in New York and attendance varied from eight to fourteen ministers. An equal number of elders were generally also present. Some of the problems discussed at these sessions were perennial and difficult to solve. At almost each meeting, for example, there were discussions about the bitter division existing among the Kings County churches on Long Island between the supporters of Arondeus and those of Van Sinderen. Quarrels between Muzelius, the anti-Coetus minister of Tappan, New York, and his pro-Coetus consistory, were also the subject of frequent debates.

Arondeus was eventually deposed and Muzelius was declared emeritus. Questions pertaining to ordinations also arose several times.

In trying to solve minor problems, the Coetus usually resorted to an exchange of correspondence. Thus, letters of admonition and advice were sent from time to time to congregations for their failure to pay ministers their promised salaries, to churches which experienced disputed consistorial elections, and to ministers who were overstepping their bounds by interfering in the affairs of a neighboring parish. In some instances, committees were appointed to investigate particular problems. Thus, a committee of two ministers was sent to the church at Acquackanonck, New Jersey, to give assistance in locating a new pastor. The suggestion was made that perhaps the Acquackanonck church should unite with that of Second River in calling and sharing a common minister. Similarly, in dealing with the Muzelius affair, Coetus decided to send a delegation of four ministers to Tappan "to get a nearer view of things, and to do what is in their power for the welfare of the congregation."[13] The dispute between Dominie Benjamin Meinema and his congregations at Fishkill and Poughkeepsie, New York, over the matter of his salary and the generally poor quality of his sermons was also referred to a committee for study.

From time to time, changes were made in the organization of the Coetus and in its manner of doing business. Thus, in September 1750, a fourth Circle was created to accommodate the churches of Orange and Ulster counties, and in September of the following year, Bergen and Staten Island were brought into the New York Circle. More elaborate rules were also drafted on such matters as the time for meetings, the election of officers, and the examination (when permitted by the Classis) of candidates for the ministry. Some of the rules for the preservation of order at meetings of the Coetus are particularly interesting, as illustrated by two of those adopted in 1748:

4. In the meeting, each [member] shall keep his own seat in the circle, and not speak except in his turn; or else pay twopence.
5. Whoever, without the permission of the President, comes in after prayer, shall pay sixpence; if he is absent from the whole session, he shall pay a shilling; if from the Coetus entirely, six shillings; and in the case of officers, these fines shall be doubled. Every one shall abstain from invective and injurious words, under penalty of not less than twopence, and not more than six shillings.[14]

The attitude of the Classis of Amsterdam toward the Coetus during these years was mixed. In some instances, it seemed to favor a strong American organization. Thus, Classis gave it considerable authority to deal with the quarrel between the Arondeus and Van Sinderen factions, and approved the decision by Coetus to depose Arondeus. Nor did Classis object to Coetus' decision of 1749 that henceforth no calls should be made to ministers in the colonies or in Holland or anywhere else unless they had "first been brought before the Coetus or the Circle, and approved by them."[15] Support for the Coetus was also demonstrated in the letter of October 2, 1747, from the Classis to Dominie Muzelius of Tappan. After describing how it had encouraged the formation of a Coetus and expressing pleasure at the progress that had been made, Classis declared that Muzelius had shown poor judgment in not joining it and urged him to reconsider:

Worthy brother, only think how important such a plan is; and how fruitful of good it may be, for the overseers of a Church in any land to unite themselves by a close bond, and assemble fraternally from time to time at a certain place, to discuss not only matters of doctrine, as indeed may be necessary; but to deliberate on the interests of their churches, to strengthen one another by their mutual counsel and actions and thus, by a common understanding, to give increased power to the execution of all profitable measures. . . . The Classis can communicate its suggestions and deliberations to all the churches in a better and easier way through the medium of such a Coetus, than by writing separately to particular churches and their officers. Therefore, brother, let us have joy over you in this matter.[16]

Had a member of the Coetus written to Muzelius, he could not have expressed it better!

A similar letter was dispatched to Muzelius on May 5, 1749, as well as to the reverends Boel, Arondeus, and Mancius, urging them once again to join the colonial body. Separate communications were also occasionally sent to the consistories of churches opposing ecclesiastical union. A special letter of commendation was sent to Dominie Theodorus Frelinghuysen of Albany expressing pleasure at his stand in favor of the Coetus and urging him to continue his efforts to induce his consistory to also support it.

On the other hand, in looking at the correspondence exchanged between the Classis and the Coetus during these years, it is obvious that the latter was still considered a subordinate body. The type of information sent to the Classis indicates that the Coetus was often merely gathering facts and asking Classis for advice on how best to act on those facts. As an example, one can cite the manner in which a decision was reached on whether John Amelius Wernich, who was serving the church at Stone Arabia, New York, was properly ordained.

It was also exemplified in discussions over whether the New Paltz church was independent of the Kingston congregation and could therefore call its own minister. In each of the above instances, Coetus supplied Classis with the information after which Classis made the decision and relayed it to the Coetus. The Coetus also repeatedly sought advice on the Arondeus and Mutzelius matters, despite its being given some special authority to deal with them.[17]

In various other ways, too, it can be shown that Classis and not the Coetus was looked upon as the senior "partner." Colonial ministers, including distinguished members of the Coetus, sometimes wrote directly to the divines in Amsterdam concerning particular questions and problems. Thus, in 1748, the Reverend Ritzema of New York wrote directly to the Classis to inquire about the propriety of baptizing sick children in their homes rather than in churches. Similarly, Dominie Haeghoort of Second River, New Jersey, in a letter of 1750 to Classis indicated that he was becoming disillusioned with Coetus' inability to force his congregation to meet its salary obligations to him, and urged Classis to intervene. Congregations and consistories sometimes also bypassed Coetus and corresponded directly with Classis, as happened with the churches at New Paltz, Rhinebeck, Claverack, and Newtown.[18]

It was especially in the matter of examining and ordaining candidates for the ministry that Coetus revealed itself as a docile body. During the years 1747 to 1754, Coetus ordained only four ministers: Benjamin Van der Linde and Johannes Leydt in 1748, Samuel Verbryck in 1749, and David Marinus in 1752. In 1748, it also reordained John Henry Goetschius, who had been irregularly ordained in 1741, and had since been serving on Long Island. None of these ordinations occurred without the prior approval of the Classis. During this same period, six candidates bypassed the Coetus and went to Holland for ordination, and eight ministers were sent directly from Europe to the colonies.

The ordination of Verbryck is particularly interesting. When he appeared before the Coetus in 1748 requesting to be examined, he was informed that permission would first have to be received from the Classis. In asking the Amsterdam body about this, Coetus promised "that nothing of this nature shall be done which will not consist with the wise approval of your Rev. Body."[19] Although the request to examine Verbryck was granted, it was done grudgingly and with the strong implication that it might be the last such request granted. When Classis learned at the time of the Verbryck petition that Coetus was planning to charge a set fee for examinations, Classis expressed alarm, declaring that "this seems to imply that you expect examinations to

Henricus Boel

Lambertus De Ronde

Johannes Ritzema

Ministers who played a prominent role in the Coetus-Conferentie schism.

take place quite frequently henceforth; but such a thought by no means agrees with the intentions of Classis."[20]

Various explanations may be given as to why the Classis of Amsterdam was so determined to retain the right of examining and ordaining ministers. It may have resulted in part from a sense of pride, although it had plenty of other churches to care for if its ego was in need of inflation. In addition to supervising the Dutch Reformed and German Reformed churches in the American colonies, it looked after churches in the colonies of Surinam, Cape Colony, Ceylon, and the East Indies. It also supervised congregations at several places where the Netherlands carried on extensive trade and where small Dutch communities had been established, such as Moscow, Constantinople, and the island of Deshima in southern Japan.

No doubt, the primary factor influencing the decision of Classis to retain supervision of examinations and ordinations was its apprehension that to do otherwise might result in an inferior colonial ministry. There was as yet no Dutch Reformed theological school in the colonies and, according to Classis, private study under ministers left something to be desired. Moreover, there was fear that the Coetus might not set its standards for ordination high enough. As grounds for this fear, attention can be directed to the case of Peter De Wint. Coetus had been greatly impressed with De Wint's learning and character when he appeared before it as a ministerial candidate in 1749, but the Classis of Amsterdam refused to grant it permission to examine and ordain him. Because De Wint had already received a call from the churches of Bergen and Staten Island, he went to Holland and submitted himself to the Classis for examination. Here he was passed and ordained but against the better judgment of the Classis. In a letter of March 2, 1751, Classis criticized the Coetus for having ever considered De Wint for the ministry. The letter reads in part as follows:

We all wished that rev. P. De Wint had given better proofs in his examination of having his senses exercised in the Word of righteousness. All the members of our Assembly were very sorry that he possessed so little knowledge of the doctrines of the truth. If matters had not already advanced as far as they had, no one could have conscientiously have admitted him to the ministry of the word for the congregations which had called him. We have seriously admonished him, with prayer for God's blessing to stir up his gifts and increase them.[21]

The Coetus was further embarrassed when it was discovered a short time later that some of the documents De Wint had submitted to the

Coetus and to the Classis had been falsified, resulting in his being deposed from the ministry in 1752.

In explaining its refusal to permit more examinations and ordinations, the Classis expressed fear that to do otherwise might produce unpleasant complications because the Coetus was under a foreign government. The following letter sent by the Classis to the Coetus on October 5, 1750, implies that the Amsterdam divines were worried that if the Dutch churches became too independent of Holland, the English government might look upon them as just another group of Dissenters:

We may well present for your consideration this thought: Whether, while you are subject to a Foreign government there may not sometimes arise unpleasant complications, should the examinations and ordinations of candidates and students be made too frequent and easy in that country. We judge, Rev. Sirs and Brethren, that a Church, in a country that was originally colonized by Hollanders is safest in expecting to receive its overseers from that land wherefrom it originally emigrated.[22]

It soon became apparent to the colonial ministers that just as the Coetus when first established in 1738 never really developed much beyond the planning stage, the attempt to reorganize it in 1747 was also having only limited success. It is therefore not surprising that at its meeting of September 1754, the main order of business was a discussion of how the Coetus could be placed on a "better footing." Although some members in attendance wished to retain the status quo, except for revising a few "defects," others desired to bring about a complete transformation and virtually form an American classis. The latter view won out, although the new body would continue to be called a Coetus. It was unanimously decided to send a circular letter explaining the reorganization plans to all the churches and solicit their comments, which in turn would be discussed at the next regular meeting. The letter summarized very precisely the major defects of the old organization:

1. The Coetus can give no satisfactory reason from the Church Order for its *present* organization, being neither a Consistorial, nor a Classical, nor a Synodical Assembly. As it exists now, it is liable to contempt from without, and to confusion within.

2. The Coetus has no power to act for the highest welfare of the Church, and to the satisfaction of the congregations located here; for it can neither give a general final decision of a case, nor constitute candi-

dates and ministers. Besides, there is the trouble and the delay in the *present* mode of procedure; for matters have to pass to and from between the Coetus and the Classis of Amsterdam before a consummation can be reached, and often it is not then reached.

So, on the other hand, the necessity for a Classis is obvious. Thereby we shall meet the wishes of nearly all the churches; and also free them from the needless and heavy expenses which are incurred by sending over the sea our young men for ordination. We shall also free them from the loss of much time, and from the great risks to which the young men expose themselves; as well as giving calls to unfit candidates.[23]

Unfortunately, the session for reorganizing the Coetus had hardly come to a close, when some of its members had a change of heart. This was particularly true of the Collegiate ministers of New York and some members of their consistory. As a consequence, Dominie Ritzema, in carrying out his instructions from the Coetus to circulate a letter describing the plan to transform that body into a classis, enclosed a memo from his consistory criticizing the proposal. Ritzema also made it clear that he himself also opposed reorganization.

What brought about the reversal on the part of the New York ministers and others? The death of the venerable Dominie Du Bois in 1751 was a severe blow to the pro-Coetus forces. Highly respected as the senior pastor of New York, he had been a strong supporter of the Coetus. But it is doubtful whether even Du Bois could have held the Coetus together after 1754 and prevented the schism. There were some fundamental differences among the ministers that were difficult to bridge, and basic to them was the degree to which the Coetus should remain a subservient body.

Nowhere were these differences more clearly shown than in the question of examining and ordaining candidates for the ministry. Like the Classis, the critics of the new Coetus were apprehensive that without careful restrictions on ministerial appointments, the result might be a less learned and less respected ministry because of the lack of satisfactory educational institutions in the colonies. Already in 1743, the five united consistories of Kings County, Long Island, in requesting a new minister, made it clear that they did not want someone who had been educated in the colonies. Disparaging remarks about American-educated ministers continued to be expressed. Thus, Dominie Ritzema, in commenting on the ordination of Jacobus Rutsen Hardenbergh by the Coetus in 1758, expressed doubt whether he could "translate a single sentence of Latin." Ritzema added that, among the Coetus leaders, "learning is not of so much consequence" in examining and ordaining ministers, but that "the single test question now is as to whether they have the Spirit." And as late as 1764, the anti-Coetus minister, Johannes Fryenmoet, pastor at Kinderhook and Claverack, referred to the recently ordained Jacobus Van Nist as "a poorly educated Coetus youth."[24]

These fears do not mean that the critics of the new Coetus were diametrically opposed to ordinations taking place in the colonies. What worried them was whether the Coetus would become lax in accepting candidates for the ministry and whether it would seek prior approval from the Classis for ordinations. They were also fearful about heterodox views being pronounced from the pulpit. Dominie Antonius Curtenius of New Jersey, who studied at the Universities of Groningen and Leiden, undoubtly expressed the views of several colonial pastors when he declared in a letter of November 5, 1754 to the Classis of Amsterdam that he opposed giving the Coetus too much authority in examining and ordaining ministers because "the door would [thereby] be opened for the introduction into our Church of Arminians and independent Presbyterians."[25] Moreover, as in the past, the more conservative ministers were fearful that any alteration in the relationship with the Classis might endanger the favored position the colonial churches had been granted by the English in the surrender guarantees of 1664 and by the several church charters, which accorded privileges to the Dutch Reformed Church that were not granted to other non-Anglican religious groups.[26]

Objections to creating an independent American classis were also associated with plans being developed at this time for establishing a college in New York City. Discussions aimed at founding such a school, to be known as King's College (present-day Columbia University), extended back several years. Because the plans called for an Episcopal school supported by public funds, the proposal evoked considerable criticism among those who wanted a non-sectarian institution. Neither the latter group nor the Anglicans, however had sufficient votes in the Assembly to get their particular plans adopted. Consequently, each side waged a vigorous press campaign for several years to win support among the Dutch Reformed people. Prominent among the anti-Anglican forces was William Livingston, a newspaper editor who had once been Dutch Reformed but had become Presbyterian because of his preferring English to Dutch sermons. Despite his efforts and those of others, a significant number of Dutch Reformed leaders in New York City showed a willingness to cooperate with the Anglicans in the matter of King's College. They were hopeful of being able to persuade the Assembly to approve a petition asking that a Dutch Reformed professor of theology, nominated by the Collegiate Consistory of New York, be appointed to the faculty of the proposed school.

The supporters of the petition therefore had a special reason for opposing the creation of an independent American classis at this time. They were fearful that if such a body were established, it probably would not be satisfied with merely having a professor of Dutch Reformed theology on the staff of an Anglican school, but might instead want to establish a college of its own and, moreover, probably would not locate it in New York City. And even if the plans for King's College did materialize, it might very well happen that the new American classis and not the Collegiate Consistory of New York would have the final decision on who should receive the theological appointment to the school, a procedure that would displease many Dutch Reformed churchmen in New York. As one writer has recently stated, the latter group wanted a professor who "would be at their beck and call"—someone who would conform to their theological beliefs and to their views on what constituted good preaching rather than someone who would listen to the evangelistic-minded leaders of the Coetus.[27]

Dominie Ritzema was especially interested in implementing his consistory's plan for King's College because he hoped to receive the appointment to fill the special Dutch chair. To his surprise and that of his consistory, when the charter for King's College was issued in 1754, it made no mention of the Dutch professorship. The consistory felt betrayed, but Ritzema, undaunted, personally petitioned the governor and his council to amend the charter so that the Collegiate Consistory could nominate someone to the position. This was agreed to, but by then the consistory had become disillusioned. Indeed, it became so chagrined at Ritzema's bypassing it and dealing directly with the governor, that it voted on August 11, 1755 to censure him.

By this time, the Collegiate Consistory was having some second thoughts on the matter anyway. It was becoming distrustful of the pro-Anglican stamp of the school and, like the leaders of the Coetus, was worried that Reformed interests might, in time, be subverted to those of the Anglicans. This fear was reflected in the annual consistorial elections of October 1755 which saw some members who had favored the Anglicans in the past being replaced by persons who were less sympathetic toward them.[28] Two other factors also contributed to a change of heart: first, the fact that the revised charter providing for the appointment of a Dutch Reformed professor made no provision for his salary, and secondly, the failure of the new charter to provide safeguards that would prevent his being arbitrarily removed from his position. The change of heart by some members of the Collegiate

Consistory did not, however, end the matter. The idea of having a professor of Dutch theology on the staff of King's College was revived from time to time and continued to intrigue some members of the anti-Coetus faction.

There were other differences, too, between the two groups of ministers. The critics of a stronger Coetus, for example, claimed that decisions on major issues should be unanimous, and when this could not be achieved, such matters should be referred to the Classis of Amsterdam or to a synod in Holland. The supporters of a strong Coetus, on the other hand, believed that a majority opinion was sufficient for action on even major issues. The critics were also more desirious than were their opponents in trying to keep things "in the Dutch way." Thus, the anti-Coetus group outlined goals such as these: to advance "the true welfare of our New Netherlands Zion;" to "preserve our Netherlandish Church pure," and to "have the tie between us and the Church of the Fatherland, instead of growing weak, to become stronger and stronger." As a final difference among the two groups, it can be noted that the anti-Coetus ministers tended to be less evangelical in their manner of preaching than their opponents.[29]

As a result of the above differences, the Dutch Reformed Church quickly became split into two opposing groups. The schism, which lasted almost eighteen years, affected not only the ministers but also the lay people who took sides in supporting the one faction or the other. The ministers who opposed the reorganized Coetus met periodically during the years after 1754 to discuss their common aims. Their assembly became known as the Conferentie, meaning "Conference." The first meeting was held in September 1755 with five ministers present: Ritzema, De Ronde, Haeghoort, Curtenius and Van der Linde.[30] The presence of Ritzema has already been explained. His colleague, De Ronde, had been a conservative minister since the time of his arrival in New York in 1750.[31] Haeghoort's membership is rather surprising in view of his earlier support for a stronger Coetus. He, however, had a reputation for being a trouble-maker, having long criticized both the old Coetus and the Classis of Amsterdam for their failure to obtain some back salary reputedly owed him by his congregation at Second River, New Jersey. Later, he was censured by the Coetus for improperly appointing a new consistory at Hackensack. He apparently did not get along well with the Conferentie either, for he remained a member of it for little more than a year. Personal pique probably also explains why the reverends Curtenius and Van der Linde joined the Conferentie, both having once been censured by the Coetus for allowing themselves to be irregularly called.

The Conferentie met more or less annually, with Ritzema serving as permanent president and De Ronde as permanent secretary. Meetings were held in the consistory room of the Garden Street Church in New York. The highest membership of the Conferentie in terms of minister attendance occurred at the October 1765 meeting when ten pastors were present.[32] An examination of the lives of these men makes it difficult to reach any conclusions regarding the general composition of the Conferentie. One cannot state, for example, that it appealed primarily to older ministers, because the oldest of them about whom there is definite information was Ulpianus Van Sinderen who was fifty-seven in 1765. Nor can it be said that it was purely a Dutch ethnic group: at least three of these ten men were born in Germany,[33] another came from Switzerland, one was born in the colonies, and three had received their ministerial training and ordination on this side of the Atlantic.[34] Although there were a few learned men among them, such as Ritzema of New York and Isaac Rysdyck of New Hackensack and Poughkeepsie, the Conferentie ministers, on the whole, seemed to be men of average attainments.

The problems discussed at the Conferentie sessions were similar to those brought before the Coetus: irregular consistorial elections, questions about ministerial salaries, and disputes between various ministers and their congregations. Although the Conferentie licensed only one man for the ministry (Garret Lydekker in 1765), it, like the Coetus, was

Garret Lydekker, the only minister licensed by the Conferentie (1765). He supported the Tory cause and after the Revolution went into exile in England where he died in 1794. (Courtesy of Sage Library, New Brunswick Seminary)

interested in the examination and ordination of ministerial candidates, *providing proper safeguards were taken*. This is clear from its report of October 12, 1758 to the Classis of Amsterdam: "The unaimous cry of all our congregations is, for liberty to admit suitable persons to the preparatory and final examinations here for the ministry, because of our great distance from Holland, and the consequent great expense and danger of the sea voyage, especially in time of war."[35]

The failure of the New York Collegiate Church and others to support the reorganized Coetus proved to be a handicap for that body at first, but with good leadership it managed not only to survive but to grow in membership. The new Coetus was initially led by the Reverend Theodorus Frelinghuysen of Albany, a son of the minister by the same name around whom so much controversy centered a few decades earlier in the Raritan Valley of New Jersey. After the Albany minister's death in 1761, the reverends Samuel Verbryck of Tappan and Jacob Rutsen Hardenbergh, pastor of several churches in central New Jersey, served very ably as leaders of the reorganized Coetus. It is interesting to note that both of these men had been licensed by the Coetus: Verbryck in 1749 and Hardenbergh in 1758.

Frelinghuysen's support for greater ecclesiastical independence stemmed in part from his own personal experience about the hazards of ocean crossings. On his return from Holland in 1745, where he had gone for ordination, his ship had been captured (King George's War was waging at this time) and he had to spend six months at sea before returning to the colonies.[36] Later, in 1753, two of his brothers died at sea of smallpox on their return from Holland, where they had gone for theological studies and ordination. Despite Frelinghuysen's support for the Coetus, he did not attend its meetings for several years because of opposition from his own congregation. The attempt after 1754 to establish a chair of Dutch theology at King's College, however, caused him to ignore the wishes of his own congregation, and he henceforth labored diligently in behalf of an independent American classis and the formation of a Dutch Reformed college.

The schism between the Coetus and Conferentie groups lasted for nearly eighteen years, and its effects were tragic for the colonial churches. Vehement language was frequently exchanged among them, with minister pitted against minister and congregation against congregation. Family relations were also strained as fathers sometimes opposed children and children opposed fathers. Some ministers refused to baptize children because their parents supported a faction opposed by the ministers. As someone has said of the two factions:

All their "Dutch" was up on both sides. . . . Whatever most trifling thing a partisan of the [Coetus] wanted was enough to make a partisan of the [Conferentie] oppose it tooth and nail even if it had not the slightest relation to the original dispute. If a Conferentie man liked anything, it was enough to make a Coetus man hate it. They had resolution and feeling enough on both sides to have been martyrs.[37]

Several congregations had serious divisions within their own midst. At Hackensack, New Jersey, for example, there were two ministers, two sets of consistories, and two congregations which took turns using the church edifice. The controversy was also particularly acute in Queens County, Long Island, and at Poughkeepsie and Fishkill, in the Hudson Valley. At times, there was violence, with ministers being assaulted and some groups being forcibly prevented from using the church buildings for worship services. A pamphlet "war" also developed between the two sides. Thus, in the summer of 1760, Dominie Leydt of New Brunswick published "True Liberty the Way to Peace," setting forth the views of the Coetus party. The Reverend Ritzema thereupon published an answer entitled "Reply to True Liberty, the Way to Peace." This brought a rather uncharitable answer from Leydt, which in turn brought a lengthy retort from Ritzema.[38]

Both the Coetus and the Conferentie sent bitter letters to the Classis of Amsterdam, each blaming the other for the way things turned out. The reaction of the Classis to these developments is well-summarized in one of its letters of January 13, 1756 to the consistory in New York:

When we read this long and generally unintelligible account of affairs, we are obliged to say that we were affected with feelings of sadness and pity, and not without some indignation. We cannot understand how there can be men, Christian men, even Christian ministers, who are able not only to originate such acts—biting and devouring one another, but who can continue in such conduct for years. They are men who profess to be followers of the meek and lowly and the loving Jesus; but who do not seem rightly to understand that LOVE is the livery of Christianity, and that hate, envy, wrath, evil passions and selfishness are of the devil; who seem never to ponder that enmity, quarrels, jealousy, anger and discord exclude from the kingdom of heaven.[39]

The above letter points out that the Classis at times tried to follow a neutral policy. This was also manifested in its letter of July 21, 1755, criticizing the ministers and the consistory of New York for withdrawing from the Coetus, declaring that by their absence they could no longer influence its members by upholding them in their "counsels" when they were reasonable "or direct them in the right way when they [were going] astray." Classis added, philosophically, that "one should never avoid one extreme by rushing into another."[40]

Most of the correspondence from Classis, however, indicates that its sympathies, and also those of the Synod of North Holland, were clearly on the side of those favoring a weak Coetus. This attitude is shown in the opening remarks of a very long letter that the Classis sent to the Coetus on June 3, 1765. It was written in answer to an earlier letter sent by the Coetus and indicates that both sides in the dispute could be rather arrogant at times:

The "Introduction" to your Revs. letter is not exactly in a fraternal spirit. When you become somewhat earnest in dealing with your own affairs in relation to the condition of the New York [and New Jersey] churches, you say;—"We do not feel disposed just now to reply to your letters, clearly perceiving, etc." We might justly retort: "We do not feel disposed to have anything more to do with your Revs. . . ." Your Revs. are building upon propositions which have no foundations. The first is that your Revs. are already constituted into a Classis, and that we are acting improperly in not acknowledging that fact. But whence did your Revs. derive that Classical power? Upon what basis does it rest? Your Revs. know that you have arrogated that position to yourselves, and that we have many a time shown you the invalidity of it. [41]

In view of the strong anti-Coetus views expressed in this letter, it is not surprising that the Conferentie party had 600 Dutch and 400 English copies of it printed for distribution. [42]

As the years went by, the Coetus acted more and more independently of the mother church in Holland and took on the appearance of an independent American classis. Stated meetings were regularly held, but those in New York were conducted in private homes instead of in one of the local Dutch Reformed churches. Disputes were solved in a terminal manner without recourse to the Classis of Amsterdam, and examinations and ordinations were soon conducted without seeking prior approval. In 1766, the success of the Coetus seemed assured when it was granted a royal charter to establish a college in New Jersey. Four years later, after an amended charter was received, it began organizing Queen's College at New Brunswick, the forerunner of present-day Rutgers University. Dominie Verbryck, one of the leading spokesman of the Coetus, labored with particular zeal in behalf of this school.

The increasingly independent spirit shown by the Coetus leaders on ecclesiastical matters was encouraged by the idea of political independence that was germinating in the colonies at this time. Thus, in a letter of June 3, 1765 to the Classis, Coetus declared that it would no longer argue on the basis of past history whether the colonial churches should remain in a subordinate position but would argue instead from "inherent rights." It also declared that "as a free people," it was a matter of their choice whether or not to correspond with the Amsterdam body.[43]

By the late 1760's, conditions were propitious for reconcilation. Ministers who had been more or less neutral in the controversy, such as Eliardus Westerlo of Albany and Archibald Laidlie of New York, worked quietly behind the scenes to soothe those who were quick-tempered and to bring opposing factions together. The influential consistory of New York also began taking a more neutral position on the issues. Meanwhile, the Conferentie party seemed to be losing its resolve to continue the struggle as its meetings became less frequent and more poorly attended. Throughout 1768 and 1769, the Classis of Amsterdam worked especially hard to bring about a reconciliation, and at one point drafted a plan of union that had considerable appeal to both sides. The Classis took a major step toward reconciliation when it informed the Coetus leaders on October 3, 1768 that because the word "subordination" had become so offensive to some of them it was "willing to modify the same, and to call it a 'Close Union,' in which you stand to the Netherland Mother Church."[44] The ecclesiastical authorities in Holland also began retreating from their former stand against permitting examinations and ordinations in the colonies. At a meeting of the Synod of North Holland in the summer of 1768, it was declared that because of the decline in usage of the Dutch language among colonists of Dutch descent there were "ministers sent from here, who, from now on will be of little use, and before long entirely useless."[45]

Fortunately for all parties concerned, a young man now appeared on the scene who was able to draw together the various strands tending toward reconciliation. His name was John Henry Livingston. Born at Poughkeepsie, New York in 1746 and brought up in the Dutch Reformed Church, he was a member of one of New York's most prestigious families. After graduating from Yale in 1762 at age sixteen, he studied law for a few years but following a period of poor health and some serious personal reflections, he decided to become a minister. His first thoughts were about entering the service of the Episcopalians or Presbyterians, but he finally decided on the church of his youth. This is rather surprising in view of Livingston's limited knowledge of the Dutch language at this time and the bitter controversy being waged in the Dutch Reformed Church. His decision was apparently influenced by the close friendship that had developed between him and the newly arrived Reverend Archibald Laidlie, who had been called to

John H. Livingston

New York in 1763 as the first Dutch Reformed pastor for the exclusive purpose of preaching in the English language. In August 1766, Livingston enrolled at the University of Utrecht, where he received the doctorate in theology in 1770. Immediately thereafter, he left for New York as an assistant to the other Dutch Reformed pastors there.

Disturbed by the ecclesiastical conflict in the Church that he hoped some day to serve, young Livingston while in the Netherlands took time from his theological studies to meet with members of the Classis of Amsterdam and the Synod of North Holland to exchange views on how to end the schism in the colonies. It is therefore not surprising that soon after his arrival in New York, he persuaded his consistory to invite all the Dutch Reformed churches to send delegates to a meeting to devise plans for reconciling the Coetus and Conferentie parties. The meeting, which took place in October 1771, was attended by twenty-two ministers and twenty-five elders representing thirty-four churches.

The background and alignment of the colonial ministry at this time is interesting. Of the thirty-four Dutch Reformed ministers serving in the colonies in 1771, fifteen had been born, educated, and ordained in Europe; eight had been brought up in the colonies but had gone to Holland for ordination; and eleven had been reared in the colonies and also ordained there. How did the thirty-four ministers feel about the issues separating the Coetus and Conferentie parties? Thirteen ministers were pro-Coetus, of whom ten were present at the reconciliation meeting in 1771; eleven were pro-Conferentie, of whom seven were present; and ten may be considered as more or less neutral, of whom five attended the meeting.

The session lasted four days, with Livingston presiding. A spirit of amity and accord prevailed as both sides tried to put personal animosities aside for the sake of peace. Although the indomitable Ritzema was conspicious by his absence, the sessions got off to an auspicious beginning, with De Ronde deliverying the opening sermon, using Ephesians 6:23 for his text: "Peace be to the brethren, and love with faith from God the Father and the Lord Jesus Christ." De Ronde had by this time been exhibiting a change of heart and was even trying, albeit not too successfully, to preach occasionally in English. A committee of twelve persons, consisting of two ministers and two elders from each faction as well as two ministers and two elders considered to be "Neutral Brethren," was appointed to draft a plan of reconciliation. As a basis for their discussions, the committee considered the ideas that had been proposed earlier by the Classis of Amsterdam, some of which Livingston had helped formulate while in Holland. Upon submission of the committee's plan to the assembly, it was adopted without a dissenting voice.

The finished document, known as the Articles of Union, embraced the following basic points: the churches would be divided into five circles, in which ministers and elders would meet together three or four times a year in special gatherings known as Particular Assemblies; each of these would send delegates once a year to a larger gathering, known as the General Assembly, representing the entire colonial church; the General Assembly would have the right to examine and ordain young men for the ministry, but their names would have to be registered in Holland; the college at New Brunswick would be placed under the control of the General Assembly and be provided with a professor of theology; and, finally, annual reports would be sent to the Classis of Amsterdam and appeals could also be directed there.

The plan satisfied the Coetus party because it gave them virtual independence from Holland. As an inducement to get the Conferentie faction to accept it, it was agreed that the plan would have no force until it had been approved by the Classis of Amsterdam. The Conferentie delegates were also delighted to note that annual reports would be sent to the Classis, which would also hear appeals. Moreover, the wording made it abundantly clear that the colonial churches would conduct themselves in a manner consistent with the government and doctrines of the Church in the Netherlands. Copies of the plan were circulated among the colonial churches for their approval.

A second meeting was convened on June 12, 1772, which was attended by twenty-six ministers and forty-three elders representing more than fifty churches. At this time, the Articles of Union were formally approved and the Dutch Reformed churches were thus once more united. Some bitterness, of course, lingered, and a few ministers and congregations remained aloof of the union for several years, but they were in a decided minority. As a sign of the changed mood that had taken place, Dominie Ritzema not only attended this meeting but his name headed the list of those signing the Articles. Moreover, he was asked to deliver the opening sermon when the General Assembly would hold its first session.

XII

The Language Question

At the same time that the Coetus-Conferentie struggle was being waged among the Dutch Reformed churches over the matter of ecclesiastical independence from the Netherlands, questions were also being raised about continuing the virtually exclusive use of the Dutch language in the worship services. For almost a century and a half, the colonial churches had been not only subject to a foreign ecclesiastical body, but on Sundays their members listened to sermons and prayers delivered in a foreign tongue and sang praises to God in the same manner. Moreover, the schools that were under the supervision of local consistories used a foreign tongue as the language of instruction. By the middle of the eighteenth century, a significant element within the churches was prepared to challenge these practices and to urge the substitution of English for Dutch, at least in a limited way. Unfortunately, another group of church-goers was equally prepared to maintain the status quo.

In retrospect, it seems almost inconceivable that until the time of the Revolution the Dutch Reformed churches continued to use the Dutch language almost exclusively. On closer examination, however, this development is not surprising considering that the Dutch language in general remained popular in New York and New Jersey throughout most of the colonial period. For a proper understanding of the language question in the churches during the eighteenth century, it is therefore necessary to first give a review of the persistence of the Dutch language in other walks of life besides its use on the pulpit.

The fall of New Netherland to England in 1664 brought no immediate transformation in the customs or appearance of the Dutch communities that had been established during the previous half century. The daily habits of the people underwent little change, and their homes often continued to resemble those in the Old Netherlands. Church life and the education of the youth went on much as before. Indeed, the persistence of Dutch traditions in the older communities of the Hudson Valley and on Long Island was still noted frequently by eighteenth century travelers and writers. This was particularly true

211

concerning the use of the Dutch language. Thus, in 1749, Peter Kalm, wrote that "the inhabitants of Albany and its environs are almost all Dutchmen. They speak Dutch, have Dutch preachers, and the divine service is performed in that language."[1] Similarly, after a visit to Long Island, Ambrose Serle, who served for two years as Lord Howe's private secretary in America, wrote in his journal on September 5, 1776: "Many Descendants of the Dutch still remain, much unmixed in New York Colony, and especially upon Long Island. The Dutch were the original settlers . . . and the Dutch Language is still very much in Use among them."[2]

In some regions it was difficult for many years to carry on public business except in the Dutch language. In 1702, for example, at the trial in New York City of Nicholas Bayard on charges of sedition and of his being a Jacobite, the defendant's counsel objected to the composition of the twelve-man jury on the grounds that scarcely one of its members was able to say the Lord's Prayer in English. Similarly, as late as about the middle of the eighteenth century, the sheriffs in some New York counties found it difficult to obtain jurors who had an adequate knowledge of the English language. And on western Long Island, the records of several towns were kept in Dutch until the Revolution.[3]

Non-Hollanders who settled among the Dutch in the older communities were often so completely assimilated into the more dominant Dutch culture that they adopted the Dutch language as their own. This was frequently the experience of the Walloons and Huguenots who arrived during the seventeenth century, and of the Palatines during the following century. As described by one writer, "The mixed elements that formed the original group of settlers soon became a harmonious whole, one in the use of Dutch as the common language and one in Dutch feeling."[4] Even in some of the Lutheran churches of New York in which Germans were in a majority, Dutch became the language of the pulpit. Justus Falckner, who was born and educated in Germany and served as a pioneer Lutheran pastor for about two decades in the Hudson Valley and northern New Jersey, wrote in 1704 to a friend in Germany: "I learned the Dutch language in a short time, so that at times now I preach three times a week. . . . My few auditors are mostly Dutch in speech, but in extraction they are mostly High Germans, also Swedes, Danes, Norwegians, Poles, Lithuanians, Transylvanians, and other nationalities."[5] In the Lutheran church in New York, "the Dutch language continued to be the sole language down to the seventeen forties," although the congregation was made up mostly of persons of German background.[6]

Inhabitants of some of the communities dating from the New Netherland period clung so tenaciously to their Dutch ways that when population growth and a desire for cheap, fertile land caused some of them to move elsewhere, the new communities, too, developed a distinctively Dutch culture. Dutchmen from Manhattan and Long Island who began settling in the river valleys of northern New Jersey after 1664 mingled with a variety of ethnic groups, but it was a Dutch atmosphere, including the Dutch language, that frequently predominated. Similar situations developed elsewhere. Thus, as late as 1776, a call for a pastor to serve the two Dutch Reformed churches that had been established in Bucks County, Pennsylvania in 1710 stipulated that the new minister would be expected to deliver half his sermons during the summer time and two-thirds of them during the winter months in the Dutch language. Even from distant Harrodsburg, Kentucky, where Dutchmen began settling shortly after the Revolution, came a request in 1795 for a minister who could preach at least some of his sermons in Dutch.[7]

Only in areas where Dutch traditions were not strongly entrenched did Dutchmen become assimilated quite quickly into the more dominant English or other culture. One of the first such instances occurred at New Castle (called New Amstel under the Dutch) in the lower Delaware Valley. Although on several occasions it appeared that a flourishing Dutch community would develop on the Delaware, only a few hundred Dutchmen settled there during the New Netherland period, and some of them moved away after 1664. The Reverend Peter Tesschenmaeker, who studied for a time at the University of Utrecht, served at New Castle from 1679 to 1682, preaching in Dutch and English. He was the community's last regular Dutch preacher.

In 1682, the ruling consistory of elders and deacons of the New Castle church reported that the congregation comprised about "one hundred fathers of families" and urged the Classis of Amsterdam to send them a new preacher. "We live here among many Lutherans," they wrote, "whose teachers preach in a very unedifying manner; and among a still greater number of Quakers who are given to errors. ...Therefore preaching and catechizing in the clean, upright, true Reformed religion is very necessary here, especially as a great many unreliable, dissolute people move in here among us."[8] The appeal for a new preacher went unheeded; there are no extant documents about the congregation after 1687, and it may be assumed that by 1700 its members had joined other denominations in the New Castle area.

The Dutch atmosphere in Monmouth County in northeastern New Jersey also yielded to English encroachment more quickly than most places. As has been noted elsewhere in this study, Dutchmen began migrating there from Long Island in 1672, and established two churches by 1699. Despite these promising beginnings, when the Reverend Gerardus Haeghoort arrived there from Holland in 1731 to take charge of these churches, he reported them as being in a very distressful condition. He attributed this partly to the fact that many of the people had become "wholly English, and had thus become estranged from the Dutch Reformed Church."[9] His successor, the Reverend Reinhardt Erickzon, who arrived in Monmouth County in 1736, supported this view.[10]

The decline of Dutch culture in places such as the lower Delaware Valley and Monmouth County, New Jersey, was the exception rather than the rule. In the older communities on Long Island and in the Hudson Valley, as well as in many of the new communities established in these regions and elsewhere, Dutch traditions often remained strong. As a consequence, almost all of the nearly one hundred Dutch Reformed churches in the colonies at the time of the Revolution were still using the Dutch language exclusively in their worship services.

The perpetuation of the Dutch language was the result of a number of factors, but certainly one of the most important was the employment of ministers who were born in Holland and received their training there. This practice served as a kind of continuing transfusion of Netherlandish ideas into the Dutch communities. Of the fifty-one new pastors who took service in the Dutch Reformed churches between 1700 and 1750, twenty-two came from Holland, ten arrived from Germany, four came from Switzerland, and seven were born in the colonies. The birthplace of eight others is uncertain. It should be noted that two of the seven ministers born in the colonies went to the Netherlands for ordination.

It is also significant that of the ten ministers who arrived from Germany, several came from areas which linguistically and culturally were hardly distinguishable from the Netherlands at the opening of the eighteenth century. In some instances, the calls to ministers of German background stipulated that they learn the Dutch language within a specified period of time. This happened, as explained in a previous chapter, in the case of George Wilhelmus Mancius, who was called to Kingston, New York in 1730. Similarly, when the Reverend John Gabriel Gebhard, who was German-born, arrived at Claverack, New York in 1776, it was stipulated that he would have to learn Dutch because of the large number of Dutchmen in his congregation. Within about a decade, according to the record, the Dutch language had "swallowed up" the German language to such a degree, that Gebhard was preaching three services in Dutch to one in German and one in English.[11]

Dutch schools in the colonies reinforced the churches as an important means for preserving the traditions of Holland, including its language. Although the authorities had been rather slow in establishing schools in New Netherland, all but two of the eleven chartered towns in the colony had common schools by 1664 and New Amsterdam also had a Latin school. Several private schoolmasters also received licenses to teach in New Netherland. Additional Dutch schools were established after 1664 in villages that were predominantly Dutch in language and of sufficient size to maintain a church, such as Kinderhook, New York and Bergen, New Jersey. The schoolmaster not only taught reading and ciphering, but, using Dutch as the language of instruction, he also taught his pupils the common prayers, the Psalms, and the Heidelberg Catechism, while the Bible and writings on piety and moral prudence served as basic textbooks. Such practices, of course, further bolstered the use of Dutch in the church services.

Instruction of the youth in the Dutch language took on added importance after the arrival of the English. To permit the ancestral tongue to fall into disuse was unthinkable as long as most preaching in the Dutch Reformed churches continued to be in Dutch, and also because the formularies of the Church were written in that language. It is therefore not surprising that in 1726, the Consistory of New York urged parents to take every available opportunity to teach the language to their children, declaring that "the true doctrine of comfort in life and in death is preached in the clearest and most powerful manner, in the Dutch tongue."[12] Similarly, when a new teacher was hired for the local Dutch school in 1733, the consistory told the congregation that the school was "absolutely necessary, useful and salutary for the Christian rearing, teaching and training of our youth, in order to gain them, from the earliest period, to the language of our Church, and to a love for the Dutch Reformed worship."[13] The situation that existed at New York after 1664 relative to religious training in the Dutch schools and the use of Dutch as the language of instruction also prevailed in other Dutch communities.[14]

Although the churches and the schools were the primary means for perpetuating Dutch traditions, including the language, other factors were also at work. One of these was intermarriage among Dutch families, a practice that was followed not only by the lower classes but also by families of wealth and influence. Sometimes such intermarriages extended through several generations. President Martin Van

Buren, for example, whose Dutch ancestors came from Holland during the New Netherland period, stated in his autobiography that his eldest son was the first Van Buren in six generations of Dutch-Americans to marry outside the Dutch line.[15] Seclusion, together with poor communications, also helped preserve things in the Dutch way. Peter Kalm reported in 1749 that the Dutch residing in New Brunswick, New Jersey, tended to remain aloof of other ethnic groups, keeping "company only with themselves, and seldom or never go(ing) amongst the other inhabitants, living as it were quite separate from them."[16] Similar situations were reported existing among the Dutch at Albany and on Long Island.[17]

As was true of the subservience of the colonial churches to the Classis of Amsterdam and the obtaining of ministers who were trained in Holland, the use of the Dutch language in divine services and in the schools gave the Dutch Reformed churches a cohesiveness during the seventeenth century that was helpful in maintaining their separate identity. This became particularly important as increasing numbers of Englishmen began arriving and as other denominations were established. But, like the dependence on the mother church in Holland, the use of the ancestral tongue was protracted beyond the time needed.

Already in the seventeenth century, there had been a few attempts to acquire ministers who could preach in English as well as Dutch. The Reverend Samuel Drisius, who was called to New Amsterdam in 1652, was competent in Dutch, French, and English. He preached in French occasionally to the Huguenots and Walloons on Staten Island, and he probably also delivered occasional sermons in English. The inhabitants of Kingston, New York in 1681 requested the Classis of Amsterdam to send them a minister who could preach in Dutch and English because they could not afford two pastors. Classis was unable to find such a person, and Kingston therefore had to satisfy itself with someone who could preach only in Dutch. A similar request was made to the Classis by the collegiate churches of Kings County, Long Island in 1695, but it too was unsuccessful. As was noted, Peter Tesschenmaeker preached in English occasionally during the latter part of the seventeenth century, as did a few other ministers, such as Theodorus Frelinghuysen of Albany, during the first half of the eighteenth century. By 1750, however, a modicum of English preaching was no longer satisfactory; some churches were requiring at least a degree of English services on a regular basis.

The mid-eighteenth century was a kind of watershed in the general use of the Dutch language in the colonies. Several of the same writers who reported considerable evidence of Dutch still being spoken about

1750, also frequently noted that changes were near at hand, if not already underway.[18] In retrospect, it is surprising that the challenge to the Dutch language did not come earlier. With the exception of ministers, together with a few professional people and an occasional farmer or artisan, very little emigration from Holland occurred after the fall of New Netherland in 1664. English emigration, on the other hand, steadily increased, not only from Old England but also from New England. The increasing number of migrants settling in the Hudson Valley and in northern New Jersey naturally had a disturbing effect on the continued use of Dutch in the conduct of daily affairs.

The first serious threat to the Dutch language came in the schools, as the growing importance of English in the everyday life of the people and the appearance of more English schoolmasters raised serious questions about the continuance of the Dutch schools in their present form. Parents could hardly be expected to send their children to schools which, as one authority stated, gave "exclusive support to an education which served one day of the week only, ignoring the economic demands of the other six."[19] This problem was recognized as early as 1726, when the consistory of the Dutch Reformed church of New York, although urging the congregation to support the local Dutch school for religious reasons, admitted that a knowledge of English was needed "in order properly to carry on one's temporal calling."[20] It is therefore not surprising that during the latter half of the eighteenth century an increasing number of Dutch children began enrolling in English language schools. Consequently, in 1757, one of the two Dutch schools in New York City was forced to close its doors; it had at the time only ten pupils. The other Dutch school in that year had only about forty-five pupils, although the school age population of the city was then slightly over three thousand.[21]

To meet the growing demand for instruction in English, some of the Dutch schools became bi-lingual. In 1758, for example, the school authorities at Flatbush, on Long Island, advertised for "a person qualified to teach Dutch and English, both Reading and Writing."[22] Before 1761, the Dutch school at Bergen, New Jersey also began teaching in both Dutch and English. In New York, too, the inevitable could be held back no longer. Although in 1755 the consistory had purposely hired a schoolmaster directly from Holland in order to obtain someone who was both Dutch and orthodox, a changed attitude had set in by 1773. In looking for a new schoolmaster in that year, the consistory decided that because "the Dutch language is constantly diminishing and is going out of use," it was only proper "to call a person who is qualified to instruct and educate the children in the English as well as

the Dutch language."[23] In some communities, however, English instruction was delayed. At Albany, for example, at the close of the
Revolution, according to one writer, "a competent English teacher was
scarcely to be found."[24]

It was not merely a decline in usage of Dutch that was creating a
problem among the churches by the middle of the eighteenth century.
The language itself, as used in the colonies, was becoming perverted
from its original conditions of sound and meaning, and was also being
combined with numerous English words and colloquial expressions.
On a boat trip from New York to Albany in 1744, for example, a
traveler observed that everyone except himself and his servant could
speak Dutch and seemed to prefer it to English, but added that it was
not a pure Dutch but a "medley of Dutch and English as would have
tired a horse."[25]

This debasement of the language created a special problem for
ministers who had been trained to preach in a pure Dutch tongue but
were placed in charge of congregations accustomed to a kind of Yankee
Dutch dialect. In 1753, the *Occasional Reverberator*, a New York City
paper, noted: "There is a vast Difference between understanding the
common barbarous Dutch spoken in our Families, and the studied and
ornamented Style of the Pulpit. The Generality of our People, that are
well enough acquainted with the former, are almost totally ignorant of
the latter."[26] It is therefore not surprising that when the Reverend
Herman Boelen arrived from Holland in 1776 to take charge of the
Queens County churches on Long Island, his parishioners had difficulty understanding him because his language was "too pure and high-
flown."[27]

The increasing use of English in the schools and in government and
trade, together with the dilution of the Dutch language, soon raised
questions about the use of Dutch in the worship services. The historian
William Smith reported about the middle of the eighteenth century:
"The Dutch congregation [of New York] is more numerous than any
other, but as the language becomes disused, it is much diminished; and
unless they change their worship into the English tongue, must soon
suffer a total dissipation."[28] These views were shared by William
Livingston, editor of a small weekly paper, the *Independent Reflector*.
Livingston himself had once belonged to the Dutch Reformed Church
but had transferred to the Presbyterian Church because of his defi-
ciency in understanding spoken Dutch, although he could read it. In
January 1754, he wrote:

In all the british Colonies, as the knowledge of the english tongue must
necessarily endure, and instead of declining, will naturally become

more perfect and improved; so every foreign Language, however generally practised and understood for a time, must, at length, be neglected and forgotten. Thus it is with the dutch tongue, which, tho once the common dialect of this province, is now scarcely understood, except by its more ancient inhabitants. . . .To prevent therefore the ruin of the dutch Churches, common sense [points] out the absolute necessity, of disuniting them from the Language, by translating their public acts of devotion, and worship into English; or the speedy introduction of the present translations now used, by several of their Churchs in Holland.[29]

The comments by Smith and Livingston illustrate the problems that faced the Dutch Reformed churches by the mid-eighteenth century, but their remarks were somewhat exaggerated. That these men overstated their case is clearly shown by the strong opposition that later developed in New York City when English preaching was finally introduced there in 1763 in one of the churches. Moreover, the long period of time in which at least a degree of Dutch preaching was continued elsewhere in New York as well as in New Jersey also indicates some exaggeration on the part of Smith and Livingston. Relying on their remarks, later writers often pointed to the language question as a cause for the transfer of membership from the Dutch Church to denominations having English services, especially the Episcopalians and Presbyterians, overlooking other causes.

Frequently overlooked in explaining such transfers of membership has been the proselytizing activities of the Society for the Propagation of the Gospel in Foreign Parts. This organization, chartered in 1701 as a missionary arm of the Episcopal Church, labored diligently to win converts among the Dutch. As early as 1704, the Society pointed out the need for religious works in the Dutch language, and in 1709, it sent fifty copies of a Dutch translation of the Prayer Book to William Huddleston, the Society's schoolmaster in New York. According to the Society's annual report for 1711, the Society printed 750 copies of the liturgy in English and "Low Dutch." The New York school soon began enrolling many pupils with Dutch names, which partly explains the influx of Dutch people into Trinity Church and its two chapels, St. George's and St. Paul's. Similar successes were achieved elsewhere as schools and missions were established at other Dutch communities, including Richmond, Schenectady, Poughkeepsie, and Yonkers in New York as well as at a few places in New Jersey. In some of these communities, the Society made a conscious effort to appoint schoolmasters and missionaries who could speak Dutch, although English was the language of instruction in the schools.[30]

The effect of the Society's activities among Dutchmen is clearly shown in the following remarks sent from Albany on September 26, 1710 by the Reverend Thomas Barclay to the Society's secretary in London:

As I did begin from my first coming to Albany, so I go on to catechise the youth, and it hath pleased God to bless my weak endeavours that way, for a great many Dutch children, who at my first arrival were altogether ignorant of the English tongue, can distinctly say our catechism, and make the responses at prayers....At Schenectady I preach once a month, where there is a garrison of forty soldiers, besides about sixteen English and about one hundred Dutch families; they are all of them my constant hearers. I have this summer got an English school erected amongst them, and in a short time, I hope, their children will be fit for catechising....In this village there has been no Dutch ministers these five years....[Similarly] at present there is no Dutch minister at Albany, neither is any expected 'till next summer....In the meantime some of the Dutch children I have baptized, and married several, and other parts of the service I have performed in the Dutch tongue, and more of them would accept my ministry; but that Mr. Du Bois, a minister of the Dutch congregation of New York, comes sometimes to Albany; he is a hot man, and an enemy to our church.[31]

The letter by the Reverend Barclay illustrates yet another reason, besides the language question, for defections from the Dutch church to other denominations, namely, a shortage of Dutch Reformed pastors. In 1704, when the four Dutch congregations in Kings County, Long Island had no minister, the Reverend William Vesey of the Episcopal Church sometimes preached to them. He reported that "some of the Dutch [were] well affected to the Church of England."[32] A similar situation was reported concerning the Dutch Reformed element at Harlem in 1709, on which occasion an appeal was even made for Dutch Common Prayer Books.[33] The problem of vacancies continued to plague the Dutch churches. In 1741, the Reverend Gualtherus Du Bois of New York wrote the Classis of Amsterdam that there were many vacant churches throughout the land and "if they can secure no Dutchman to preach to them, some will assuredly go over to the Independents, and others to the Episcopalians. This some have already done."[34] A similar warning was directed to the Classis by a pastor from Freehold, New Jersey in 1746.[35]

The quarreling that occurred from time to time in the Dutch Reformed Church must also be considered in explaining why some persons transferred their membership to other denominations. In 1748, the Reverend Du Bois of New York informed the Classis of Amsterdam that "the Dutch churches here are gradually beginning to languish," but attributed it only in part to a "distaste for true piety" and a "neglect of the Dutch language," adding that it was also the result of internal strife.[36] As described elsewhere, for example, the discord among the Kings County churches resulted in some defections to the Episcopalian Church. Disagreements at Poughkeepsie and Fishkill, New York and in the Raritan Valley of New Jersey also affected the Dutch churches adversely. It goes without saying, of course, that the Coetus-Conferentie controversy, described in the previous chapter, especially hurt the growth of the Church, since it involved the entire denomination and lasted in a serious form for almost two decades.

It is thus apparent that several factors besides the language question contributed to the loss of some church members to other denominations. Nevertheless, as time went by, the need to introduce at least partial English preaching became increasingly mandatory for the future growth of the Dutch Reformed Church. This was necessary not only in order to retain young people among its membership, but was also required if the Church expected to increase its membership from among new arrivals coming into the old centers of Dutch culture.

As might be expected because of its cosmopolitanism, the first serious challenge to Dutch preaching occurred in New York, where from time to time before the Revolution petitions requesting the introduction of English preaching were sent to the consistory. The arguments used by the petitioners were virtually the same as those raised by Smith and Livingston but at first elicited no favorable response. The older church members who understood Dutch better than English resisted the change, as did those who had a nostalgia for the old way of doing things. Moreover, the Reverend Lambertus De Ronde, one of the two Dutch preachers in the city, was not strongly in favor of English preaching, although he did write a few religious treatises in English, one of the first Dutch preachers to do so. The distinguished Reverend Johannes Ritzema, the city's other Dutch preacher, eventually came out in favor of English preaching, but is reported to have said on an earlier occasion that rather than allow English preaching in a Dutch Reformed church, "he would lay his head upon a block, and say, 'Cut it off.'"[37]

Undaunted by earlier failures, the pro-English party on May 3, 1762, presented another petition to the Collegiate Consistory. On this occasion, the reasonableness of the request was acknowledged but the consistory decided to "delay a little" because there were many members to whom they also owed consideration, who opposed any concessions to English preaching. Members of the consistory did, however, begin discussing the matter seriously among themselves and with other church members. The discussions were frequently heated and bitter. Among the important questions raised was whether, if English preaching were introduced, there should be two separate consistories (one for the Dutch group and another for the English group) and whether the English preacher should be paid from the same funds as the Dutch preachers.[38]

Despite opposition, the Dutch ministers and some of the consistory members of New York began corresponding with their ecclesiastical superiors in Holland about the language question. Finally, in July 1763, the consistory sent a formal request to the Classis of Amsterdam asking for assistance in obtaining a minister qualified to preach and catechize in the English language. The request specifically stated that the person selected should be a member in "full communion" with the Dutch Reformed Church, that he be ordained by the Church in Holland, and that he subscribe to the doctrinal standards of the Church.[39]

Classis recommended the Reverend Archibald Laidlie, a Scotsman who had been preaching the past four years at the English church in Vlissingen (Flushing), a seaport town a few miles from Middleburg in the southern part of the Netherlands.[40] Hopefully, Laidlie's having a knowledge of Dutch customs and some acquaintance with the language, together with channeling the request through the Classis of

Archibald Laidlie. (Courtesy of the New York Historical Society, New York City)

Amsterdam, would make him acceptable to the pro-Dutch party in New York. Laidlie was quickly ordained by the Classis of Amsterdam in December 1763, after which he shortly set sail for America. According to the pastoral call sent him by the New York Consistory, he would preach two sermons in English per week, "either both times on Sunday, or once on Sunday and once in the week, according to the pleasure of the Consistory."[41] Because of the lack of an English Psalmbook, congregational singing would continue to be in Dutch for the present. Laidlie arrived in New York City on March 29, 1764, after a voyage of about six weeks.[42]

The opponents of English preaching were not prepared to accept Laidlie. Even before his arrival, they presented the consistory with a petition signed by one hundred ten male church members who opposed English preaching. They also sent several appeals to the Classis of Amsterdam. The latter gave them little satisfaction; it declared that the "Everlasting Gospel" could be preached as well in one language as in another and reprimanded Laidlie's critics for confusing zeal for sound doctrine with zeal for maintaining the use of Dutch in the church services.[43] The pro-Dutch party also appealed for help from the local authorities. About a year after Laidle's arrival in New York, they took their case to court on the plea that, according to the church's charter, the congregation as a whole and not the consistory should have the final decision as to whether English preaching should be introduced. The lawsuit went against the pro-Dutch forces. Undaunted, in July 1767 the opponents of English preaching sent a long remonstrance listing their grievances to the provincial governor of New York, Sir Henry Moore. The latter asked the pro-English party to deliver an answer, which they did in great detail. The governor was impressed by their response and dismissed the petition that had been made by the pro-Dutch group.[44]

Meanwhile, the number of hearers who gathered in Laidlie's church to listen to English preaching continued to increase. Upon arrival in New York, he was assigned to the so-called New Church on Nassau Street, later called the Middle Dutch Church. Although new galleries had just been installed in this church, a larger edifice had to be built three years after his arrival. It was located at Fulton and William streets and became known as the North Dutch Church. This expansion was not only a tribute to the ability of the Reverend Laidlie, but also clearly showed the need for a Dutch Reformed minister in New York who could preach in the English language. This was further demonstrated on March 31, 1769, when a second English-preaching pastor was called to assist in the city. He was the Reverend John H.

Livingston, whose role in the settlement of the Coetus-Conferentie problem has already been discussed. Henceforth, Dutch preaching in New York was gradually phased out, with the last Dutch sermon preached there on a regular basis apparently occurring in 1803.[45]

The introduction of English preaching in New York was followed by the gradual appearance of English preaching among Dutch Reformed churches elsewhere. The collegiate churches of Brooklyn, Bushwick, Flatbush, Flatlands, Gravesend, and New Utrecht in Kings County, Long Island, followed a procedure similar to that of New York. Two ministers were employed: the Reverend Martinus Schoonmaker, who preached in Dutch during his entire pastorate there from 1784 to 1824, and the Reverend Peter Lowe, who was called to assist Schoonmaker in 1787 with English preaching. Similarly, at Albany the Reverend John Bassett arrived in 1787 to begin English preaching as an assistant to the Reverend Eilardus Westerlo, who since 1782 had been trying with great difficulty to preach an occasional sermon in English.[46]

Most churches, however, were prevented from supporting two pastors because of the shortage of funds and the lack of facilities. In such instances, a rotation plan was introduced in which the minister conducted some of the services in English, while the remainder continued to be in Dutch. This generally meant that at first only one or two sermons per month were in English, with their number gradually increasing at the expense of Dutch preaching. Among some churches, the transition was slow. As late as 1785, the congregation at Tarrytown, New York was still so strongly Dutch in its customs that it stoutly resisted Dominie Stephen Van Voorhees when he had "the temerity to use the English language at a baptismal service."[47] At Paramus, New Jersey, English preaching was not introduced until 1811, and then only on a part-time basis, while at Tappan, New York, Dutch preaching maintained its ascendancy until after 1820, and was continued once a month until at least 1835.[48]

Among other churches, the process evolved more rapidly. As early as 1795, for example, at Second River, New Jersey, only the morning service on the first Sunday of each month was still being preached in the Dutch language. According to the record, this was done "to gratify the aged, who loved to hear the word in their mother tongue."[49] At Schenectady, New York, when English was introduced on a fifty-fifty basis in February 1794, the congregation objected to that much English. It was, therefore, changed in June to one sermon in four being in English. This lasted only briefly; in 1799, the decision was again made to divide services equally between Dutch and English. Henceforth,

English preaching became increasingly popular, and stated Dutch preaching ended at Schenectady in 1804.[50]

Financial contributions by church members sometimes determined the ratio of English to Dutch sermons. Thus, the consistory minutes of the Reformed Church at Readington, New Jersey, for January 27, 1785, read as follows:

A new subscription list having therefore been circulated, according to which the service should be conducted in the Dutch or English language in proportion to the sum subscribed for each language; it appeared upon a comparison of the subscriptions that the English so far exceeded the Dutch as to have eight more services.[51]

Some churches had to delay the introduction of English because their pastors were unable to preach adequately in that language, but in a few instances such ministers had to seek service elsewhere or resign. In 1774, the Reverend Henricus Schoonmaker, for example, finding it difficult to continue preaching at Poughkeepsie and Fishkill, New York because of demands for more preaching in English, took charge of the church at Acquackanonck, New Jersey, where Dutch preaching was still the order of the day. Similarly, the inability of the Reverend John M. Van Harlingen to officiate in the English language apparently led to his resignation in 1795 from the pastorate at New Millstone, New Jersey and the calling of the Reverend James P. Cannon as his replacement.

On a few occasions, when ministers were not fluent in Dutch but were called upon to preach in it now and then, stipulations were made that they learn the old language. This did not always work out. Thus, when the Reverend Peter Studdiford assumed the pastorate at Readington, New Jersey in 1786, it was with the understanding that he would improve his skill in Dutch and occasionally preach in that tongue. When the task proved too much for him, causing considerable displeasure among some of the older people, the consistory on October 2, 1789, permitted Studdiford to preach only in English, but promised "for the sake of the Dutch friends, to try to get Dutch preaching as often as convenient by an Exchange of Service with . . . Neighboring Ministers."[52] This was also the solution followed at Kingston in 1808 when the Reverend John Gosman proved unable to handle the Dutch language. The Reverend Henry Ostrander from nearby Kaatsbaan came once a month to preach to those who wanted to hear sermons in the ancient tongue.[53]

The introduction of English into the Reformed Church took other forms besides its usage in the Sunday sermons. As early as 1763, a year before the arrival of the Reverend Laidlie, Dominie Lambertus De Ronde, one of the two Dutch pastors in New York City, advertised religious works written by him in the English language.[54] In that same year, the consistory of the New York churches approved a plan for arranging the Psalms in English rhyme, but using Dutch musical scores. Approval was later given for the purchase of two thousand of these English Psalm books.[55] A committee was also established to supervise the translation of the popular *Voorbeeld der Godlyke Waarheden voor eenvoudigen, die zich bereiden tot de belydenisse des geloofs*, a standard catechism written by the Dutch theologian Abraham Hellenbroek (1658–1731). The first American printing appeared in 1765, and several more editions followed.

It is interesting to note that despite the Americanization of the Dutch Reformed churches and the virtual disappearance of Dutch language services in the late eighteenth and early nineteenth centuries,

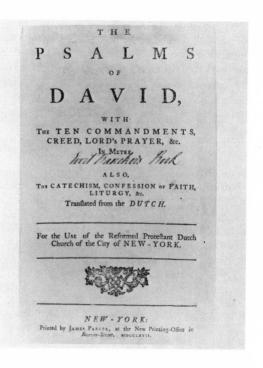

Title page and portion of Psalm I from the Psalm Book published in 1767 at the request of the Collegiate Church of New York. (Courtesy of Sage Library, New Brunswick Seminary)

the Dutch tongue displayed remarkable tenacity in domestic circles in some areas of New York and New Jersey. This is clearly shown in the observations made by numerous travelers and visitors down to the time of the Civil War and even longer.[56] As a consequence, when a new wave of immigrants from the Netherlands began arriving in New York and New Jersey about the middle of the nineteenth century, they were at first preached to on a part-time basis by ministers whose antecedents dated back to the colonial period, but who were still sufficiently acquainted with Dutch to make themselves understood by the immigrants. These preachers included Thomas De Witt of New York, Wilhelmus Eltinge of Paramus, New Jersey, and John Berdan of Acquackanonck, New Jersey.[57]

XIII

Epilogue

It is often said by historians that one can better appreciate the present by examining the past. It is in this light that this study was undertaken. By knowing something about the formative years of the Dutch Reformed Church during the colonial period, it is easier to understand the status of the Reformed Church in America today. Because this period covered nearly a century and a half and was often complex in nature, it should prove helpful to recapitulate in summary form the major developments that have been described in this study—developments that saw a small band of worshippers meeting in a mill loft in New Amsterdam in 1628 grow into a Church of almost one hundred congregations by the close of the colonial period.

In contrast to some of the English colonies, New Netherland was not founded as a place of refuge for the religiously oppressed, but was established for the specific purpose of extending the Dutch commercial empire. Nevertheless, the religious needs of the settlers were not overlooked. Numerous letters and other documents of this period attest to the fact that the divines in Holland kept a watchful eye on what transpired across the Atlantic and from an early date fostered the Dutch Reformed Church there. By the time New Netherland fell to the English in 1664, eleven Dutch Reformed congregations had been organized on American soil, all but two of which were located in the colony of New York. The conditions confronting the churches were those of the wilderness frontier: communities were generally isolated, living conditions were harsh, ministerial salaries were irregularly paid, and most of the people were of a rough and boorish background. Nevertheless, despite primitive conditions, most of the ministers were well-educated and dedicated men.

It is a tribute to the ministers of the New Netherland period and their immediate successors, working under the watchful eye of the Classis of Amsterdam, that the Dutch Reformed churches were able not only to survive the English takeover, with all its attendant problems, but were able to continue to expand in numbers and membership. As a consequence, their status at the opening of the eighteenth century was different in many respects from what it had been when the first preachers arrived from Holland about a century earlier. In 1714 there were thirty-five churches in the colonies of which twenty-three were in New York, ten were in New Jersey, and two were in Pennsylvania. There were also a number of preaching stations. Moreover, whereas the first colonial pastors, such as Michaelius and Megapolensis, had preached to very small congregations in makeshift churches, by 1714 some congregations had a hundred or more members and were worshipping in substantial buildings. Growth continued, so that the number of churches reached forty-five by 1740 and slightly less than a hundred at the time of the American Revolution. Expansion occurred not only in the older settlements, but also in new areas as the frontier was pushed outward into the Mohawk and Schoharie valleys and into northern New Jersey.

Despite this growth, several serious questions confronted the Church during the eighteenth century. Should the preaching, for example, remain formal with considerable emphasis on doctrine or should the sermons become more evangelical? Should the colonial churches remain under the jurisdiction of the Classis of Amsterdam or should they strike out on their own and form an independent classis? Should the churches substitute the English language for Dutch in the worship services and thereby appeal to a wider constituency? Answers to these questions were slow in coming and their solutions seriously disturbed the tranquility of the churches on several occasions, even leading to a schism that lasted amost two decades.

With the adoption of the Articles of Union in 1772, the Dutch Reformed churches in the colonies became independent in fact if not in name. Although they were quite subtle in asserting their independence at first, they became bolder after the Revolution. Thus, according to the Articles of Union, the term *vergadering*, which is usually translated as "meeting," "assembly," or "body," was used to designate the ecclesiastical bodies to be established among the churches, with the qualifying adjectives *algemeen* ("general") and *bijzonder* ("particular") to distinguish between the main and subordinate bodies. This terminology frequently proved confusing in the minutes and was "to an extent unintelligible to other persuasions." Therefore, the General Body meeting at New York in October 1784 resolved "henceforth to apply to the General Body the name of Synod and to the Particular Bodies the name of Classis."[1]

General Synod took an even more significant step in 1788 when it appointed a committee to supervise the translation of the standards of doctrine, the liturgy, and the rules of church order as these existed in the mother church in Holland. In order to accommodate the Articles of the Synod of Dort to the American scene, especially those that pertained to church government, seventy-three Explanatory Articles were added. The report of this committee was adopted in 1792 and published in the following year under the title of "The Constitution of the Reformed Dutch Church in the United States of America."[2] In 1794, General Synod took another step toward Americanizing the Church by deciding henceforth to keep its minutes in the English language, although both English and Dutch language clerks were chosen for the session that year.

Meanwhile, in 1792, the last Netherlander to be called until the advent of a new wave of Dutch immigrants in the mid-nineteenth century, arrived in the United States. His name was Peter Van Vlierden and he came (by way of a Dutch church in the West Indies) in response to a call from the congregation at Oakhill (Durham), New York. A few years later, in 1806, General Synod accepted a report from a special committee recommending that henceforth no consistory be permitted to call a foreigner, no matter of what denomination, to preach without prior approval from the officers of the classis to which the consistory belonged. The Americanization process was thus virtually complete.

The general celerity with which most churchgoers accepted these various changes, once concerted attempts had been made to introduce them and the initial opposition had been overcome, indicates that the modifications were overdue. It must be noted, however, that several new factors had entered the picture since 1772 to speed the process of change. It cannot be overlooked that the Revolution, the winning of Independence from England, and the formation of a new American government had a leveling effect on the people and encouraged the Americanization movement. Thus, Jedidiah Morse, the "father of American Geography," remarked as early as 1794 that although the counties inhabited by the Dutch "still retain many modes, particularly in their religion, which are peculiar to Hollanders," they were adopting "English manners in a great degree." He added that "the revolution, and its consequences, have had a very perceptible influence in diffusing a spirit of liberality among the Dutch, and in dispelling the clouds of ignorance and national prejudice."[3] Moreover, the wars of the French Revolution and Napoleonic era, which began in the early 1790's and lasted until 1815, also quickened the Americanization process by interrupting contacts with Europe for almost a quarter of a century.

The events experienced by the Dutch Reformed Church during the eighteenth century as it was transformed from a group of churches dependent on a foreign ecclesiastical body into an independent American denomination were not unique. Other religious groups in the colonies went through similar experiences, and some of these, too, were bitter at times. The German Reformed churches, for example, which had been placed under the jurisdiction of the Reformed Church in the Netherlands in 1728, gradually became independent beginning with the establishment of their own Coetus in 1747. In its annual meetings in Philadelphia, this body gradually asserted rights and privileges reminiscent of those being affirmed by the Dutch Reformed Coetus in its meetings in New York. Similarly, many Lutherans advocated a loosening of ecclesiastical ties with the Lutheran Church in Germany. Their reasons were virtually the same as those voiced by the Dutch Reformed churches, namely, poor communications and a conviction that the spiritual leaders in the homeland failed to appreciate the special problems facing the American Lutherans. In 1748, a group of Lutherans formed their own synod, a step that caused a split similar to that of the Dutch Reformed during the 1750's and 1760's. Unity among the Presbyterians was also strained from time to time as conservative and liberal clergymen responded in opposing ways to the "Great Awakening" and to revivalist-type preaching. They also differed among themselves over maintaining strong ties with Presbyterian institutions in Great Britain, such as the Irish Synod and the General Assembly in Scotland, as well as with the universities there. The Anglicans, too, were divided among themselves over the question of establishing a colonial bishop who could ordain ministers and decide ecclesiastical disputes without referral to the Church of England.[4]

Nor was the transition unique that saw the change from Dutch to English preaching in the Dutch Reformed churches. Similar developments took place among other denominations during the eighteenth century, with the result that sermons in the traditional tongue were gradually replaced by those in English among Welsh Quakers, French Huguenots, Swedish Lutherans, German Lutherans, and German Reformed. The process among the Welsh churches occurred quite early, but the transition among most other groups took place at about the same time that it did among the Dutch Reformed, with it being slowest among the German Reformed churches. These various movements were similar to those which occurred in the Dutch Reformed churches in terms of their causes and in the adverse reaction of the conservatives to change.[5]

In reviewing the course of development of the Dutch Reformed Church during the colonial period, one can grieve at mistakes that were made and at opportunities that were lost. As examples, one can cite the intolerant spirit manifested by some of the ministers of the New Netherland period toward Lutherans, Quakers, Jews, and others, and the polarization of views and the bitter discord that developed between the adherents of a formalized approach to preaching and those who favored a more evangelical approach. One can also lament the prolonged ecclesiastical vassalage to the Classis of Amsterdam which, though necessary at first, eventually caused hardships for the colonial churches in settling disputes promptly and in supplying vacant pulpits. Similarly, the delay in substituting English for the Dutch language restricted the Church's growth, as members in some areas transferred to religious bodies having English preaching.

On the other hand, such a review of the history of the Church can be a pleasant exercise in historiography by examining how some of its antiquated views were eventually corrected and how it gradually solved some of its perennial problems, such as the shortage of ministers. A study of the relations of the Church with the Indians and the blacks especially brings into sharp focus the great distance in time that separates the colonial Church from that of today. During the seventeenth and eighteenth centuries, the Church concerned itself only in a limited way with the rights of minorities and, more significantly, condoned the practice of slavery and even racism. In regard to missions, it made only feeble efforts to Christianize the Indians, with the exception of those in the Albany area, and left the proselyting of blacks largely up to individual slaveowners. By contrast, the Reformed Church of today has taken a strong stand on behalf of civil rights and carries on an extensive domestic and overseas mission program. Moreover, within its administrative organization today, there is a Black Council, an Hispanic Council, and an American Indian Council.

An examination of the concern for an educated ministry that was frequently expressed by the colonial ministers and particularly by the supporters of the Conferentie party also has a happy ending. In 1766, King George III granted his "loving [colonial] subjects of the Church of the Netherlands" permission to establish a school, to be called Queen's College, in the province of New Jersey. The charter was reissued in 1770 in slightly different form, stipulating that the college was "for the education of youth in the learned languages, liberal and useful arts and sciences, and especially in divinity; preparing them for the ministry, and for other good offices."[6] The school was located at New Brunswick, New Jersey, and was the eighth college to be established in the original thirteen colonies. In 1825, the name was changed to Rutgers College, in honor of Henry Rutgers, a prominent Reformed layman and philanthropist from New York City.

This concern for higher education and an educated ministry continued beyond the colonial period. Thus, in 1784, General Synod appointed the distinguished John H. Livingston as professor of theology, thereby creating one of the first theological seminaries in the United States. Other staff appointments came later and in 1810, the seminary, which had been in New York and Flatbush (frequently in Livingston's home), was moved to New Brunswick. In 1795, through the efforts of Dominie Dirck Romeyn, Dutch Reformed churchmen joined with Presbyterians and Congregationalists in founding Union College at Schenectady, New York. As churches were founded farther westward, especially after the appearance of a new wave of immigrants from the Netherlands beginning in the late 1840's, additional schools were established, including Hope College and Western Theological Seminary at Holland, Michigan, Central College at Pella, Iowa, and Northwestern College at Orange City, Iowa.

The story of the Dutch Reformed Church during the colonial period was obviously one of change, but one must be careful not to exaggerate the modifications that occurred. As one historian has stated, "Our modern viewpoint tends to overweigh the element of change while underestimating the influence of continuity."[7] Even the achievement of ecclesiastical independence in 1772 and the other changes that followed did not signify a complete break with the past. Various traditions and practices remained to remind one of the Church's Old World heritage. In matters of doctrine, for example, the intensely Calvinistic standards that had been accepted in Holland during the Protestant Reformation, including the Belgic Confession, the Heidelberg Catechism, and the Canons of Dort, were retained by the new denomination. Thus, it happened that a Dutch immigrant who had just arrived from the Netherlands could report with amazement in 1848 that the New Jersey church in which he worshipped was still remaining "faithful to the ancient rules and confessions."[8] The new denomination also retained much of the polity of the mother church in Holland, with its various representative bodies known as consistories, classes, particular synods, and general synod.

The memory of the Dutch background of the Church was especially kept alive for many years in its name. At first, the new denomination was known as the "Dutch Reformed Church in North America," and as the "Reformed Dutch Church in the United States of America," but in 1819, it was incorporated as the "Reformed Protestant Dutch Church in North America." Not until 1867, almost a century after achieving ecclesiastical independence from Holland, was the term "Dutch" dropped from the official title, at which time the present name of

"Reformed Church in America" came into use. Even at that late date, the change in name caused friction within the Church.

That the memory of the Dutch background of the Church was kept alive for so many years presents a curious anomaly. On the one hand, it is understandable why the Church was referred to as the *Dutch* Reformed Church. After all, it had been founded by the Reformed Church of the Netherlands and was subject to the ecclesiastical jurisdiction of the Classis of Amsterdam during most of the colonial period. The Dutch background of many of its ministers and the extensive use of the Dutch language in the worship services also explain why it continued to be looked upon as a "Dutch" religious body. On the other hand, despite some early acts of intolerance toward non-Reformed groups and the failure to attract a significant number of Indians and blacks, it had from the beginning of its founding a polyglot membership that included Germans, Scandinavians, Frenchmen, Walloons, English, and others as well as Dutchmen.

Given the pluralistic makeup of the churches, the prolongation of matters "in the Dutch way" for such a long period of time is a tribute to their strength and influence and can be understood only in that light. A community church during the colonial period meant much more to the people then than now. It was the heartbeat of a neighborhood and the center of its cohesiveness, as the Sunday services and other church functions drew people together from miles around. The colonists gathered on these occasions not only to worship God but also to visit friends, to make new acquaintances, and to exchange news and gossip. The minister, too, was usually a more influential personage in that age than he is today. As one of the few educated persons in a community, his weekly sermons and pastoral visits were one of the major sources of intellectual stimuli for the colonists. The church also influenced the intellectual climate of a community through the role it played in selecting schoolmasters and in determining school curricula.

Considering these factors, it is not surprising that when a community had only one church and it happened to be Dutch Reformed the local populace, no matter what its ethnic background, generally attended Dutch church services, adopted Dutch as its everyday language, and observed Dutch customs and traditions. Thus, as one writer has stated, and as this study has pointed out several times, the Dutch Reformed Church during the colonial period often represented "not so much an ethnic as a cultural identity,"[9] an identity that, having engrained itself among the people of a community for several generations, was not likely to be erased within a brief period of time. The success of the Dutch Reformed Church in bringing so many different ethnic groups under its ecclesiastical umbrella during the colonial period, *without losing sight of its primary purpose*, should be an inspiration to the Church today in ministering to the needs of an American society that seems to emphasize increasingly its ethnic pluralism rather than the "melting pot" dream of a generation ago.

This is not to say that in subscribing to pluralism the Church was not at times sluggish in discarding practices that had become archaic and were hampering its growth. A study of the Church's experience in this regard and its slowness to come to terms with various changes taking place in colonial society can be useful in examining the adjustments that are being called for in ministering to today's rapidly changing world. Persons who disfavor change must take care not to become obstructionist as happened in the case of some individuals who opposed the work of pastors like Bertholf and Frelinghuysen, or who sided with the ultra-reactionaries among the Conferentie ministers. On the other hand, persons advocating change must guard against repudiating traditions that have been a source of strength in the past and can be a foundation on which to continue to build in the future.

Footnotes

Chapter I

1. Until 1772, the Dutch Reformed churches in America were subject, at least theoretically, to the Classis of Amsterdam. After achieving their independence in 1772, the new denomination became known as the "Dutch Reformed Church in North America" and as the "Reformed Dutch Church in the United States of America." In 1819, it was incorporated as the "Reformed Protestant Dutch Church in North America." An attempt was made about 1840 to drop the term "Dutch" from the official title, but the proposal failed. It was not until 1867 that the present name of "Reformed Church in America" came into use.

2. One of the best single-volume histories of the Netherlands in English is Bernard H. M. Vlekke, *Evolution of the Dutch Nation* (New York: Roy Publishers, 1945). The best history in Dutch is J. A. Van Houte and others, eds., *Algemene Geschiedenis der Nederlanden* (12 vols.; Utrecht: W. De Haan, 1949–58).

3. J. Reitsma and J. Lindeboom, *Geschiedenis van de Hervorming en de Hervormde Kerk der Nederlanden* (5th rev. ed.; 's-Gravenhage: Martinus Nijhoff, 1949) has extensive bibliographies on the history of the Reformed Church in the Netherlands.

4. For a general account of Dutch commerical activity overseas during early modern times see Charles R. Boxer, *The Dutch Seaborne Empire* (New York: Knopf, 1965). For detailed studies pertaining solely to New Netherland see Thomas J. Condon, *New York Beginnings: The Commerical Origins of New Netherland* (New York: New York University Press, 1968); Simon Hart, *The Pre-history of the New Netherland Company* (Amsterdam: City of Amsterdam Press, 1959); and C. A. Weslager, *Dutch Explorers, Traders and Settlers in the Delaware Valley 1609–1664* (Philadelphia: University of Pennsylvania Press, 1961).

5. Ten thousand has been the figure most commonly accepted until recent years. Historians now put it at about eight thousand or even less. See Alexander C. Flick, ed., *History of the State of New York* (10 vols.; New York: Columbia University Press, 1933–37), II, 35–36; Boxer, *The Dutch Seaborne Empire*, 228; Evarts B. Greene and Virginia D. Harrington, *American Population before the Federal Census of 1790* (Gloucester, Mass.: Peter Smith, 1966), 88.

Chapter II

1. As early as April 5, 1598, the Reverend Petrus Plancius in-

formed the consistory of Amsterdam that shipowners planning voyages to the Far East were willing to pay for the support of some ship chaplains. Plancius was a minister of Amsterdam, but was also a geographer of some note and a strong proponent of an energetic colonial policy.

2. A *ziekentrooster* was also called a *krankenbezoeker*, which has virtually the same translation. Because a comforter of the sick was instructed to admonish sinners to repent and refrain from further sins, the documents also occasionally refer to him as a *vermaaner*, meaning "admonisher." For a more detailed description than is given here of the office of comforter of the sick, see Gerald F. De Jong, "The *Ziekentroosters* or Comforters of the Sick in New Netherland," *The New-York Historical Society Quarterly*, LIV (October 1970), 339–359.

3. He wrote his name in different ways: Bastiaen Jansz. Krol, Bastiaen Jansz. Crol, Bastiaen Krol, Bastiaen Crol, and Sebastian Jansen Krol. For a careful study of New Netherland's first comforter of the sick, see A. Eekhof, *Bastiaen Jansz. Krol: Krankenbezoeker, Kommies en Kommandeur van Nieuw-Nederland, 1595–1645* (The Hague: Martinus Nijhoff, 1910).

4. An examination of the backgrounds of 102 comforters of the sick reveals that 18 of them were former tailors. Schoolteachers were next with 14, followed by former ministers, 9; fabric workers, 7; shoemakers, 5; former soldiers, 5; and former priests, 2. The remainder came from a variety of backgrounds but mostly from the working class. C. A. L. Van Troostenburg de Bruyn, *De*

Hervormde Kerk in Nederlandsch Oost-Indie onder de Oost-Indische Compagnie, 1602–1795 (Arnhem: H. A. Tjeenk Willink, 1884) 336–337.

5. Eekhof, *Bastiaen Jansz. Krol*, xi. See also 29–30.

6. *Ibid.*, xxi-xxiii.

7. *Ibid.*, 32–33; Edward T. Corwin, ed., *Ecclesiastical Records of the State of New York* (7 vols.; Albany: James B. Lyon, 1901–16), I, 43.

8. J. Franklin Jameson, ed., *Narratives of New Netherland, 1609–1664* (New York: Barnes and Noble, 1959), 83–84.

9. Although it was never recognized by the Dutch Reformed Church as an official writing, Van Hille's work was regularly published in the older Dutch editions of the liturgy of the church. It also appeared in the first two English editions published in America in 1793 and 1815. For a brief description of the life of Van Hille, see J. P. De Bie and J. Loosjes, eds., *Biographisch Woordenboek van Protestantsche Godgeleerden in Nederland* (5 vols.; The Hague: Martinus Nijhoff, 1907–43), IV, 31–34. For an analysis of the *Ziekentroost*, the writer relied on the 1793 edition found in *The Constitution of the Reformed Dutch Church in the United States of America* (New York: William Durell, 1793), 198–218.

10. Van Troostenburg de Bruyn, *Hervormde Kerk in Nederlandsch Oost-Indie*, 111n.

11. *Ecclesiastical Records*, I, 128. In 1645, officials in the Dutch colony in Brazil requested seven additional ministers, and in 1647, five or six more comforters of the sick. *Ibid.*, 191, 222.

12. The date as given on the plaque

is in error, because Krol arrived in 1624.

13. For a more detailed account of the life of Michaelius than is given here, see A. Eekhof, *Jonas Michaelius: Founder of the Church in New Netherland* (Leyden: A. W. Sijthoff, 1926).

14. The word "dominie" is derived from the Latin *dominus*, meaning lord or master. In the Netherlands, England, and Scotland, it was used as a title for learned men, especially clergymen. In the United States, where the Scottish practice of spelling it "dominie" (rather than the Dutch "domine") came to be accepted, its use has been restricted largely to ministers of churches having a Dutch background.

15. Ordinarily, the organization of a new church was undertaken by a special committee from the classis in which the proposed new church would be located. The committee would be authorized to meet with the people who would be the charter members, examine the papers of those who were already communicant members of a church, and hear the confession of faith of those who wished to be communicant members. It would also supervise the election of a consistory, and then declare the church officially organized. This procedure was, of course, frequently impossible in the Dutch colonies.

16. Eekhof, *Jonas Michaelius*, 130.

17. *Ibid.*, 108–109.

18. Brief accounts of the life of Bogardus are found in P. C. Molhuysen and P. J. Blok, eds., *Nieuw Nederlandsch Biografisch Woordenboek* (10 vols.; Leiden: A. W. Sijthoff, 1911–37), I, 386–389 and in Edward T. Cor-

win, *A Manual of the Reformed Church in America* (4th ed., rev.; New York: Board of Publication of the Reformed Church, 1902), 330–332.

19. *Ecclesiastical Records*, I, 196.

20. Ellis Lawrence Raesly, *Portrait of New Netherland* (New York: Columbia University Press, 1945), 206.

21. *Ecclesiastical Records*, I, 198.

22. Flick, *History of the State of New York*, II, 5.

23. Edmund Bailey O'Callaghan and Berthold Fernow, eds., *Documents Relating to the Colonial History of the State of New York* (15 vols.; Albany: Weed, Parsons and Company, 1856–87), I, 299.

24. A brief account of the life of Backerus is found in Corwin, *Manual of the Reformed Church*, 300–301.

25. *Ecclesiastical Records*, I, 234.

26. The best account of the patroon system and the role played by Kiliaen Van Rensselaer is that by Samuel G. Nissenson, *The Patroon's Domain* (New York: Columbia University Press, 1937). A copy of the charter is found in A. J. F. Van Laer, ed., *Van Rensselaer Bowier Manuscripts Being the Letters of Kiliaen Van Rensselaer, 1630–1643...* (Albany: University of the State of New York, 1908), 136–153.

27. For a lengthy account of the life of Megapolensis see Gerald F. De Jong, "Dominie Johannes Megapolensis: Minister to New Netherland," *The New-York Historical Society Quarterly*, LII (January 1968), 7–47.

28. A copy of the contract is found in *Van Rensselaer Bowier Manuscripts*, 606–608. A slightly different translation is given in *Ecclesiastical Records*, I, 143–145.

29. *Van Rensselaer Bowier Manuscripts*, 662–663, 828–829. Con-

trary to what some writers have stated, a new church was not built at Rensselaerswyck until 1656. *Ecclesiastical Records*, I, 426.

30. *Narratives of New Netherland*, 262.
31. *Ecclesiastical Records*, I, 231.
32. *Ibid.*, 262.
33. *Ibid.*, 236.
34. A brief account of the life of Drisius is found in Corwin, *Manual of the Reformed Church*, 433–435. For a longer account, see A. Eekhof, *De Hervormde Kerk in Noord-Amerika, 1624– 1664* (2 vols.; 's-Gravenhage: Martinus Nijhoff, 1913), I, 178– 183.
35. Edmund Bailey O'Callaghan, *History of New Netherland; or, New York under the Dutch* (2 vols.; New York: D. Appleton & Company, 1846–48), II, 567. For an account of the life of Schaats, see Eekhof, *Hervormde Kerk*, I, 142–165.
36. *Ecclesiastical Records*, I, 383.
37. Eekhof, *Jonas Michaelius*, 110.
38. *Ibid.*
39. *Narratives of New Netherland*, 168–171.
40. Eekhof, *Jonas Michaelius*, 71.
41. *Van Rensselaer Bowier Manuscripts*, 607. A schepel was equal to about one bushel, and a morgen was approximately two-thirds of an acre.
42. Eekhof, *Jonas Michaelius, 111.*
43. *Ecclesiastical Records*, I, 382– 386. But a "handsome parsonage" was finally built for Schaats in 1656. *Ibid.*, 395.

Chapter III

1. In order to avoid confusion, the towns of New Netherland are generally referred to by the names and spellings which came into use after the English con-

quest of the colony. The dates for the founding of these towns are approximate. It is impossible to give exact dates not only because of the uncertainties when the first settlers arrived but also because the dates for the plotting of a town and the formal incorporation may differ by several years.
2. For a more detailed description than is given here of the early history of the Reformed Church on Long Island see Gerald F. De Jong, "The Formative Years of the Dutch Reformed Church on Long Island," *Journal of Long Island History*, VIII (Summer-Fall, 1968), 1–16, and IX (Winter-Spring, 1969), 1–20.
3. *Documents Relating to New York*, XIV, 252.
4. *Ecclesiastical Records*, I, 331.
5. An account of the life of Polhemus is found in Eekhof, *Hervormde Kerk*, I, 188–205.
6. For a description of this church see Thomas M. Strong, *The History of the Town of Flatbush, in Kings County, Long Island* (New York: Thomas R. Mercier, 1842), 74–76.
7. *Documents Relating to New York*, XIV, 381.
8. On the life of Selyns before his arrival in New Netherland see Eekhof, *Hervormde Kerk*, I, 206–211.
9. *Ecclesiastical Records*, I, 487.
10. The Dutch word *bouwerij* or *boerderij*, meaning "farm," was corrupted into bowery. Hence arose the name for that part of New York City which stands near the old Stuyvesant farm.
11. A record of 1683 shows that the church paid twelve guilders for two skins for the drum. David S. Sutphen, e.a., *Historical Discourse* [on the] . . . *Reformed Dutch Church of New Utrecht* (n.p.: The Consistory, 1927), 36.

12. Peter Ross, *A History of Long Island* (2 vols.; New York: Lewis Publishing Co., 1902), I, 312–313.
13. *Ecclesiastical Records*, I, 488.
14. *Ibid.*, 434–435.
15. An account of the life of Blum is found in Eekhof, *Hervormde Kerk*, I, 227–244.
16. *Ecclesiastical Records*, I, 465–466.
17. Edmund B. O'Callaghan, *The Documentary History of the State of New York* (4 vols.; Albany: Weed, Parsons and Company, 1849–51), III, 582.
18. For a careful study of the Dutch on the Delaware see Weslager, *Dutch Explorers in the Delaware Valley*.
19. *Ecclesiastical Records*, I, 457.
20. Isaac N. Stokes, *Iconography of Manhattan Island* (6 vols.; New York: R. H. Dodd, 1915–28), IV, 55.
21. *Ecclesiastical Records*, I, 318.
22. *Documents Relating to New York*, I, 110–111.
23. *Narratives of New Netherland*, 260.
24. At least one of the colonial ministers sided with the directors on the matter of intolerance. Dominie Polhemus wrote the Classis on April 21, 1664: "The Quakers also are compelled to go before the court, and be put under oath; but such compulsion is displeasing to God." *Ecclesiastical Records*, I, 544.
25. *Ibid.*, I, 349.
26. *Ibid.*, 343–344.
27. *Ibid.*, 317–318. According to one study, the Lutherans at this time numbered about fifty families on Manhattan Island. Lars P. Qualben, *The Lutheran Church in Colonial America* (New York: T. Nelson and Sons, 1940), 129–130.
28. *Ecclesiastical Records*, I, 322.
29. *Ibid.*, 387–388, 449, 454.
30. *Ibid.*, 460.
31. *Ibid.*, 396. As late as 1664, Dominie Selyns, who was more tolerant of clergymen of other denominations than were Megapolensis and Drisius, made a similar reference to the unchristian behavior of Lokenius. *Ibid.*, 550.
32. *Documents Relating to New York*, XIV, 156.
33. *Ibid.*, 336–337.
34. *Ecclesiastical Records*, I, 400.
35. For a discussion of this, see Raesly, *Portrait of New Netherland*, 231–233.
36. *Ecclesiastical Records*, I, 400.
37. *Ibid.*, 530.
38. Raesly, *Portrait of New Netherland*, 214.
39. *Ecclesiastical Records*, I, 335–336.
40. *Documents Relating to New York*, XIV, 351. The Classis of Amsterdam, however, as early as 1646, had been urging restrictions on the Jews as well as Roman Catholics in the Dutch colony of Brazil. *Ecclesiastical Records*, I, 204–206.
41. This is discussed later in Chapter IX.
42. *Ecclesiastical Records*, I, 438.
43. *Ibid.*, 439.
44. Eekhof, *Hervormde Kerk*, II, 42–54. A copy of the letter is found in the appendix of Eekhof's work.
45. *Ecclesiastical Records*, I, 397.
46. *Ibid.*, 446.
47. *Documents Relating to New York*, XIV, 371, 376.
48. *Ibid.*, 479.
49. A. J. F. Van Laer, ed., *Documents Relating to New Netherland 1624–1626 in the Henry E. Huntington Library* (San Marino, Calif.: Henry E. Huntington Library and Art Gallery, 1924), 187, 207.

50. Eekhof, *Jonas Michaelius*, 11.
51. *Documents Relating to New York*, XIV, 444, 471; II, 51.
52. *Van Rensselaer Bowier Manuscripts*, 805–846. See also Mildred P. Wheeler, "Early Dutch Life at Fort Orange and Beverwyck," *The Dutch Settlers Society of Albany Yearbook*, XXI and XXII (1944–45), 5–12.
53. Edmund Bailey O'Callaghan, ed., *Laws and Ordinances of New Netherland 1638–1674* (Albany: Weed, Parsons and Company, 1868), 93.
54. *Ecclesiastical Records*, I, 236.
55. *Ibid.*, 383–384.
56. O'Callaghan, *Laws and Ordinances of New Netherland*, 258–259, 448–449. Similar decrees were issued in 1641, 1647, 1648, 1657, 1658, 1661.
57. For a discussion of education in New Netherland see William Heard Kilpatrick, *The Dutch Schools of New Netherland and Colonial New York* (Washington, D. C.: Government Printing Office, 1912).
58. *Van Rensselaer Bowier Manuscripts*, 151. See also *Narratives of New Netherland*, 353; Daniel J. Pratt, *Annals of Public Education in the State of New York from 1626 to 1746* (Albany: The Argus Company, 1872), 39.
59. *Narratives of New Netherland*, 398.
60. For an account of this school see Henry W. Dunshee, *History of the School of the Collegiate Reformed Dutch Church in the City of New York from 1633 to 1883* (2nd ed., rev.; New York: Aldine Press, 1883).
61. Edmund Bailey O'Callaghan, ed., *The Register of New Netherland, 1626 to 1674* (Albany: J. Munsell, 1865), 129.

Chapter IV

1. *Documents Relating to New York*, II, 509.
2. John Romeyn Brodhead, *History of the State of New York* (2 vols.; New York: Harper, 1853–71), I, 741; O'Callaghan, *History of New Netherland*, II, 527.
3. As quoted in *ibid.*, 526.
4. *Documents Relating to New York*, II, 500.
5. *Ibid.*, XIII, 416. See also II, 377.
6. *Ibid.*, XIII, 405; *Ecclesiastical Records*, I, 588, 601, 603–604, 647–648, 686. It is possible that the West India Company, which was in difficult economic straits at this time, was merely using the alleged treachery of the dominie as an excuse to keep from paying his back salary.
7. *Ecclesiastical Records*, I, 595–597.
8. In discussing relations between the Dutch Reformed churches and the English authorities during this period, the writer relied heavily on John Webb Pratt, *Religion, Politics, and Diversity: The Church State Theme in New York History* (Ithaca, N. Y.: Cornell University Press, 1967), 26–48.
9. *Ecclesiastical Records*, I, 602.
10. *Ibid.*, 654.
11. George De Vries, "Church and State in New York: An Historical Account," *The Reformed Journal*, November 1975, 19.
12. Bruce M. Wilkenfeld, "The New York City Common Council, 1689–1800," *New York History*, LII (July 1971), 249–273.
13. Harry Julius Kreider, *Lutheranism in Colonial New York* (New York: Arno Press, 1972), 70–71.
14. *Ibid.*, See also *Centennial Discourses*, 9.

15. Pratt, *Religion, Politics, and Diversity*, 31.

16. In 1690, "the proportion of Anglicans to other sects—Dutch Reformed, Lutheran, Presbyterian, Quakers—was only one to forty." Carl Bridenbaugh, *Mitre and Sceptre: Transatlantic Faiths, Ideas, Personalities, and Politics 1689–1775* (New York: Oxford University Press, 1962), 117.

17. The difference between licensing to preach and ordination is discussed in Chapters VII and IX.

18. On the problems concerning Nicholas Van Rensselaer see Brodhead, *History of the State of New York*, II, 272, 288, 300.

19. Raesly, *Portrait of New Netherland*, 225.

20. D. M. Ellis, e.a., *A Short History of New York State* (rev. ed.; Ithaca, N. Y.: Cornell University Press, 1967), 63.

21. *Ecclesiastical Records*, I, 602. See also 587.

22. The Lutherans had as much difficulty as the Reformed in obtaining a minister. When granted permission by the English governor in December 1664 to call a pastor, it took five years before they finally succeeded in getting one, and he proved to be a disappointment. See Qualben, *The Lutheran Church in Colonial America*, 133.

23. For a detailed account of the Leisler troubles see Jerome R. Reich, *Leisler's Rebellion: A Study of Democracy in New York, 1664–1720* (Chicago: University of Chicago Press, 1953).

24. Corwin, *Manual of the Reformed Church*, 62–63; Reich, *Leisler's Rebellion*, 58–59, 63–68.

25. *Ecclesastical Records*, II, 1007.

26. Dominie Peter Tesschenmaeker, who had been serving the church at Schenectady since 1682, was killed by the Indians in February 1690; Dominie Laurentius Van den Bosch of Kingston had earlier been deposed in 1689 for scandalous behavior; and Schaats of Albany was in his mideighties.

27. *Ecclesiastical Records*, II, 1042.

28. *Ibid.*, 1050–1051. See also 1089.

29. *Ibid.*, 1102, 1044.

30. *Ibid.*, 1056, 1059, 1246–1261.

31. Henry C. Murphy, *Anthology of New Netherland* (New York: n.p., 1865), 114.

32. Edward Tanjore Corwin, the distinguished historian of the Reformed Church during the early twentieth century, was completely in error to characterize Leisler's regime as "a reign of terror, with robberies and murders and exiles." "The Ecclesiastical Condition of New York at the Opening of the Eighteenth Century," *Papers of the American Society of Church History*, Second Series, III (1912), 86. Both of the Huguenot pastors of New York, Pierre Daillé and Pierre Peiret, also opposed Leisler. John A. F. Maynard, *The Huguenot Church of New York: A History of the French Church of Saint Esprit* (New York: n.p., 1938), 72.

33. Corwin, *Manual of the Reformed Church*, 64, states that the reburial was objected to by the clergy of all denominations in the city.

34. Documents on the Ministry Act are found in *Ecclesiastical Records*, II, 1073–1079.

35. The charter is found in *ibid.*, 1136–1165.

36. *Ibid.*, 1172.

37. *Ibid.*, 1168–1169.

38. On the events that led to the charter see Pratt, *Religion, Politics, and Diversity*, 37–46.

39. *Ibid.*, 45.

40. *Ibid.*, 49.

41. *Ecclesiastical Records*, III, 1507.

42. *Ibid.*, 1616. See also 1652, 1659–1660.
43. The events relating to Cornbury's religious policy are well summarized in H. J. Westerling, "De Nederduitsch Gereformeerde Kerk in de Provincien New York en New Jersey onder het Engelsche Bewind," *Nederlandsch Archief voor Kerkgeschiedenis*, Nieuwe Serie, XVI (1920–21), 209–212. See also *Ecclesiastical Records*, III, 1615–1619, 1657–1662.

Chapter V

1. *Ecclesiastical Records*, II, 829.
2. Albert Cook Meyers, ed., *Narratives of Early Pennsylvania, West-New Jersey and Delaware 1630–1707* (New York: Scribners, 1912), 238.
3. Maynard, *The Huguenot Church of New York*, 64.
4. William Henry Foote, *The Huguenots; or, Reformed French Church* (Richmond, Va.: Presbyterian Committee of Publication, n.d.), 507–508. According to another writer, the tendency on the part of the Huguenots to become "denationalized" was perhaps partly due to "a deliberate attempt to throw off the characteristics of a country from which they felt they had been unjustly driven." Maldwyn Allen Jones, *American Immigration* (Chicago: University of Chicago Press, 1960), 51–52.
5. Corwin, *Manual of the Reformed Church*, 994; Thomas Jefferson Wertenbaker, *The Founding of American Civilization: The Middle Colonies* (New York: Cooper Square Publications, 1963), 104.
6. *Ecclesiastical Records*, II, 866–867. See also 959, 1172–1173.
7. In 1704, the French Reformed congregation built a more elaborate church edifice, known as "Le Temple du Saint Esprit," on the corner of Nassau and Pine Streets.
8. For a general discussion of the migration of Dutch farmers from the old New Netherland settlements and the founding of new communities see Gerald F. De Jong, *The Dutch in America* (Boston: Twayne Publishers, 1975), 48–62.
9. One of the best historical accounts of the Schenectady church is John J. Birch, *The Pioneering Church of the Mohawk Valley* (Schenectady: The Consistory of the First Reformed Church, 1955). Corwin gives 1680 as the date for the founding of this church, but it might have been earlier. The exact date cannot be determined because the early documents were lost in the fire following the Indian raid of 1690.
10. *Ecclesiastical Records*, II, 788.
11. *Ibid.*, I, 735–736.
12. *Ibid.*, 729.
13. *Ibid.*, 688, 701.
14. New Lotts, however, did not get its own church building, nor was it even recognized as a separate congregation, until 1824. Strong, *History of the Town of Flatbush*, 103–104.
15. *Ibid.*, 74, 102, 112.
16. *Ecclesiastical Records*, II, 757, 760, 776, 793, 838.
17. *Ibid.*, I, 729.
18. *Ibid.*, 688.
19. *Ibid.*, II, 761.
20. *Ibid.*, 781–782, 785, 801–802.
21. *Ibid.*, 797–799.
22. *Ibid.*, 810.
23. *Ibid.*, 911.
24. *Ibid.*, 922.
25. *Ibid.*, 1119–1120.
26. The documents on this controversy are found in *ibid.*, II, 1189–1212, 1286–1288, 1296–

1298. It is interesting to note that the anti-Leislerian faction had sent letters to the consistories of several other Dutch Reformed churches in the colonies to solicit their support in the matter. Of the nine replies received, only the Kingston church withheld support. It is probable that Kingston's decision was influenced by its pastor, the Reverend John Nucella, who had hoped to receive the New York call that was sent to Verdieren.

27. *Ecclesiastical Records*, II, 1117–1121.

28. *Ibid.*, I, 701–702, 713–716.

29. *Ibid.*, 740.

30. *Ibid.*, II, 1104, 1304–1305, 1346. It is also likely that he received a university education because his father was a minister in Amsterdam.

31. Murphy, *Anthology of New Netherland*, 130.

32. In 1686, Dominie Selyns prepared a list of the names of the communicant members of his church, arranged according to the streets on which they lived. He undoubtedly used it as a guide in locating church members when making pastoral calls. The manuscript, which is pocket size, has been published by the Holland Society of New York under the title *Records of Dominie Henricus Selyns of New York 1686–7* (New York: Holland Society, 1916).

33. As quoted in *Centennial Discourses: A Series of Sermons Delivered in the Year 1876, by the Order of the General Synod of the Reformed (Dutch) Church in America* (2nd ed.; New York: Board of Publication of the Reformed Church in America, 1877), 51.

34. His last name is also written Bertholff, Barthof, and Barth-

olff, while spellings of his first name also include Guiliem and Guilliam. For a general account of Bertholf's life see David Cole, *History of the Reformed Church of Tappan, N.Y.* (New York: Stettiner, Lambert, & Co., 1894), 8–20, and Adrian C. Leiby, *The United Churches of Hackensack and Schraalenburgh, New Jersey 1686–1822* (River Edge, N. J.: Bergen County Historical Society, 1976), 7–58.

35. For Bertholf's reasons for bypassing the Classis of Amsterdam see Chapter X.

36. Corwin, *Manual of the Reformed Church*, 318.

37. Tercentenary Committee on Research, *Tercentenary Studies 1928: Reformed Church in America, A Record of Beginnings* (n.p.: Published by the Church, 1928), 193.

38. Despite their success as preachers, Bertholf and Freeman were not fully accepted by some of the other Dutch Reformed ministers. This matter is discussed fully in Chapter X. Freeman's work as a missionary among the Indians is discussed in Chapter IX.

39. *Ecclesiastical Records*, II, 1131.

40. Bartlett B. James and J. Franklin Jameson, eds., *Journal of Jasper Danckaerts* (New York: Scribners, 1913), 45. See also 197, 215. It should be noted that as a Labadist preacher, Danckaerts was prone to find fault among religious leaders whose theological views differed from his own. The Labadists were adherents of a Dutch quietist sect founded about 1660 that worshipped in an austere Calvinist manner and practiced communal living.

41. *Ecclesiastical Records*, I, 555. He had been accused of similar

acts in Holland in 1661 before going to America. *Ibid.*, 506.

42. Corwin, *Manual of the Reformed Church*, 811; Westerling, "De Nederduitsch Gereformeerde Kerk," 212.

43. James, *Journal of Jasper Danckaerts*, 228–229.

44. *Ecclesiastical Records*, I, 711–719, 721–722; II, 771–780, 790–795. The statement in Sutphen, *Historical Discourses*, 6, that Van Zuuren "while in pastoral work... displayed the excellent qualities of energy, tact, and affection" is too flattering.

45. *Ecclesiastical Records*, II, 828.

46. Shortly after the Dutch vacated the Church in the Fort, repairs totalling 900 pounds were made by the Anglican congregation worshipping there. Daniel Van Pelt, *Pictures of Early Church Life in New York City* (New York: Board of Publications, 1895), 37.

47. Thomas De Witt, *A Discourse Delivered in the North Reformed Dutch Church (Collegiate) in the City of New York* (New York: Board of Publication of the Reformed Protestant Dutch Church, 1857), 27.

48. Charlotte R. Bangs, *Reminiscences of Old Utrecht and Gowanus* (n.p.: n.p., 1912), 102.

49. John Pershing Luidens, "Americanization of the Dutch Reformed Church," unpublished Ph.D. dissertation, University of Oklahoma, 1969, 51.

50. For a description of churches built in the Netherlands during this period, see M. D. Ozinga, *Protestantsche Kerken hier te Lande Gesticht 1596–1793* (Amsterdam: H. J. Paris, 1929). The Willemstad church was the first Protestant church built in the Netherlands.

51. Leiby, *The United Churches of* *Hackensack and Schraalenburgh*, 44–45.

Chapter VI

1. On the early Palatine emigration to America see Walter Allen Knittle, *Early Eighteenth Century Palatine Emigration* (Philadelphia: Dorrance and Company, 1937). For the religious life of the German colonists see James I. Good, *Historical Handbook of the Reformed Church in the United States* (2nd ed.; Philadelphia: Heidelberg Press, 1901) and the carefully documented study by John B. Frantz, "The Awakening of Religion among the German Settlers in the Middle Colonies," *William and Mary Quarterly*, XXXIII (April 1976), 266–288.

2. Kreider, *Lutheranism in Colonial New York*, 35.

3. *Ecclesiastical Records*, III, 2002–2003. See also Knittle, *Early Eighteenth Century Palatine Emigration*, 196. For a good account of the dependence of the German Reformed Church on the divines in Holland see Good, *Historical Handbook*, 49–75.

4. Wertenbaker, *Middle Colonies*, 105. See also Jones, *American Immigration*, 50; Helen Wilkinson Reynolds, *Dutch Houses in the Hudson Valley before 1776* (New York: Dover Publications, 1965), 297.

5. The work of these ministers is described in greater detail later in this and in the following chapter.

6. F. N. Zabriske, *History of the Reformed P. D. Church of Claverack: A Centennial Address* (Hudson, N.Y.: Stephen B. Miller, 1867), 25.

7. As an example of these various

problems, one can cite the twenty-four Dutch Reformed churches that made up the Classis of Montgomery in north-central New York at the time of its organization in 1800 as they are listed in a study published in 1916. The list includes such information as whether a church later became extinct or merged with another denomination, changed its name, and so forth: "1. Amsterdam (not present Amsterdam); 2. Andrustown (merged in Columbia); 3. Canajoharie (Sand Hill); 4. Charlestown (extinct); 5. Chenango (Presb. and extinct); 6. Chukonot (Florida); 7. Coenradstown (merged in Columbia); 8. Conewago (Caughnawaga, i.e. Fonda); 9. Curriestown (Currytown); 10. Duanesborough (Presb. and extinct); 11. Fonda's Bush (Presb.); 12. German Flatts (Fort Herkimer); 13. Herkimer; 14. Lower Schoharie (Schoharie); 15. Mayfield (Presb.); 16. New Rhinebeck (Lawyersville); 17. Owasco Lake (Owasco): 18. Remsen's Bush (Florida); 19. Sacondaga (extinct); 20. Schoharie Kill (extinct); 21. Sharon (Schoharie Classis); 22. Snellsbush (Manheim); 23. Stone Arabia; 24. Upper Schoharie (Middleburgh)." W. N. P. Dailey, *The History of Montgomery Classis R. C. A.* (Amsterdam, N.Y.: Recorder Press, 1916), 10.

8. The church at Fordham in the Bronx, organized in 1696, was looked upon for many years as a stepchild of the Collegiate Church because it was located on property (Fordham Manor) that was deeded to the Garden Street Church by Dominie Selyns' second wife. The Manhattan ministers, however, supplied it very irregularly during the eighteenth century. According to Corwin, a German Reformed church organized on Manhattan Island in 1758 became Dutch Reformed in 1763, but there is some confusion about whether it ever was a part of the collegiate system. *Manual of the Reformed Church*, 1003.

9. *Ecclesiastical Records*, IV, 2632.

10. As described in Corwin, *Manual of the Reformed Church*, 440. See also *Ecclesiastical Records*, II, 1346–1347.

11. As quoted in "The Rev. Archibald Laidlie, D. D. 1727–1779," *Year Book of the Collegiate Reformed Church* (1886), 79.

12. For more detailed information on the internal strife occurring on Long Island at this time see Chapter X.

13. Jacob Brodhead, *Sermon Preached in the Central Reformed Protestant Dutch Church of Brooklyn* (Brooklyn: I. Van Andem, 1851), 12.

14. Lucas Boeve, *The Reformed Protestant Dutch Church of Kingston, New York* (n.p.: Ladies Aid Society of the Church, 1924), 20–21.

15. Corwin, *Manual of the Reformed Church*, 599.

16. Edward A. Collier, *A History of Old Kinderhook* (New York: G. P. Putnam's Sons, 1914), 270–271.

17. *Tercentenary Studies*, 293.

18. As quoted in A. P. Van Gieson, *Anniversary Discourse and History of the First Reformed Church of Poughkeepsie* (Poughkeepsie, N.Y.: Published by the Consistory, 1893), 35.

19. *Ecclesiastical Records*, IV, 2730.

20. George S. Roberts, *Old Schenectady* (Schenectady: Robson and Adee, n.d.), 98.

21. Birch, *The Pioneering Church in*

the Mohawk Valley, 45, 47, 76, 87. It should be noted, however, that not all these baptisms were performed in the Schenectady church, even though they might be listed in its records; some took place in neighboring preaching stations visited by the Schenectady pastor. Such a practice was not unusual. For example, the baptisms and marriages performed at Kinderhook were recorded at Albany until 1716, although it had been a preaching station since about 1680 and was organized as a congregation in 1712.

22. As quoted in Corwin, *Manual of the Reformed Church*, 907.

23. Peter Kalm; *The America of 1750: Peter Kalm's Travels in North America*, ed. by Adolph B. Benson (2 vols.: New York: Wilson-Erickson, 1937), II, 602. See also I, 350–359.

24. As quoted in Codman Hislop, *The Mohawk* (New York: Rinehart & Company, 1948), 215.

25. A mimeographed history of the Schoharie church compiled in 1971 by the Reverend Robert W. Jackson and others was helpful in trying to disentangle the confused religious history of this area during the early eighteenth century.

26. *Christian Intelligencer*, September 5, 1888, 8–9; Dailey, *History of Montgomery Classis*, 58, 68, 86. On the other hand, Manheim, which was mostly German, "did not keep up either the German language or adopt English but used what was called Mohawk Dutch." *Ibid.*, 67.

27. Corwin, *Manual of the Reformed Church*, 691.

28. John C. Wilcox, ed., *The Old Church on the Green* (Hackensack: Published by the Congre-

gation, 1964), 16; Eugene H. Keator, *1736–1936: Historical Discourse Delivered at the First Reformed Church of Pompton Plains* (Paterson, N. J.: Lont & Overkamp, 1936), 66; *Tercentenary Studies*, 263.

29. For an excellent summary of the Church in New Jersey during the eighteenth century see Herman Harmelink III, e.a., *The Reformed Church in New Jersey* (n.p.: Published for the Synod of New Jersey, 1969), 7–24.

30. Adrian C. Leiby, *The Revolutionary War in the Hackensack Valley: The Jersey Dutch and the Neutral Ground, 1775–1783* (New Brunswick, N. J.: Rutgers University Press, 1962), 9.

31. Mellick, *The Story of an Old Farm*, 264. See also Leiby, *The United Churches of Hackensack and Schraalenburgh*, 44–45.

32. Harmelink, *Reformed Church in New Jersey*, 7, 17, 18, 22.

33. *Ecclesiastical Records*, IV, 2508.

34. *Ibid.*, 2509.

35. *Tercentenary Studies*, 268.

36. *Ibid.*, 346.

37. Amelia Stickney Decker, *The Ancient Trail: The Old Mine Road* (Trenton, N. J.: Petty Printing Company, 1942), 65.

38. Besides Southampton and Northampton (as well as Neshaminy), the churches have been known as Bensalem and Shameny as well Feasterville and Richboro. In 1816, a new church was built at Churchville, centrally located between the Southampton and Northampton churches. Henceforth, the one building replaced the two older structures. One of the best accounts of the Dutch Reformed churches in Bucks County is found in pertinent sections of the exhaustive *History of Bucks County*, edited by J. H. Battle

(Philadelphia: A. Warner & Co., 1887).

39. *Ibid.*, 489–490.

40. *Christian Intelligencer*, March 20, 1901, 180–181.

41. For a brief description of the Conewago and Hanover churches see A. Van Doren Honeyman, *Joannes Nevius and His Descendants A. D. 1627–1900* (Plainfield, N. J.: Honeyman & Company, 1900), 167–171.

42. For more detailed information on the Dutch Reformed church that was established in Kentucky see Percy Scott Flippen, "The Dutch Element in Early Kentucky," *Proceedings of the Mississippi Valley Historical Association*, IX, Part I (1915–16), 135–150, and A. H. Scomp, *Historic Sketch of the Old Meeting House* (Harrodsburg, Ky.: Harrodsburg Herald, 1900).

Chapter VII

1. Paul Zumthor, *Daily Life in Rembrandt's Holland*, translated from the French by Simon Watson Taylor (New York: Macmillan, 1963), 110–113 contains some information on ministerial training in the Netherlands. For material in Dutch see G. D. J. Schotel and H. C. Rogge, *De Openbare Eeredienst der Nederl. Hervormde Kerk in de Zestiende, Zeventiende en Achttiende Eeuw*, (2nd ed., rev.; Leiden: A. W. Sijthoff, n.d.), especially Chapter XIV, "Godgeleerde Studenten en Proponenten."

2. *Ecclesiastical Records*, II, 1104, 1113–1114.

3. Murphy, *Anthology of New Netherland*, 82.

4. *Ecclesiastical Records*, VI, 3807.

5. *Ibid.*, II, 1113–1114, 1315; VI, 3801, 3805, 3807.

6. *Ibid.*, V, 3499. See also VI, 3950.

7. *Ibid.*, IV, 2976.

8. *Ibid.*, V, 3289. See also IV, 3004, 3009–3010. In accordance with their instructions, the reverends Goetschius and Curtenius appeared at Acquackanonck on October 8, 1752 to install and ordain Marinus. *Christian Intelligencer*, January 9, 1889, 8.

9. In addition to scattered references in many of the works previously cited, the following special works were of use to the writer in researching the training of ministers in the colonies before the founding of New Brunswick Seminary: William Orpheus Shewmaker, "The Training of the Protestant Ministry in the United States of America before the Establishment of Theological Seminaries," *Papers of the American Society of Church History*, Second Series, VI (1921), 75–197; Robert W. Henderson, *The Teaching Office in the Reformed Tradition: A History of the Doctrinal Ministry* (Philadelphia: Westminster Press, 1962).

10. *Ecclesiastical Records*, IV, 2904. See also 2900–2901.

11. *Ibid.*, IV, 2935–2937. In view of the bitter arguments that developed between Leydt and Ritzema, the latter probably later regretted having interceded in his behalf.

12. *Ibid.*, V, 3693.

13. Franklin Bowditch Dexter, ed., *The Literary Diary of Ezra Stiles*, (3 vols.; New York: Charles Scribner's Sons, 1901), III, 240.

14. For examples of lengthy calls see *Ecclesiastical Records*, IV, 2497–2502, 2738–2740; Birch, *Pioneering Church*, 78–81; Keator, *1736–1936 Historical Discourse*, 83–85.

15. For an itemized list of Van

Schie's expenses see Van Gieson, *Anniversary Discourse*, 43–44. For a copy of the call see *Ecclesiastical Records*, IV, 2497–2502.

16. On Vrooman's expenses see Birch, *Pioneering Church*, 81–83; Roberts, *Old Schenectady*, 85–86.

17. As quoted in *Tercentenary Studies*, 294–295.

18. *Ibid.*, 327; Keator, *1736–1936 Historical Discourse*, 84; *Christian Intelligencer*, September 19, 1888, 8–9, and January 9, 1889, 8.

19. *Ecclesiastical Records*, V, 3445–3446. See Keator, *1736–1936 Historical Discourse*, 84 for a description of a similar arrangement for the combined churches of Acquackanonck, Pompton Plains, and Totowa.

20. As quoted in *Christian Intelligencer*, January 9, 1889, 8.

21. As quoted in *ibid*, October 3, 1888, 3.

22. William Smith, *History of New York* (Albany: Ryer Schermerhorn, 1814), 349.

23. *Ecclesiastical Records*, VI, 3855. For the salaries of the New York City ministers see *ibid.*, III, 2079; IV, 2772; V, 3489.

24. *Ibid.*, V, 3200, 3446, 3733; VI, 3984.

25. *Christian Intelligencer*, September 5, 1888, 8–9; October 3, 1888, 3.

26. *Ecclesiastical Records*, IV, 2506–2513, See also *ibid.*, VI, 3938; Boeve, "The Reformed Protestant Dutch Church of Kingston," 19.

27. *Ecclesiastical Records*, IV, 2590. Zumthor, *Daily Life in Rembrandt's Holland*, 86–87, gives some indication of ministerial salaries in the Netherlands at the close of the seventeenth century.

See also *Ecclesiastical Records*, I, 702, 713–714.

28. *Christian Intelligencer*, May 16, 1888, 9; Carl Horton Pierce, *New Harlem Past and Present* (New York: New Harlem Publishing Company, 1903), 19.

29. Battle, *History of Bucks County*, 486; Birch, *Pioneering Church*, 77; *Ecclesiastical Records*, IV, 2770; *Christian Intelligencer*, January 9, 1889, 2, 8.

30. Battle, *History of Bucks County*, 486, 490; *Ecclesiastical Records*, III, 1487; *Tercentenary Studies*, 311.

31. William E. Compton, ed., *The History of the Schenectady Classis, Reformed Church in America 1681–1931* (Altamont, N. Y.: The Enterprise Print, n.d.), 16. Roberts, *Old Schenectady*, 98–99; Birch, *Pioneering Church*, 58, 171, 173. The loaning of money by the churches, especially from the poor fund, was not unusual. Edward Payson Johnson, *Our Two Hundred and Fifty years: A Historical Sketch of the First Reformed Church, Albany, New York*. (n.p.: Published by the Officers of the Church, 1899), 22; *Ecclesiastical Records*, V, 3729.

32. Boeve, "The Reformed Protestant Dutch Church of Kingston," 19; Cole, *History of the Reformed Church of Tappan*, 3, 25, 77, 79; Dailey, *History of Montgomery Classis*, 39, 44, 45, 68, 86, 88–89; *Ecclesiastical Records*, III, 2222; IV, 3085; V, 3725, 3726–3727, 3729, 3737–3738, 3747–3749, 3758–3759.

33. In obtaining information on pews and their rental, the writer relied heavily on the better church histories, such as Birch, *Pioneering Church* and Keator, *1736–1936 Historical Discourse* as well as articles in the *Christian Intelli-*

gencer, including September 19, 1888, 8–9; October 3, 1888, 3; January 2, 1889, 2; and January 9, 1889, 2, and the *Ecclesiastical Records* (viz., IV, 2516–2519).

34. Strong, *History of the Town of Flatbush*, 92; Dailey, *History of Montgomery Classis*, 78; George Warne Labaw, *Preakness and the Preakness Reformed Church, Passaic County, New Jersey, A History 1695–1902* (New York: Board of Publication of the Reformed Church in America, 1902), 180–182; Birch, *Pioneering Church*, 53.

35. *Ecclesiastical Records*, IV, 2563. See also V, 3243.

36. For a discussion of Dutch works published in the colonies see the very careful study by Hendrik Edelman, *Dutch-American Bibliography 1693–1794* (Nieuwkoop, The Netherlands: D. De Graaf, 1974).

37. This is discussed in Chapter IX.

38. For two interesting forged letters sent to the synods of North and South Holland in 1756 in behalf of a *ziekentrooster* of New York City who was seeking ordination as a minister see *Ecclesiastical Records*, V, 3681, 3684–3685.

39. *Ibid.*, IV, 2740, 3138; VI, 3935–3939. *Tercentenary Studies*, 107; Keator, *1736–1936 Historical Discourse*, 88–89. During Morgan's pastorate from 1709 to 1731 at Freehold and Middletown, various accusations were brought against him, such as, in 1728, "practicing astrology, countenancing promiscuous dancing, transgressing in drink." Corwin, *Manual of the Reformed Church*, 634. These were never sustained, but in 1736, while serving two nearby Presbyterian churches, he was suspended for two years because of intoxication.

40. *Ecclesiastical Records*, IV,

2738–2739; Corwin, *Manual of the Reformed Church*, 440; Dexter, *Diary of Ezra Stiles*, III, 476; Harmelink, *Reformed Church in New Jersey*, 24; John B. Drury, *The Reformed (Dutch) Church Rhinebeck, New York: An Historical Address Delivered at the 150th Anniversary of Its Organization* (n.p.: n.p., 1881), 20.

Chapter VIII

1. Alexander Hamilton, *Hamilton's Itinerarium: Being a Narrative of a Journey from . . . May to September, 1774*, edited by Albert Bushnell Hart (Saint Louis: William K. Bixby, 1907), 87. For a careful account of population statistics during the colonial period see Evarts B. Greene and Virginia D. Harrington, *American Population before the Federal Census of 1790* (Gloucester, Mass.: Peter Smith, 1966), especially 88–105.

2. William Smith, *The History of New York from Its Discovery to the Appointment of Governor Cole in 1762* (2 vols.; New York: New York Historical Society, 1829), I, 264, 267; *Tercentenary Studies*, 291.

3. *Ecclesiastical Records*, IV, 3136.

4. *Acts and Proceedings of the General Synod of the Reformed Protestant Dutch Church in North America*, Vol. I, *1771 to 1812: Preceded by the Minutes of the Coetus (1738–1754) and the Proceding of the Conferentie (1755–1767), and followed by the Minutes of the Original Particular Synod (1794–1799)*, (New York: Board of Publications of the Reformed Protestant Dutch Church, 1859), cix.

5. Birch, *Pioneering Church*, 45; Coulbourn, *Reformed Dutch*

Church of Claverack, 9; Roberts, *Old Schenectady*, 87.
6. *Ecclesiastical Records*, IV, 2590.
7. *Ibid.*
8. *Ibid.* Although Poughkeepsie and Fishkill had been without a settled pastor before Van Schie's arrival, they had been ministered to quite regularly by neighboring pastors, particularly from Kingston.
9. Taylor's *Journal* covering the period from July 20 to October 12, 1802 is found in O'Callaghan's *Documentary History of the State of New York*, III, 673–696.
10. *Ecclesiastical Records*, IV, 2509–2510, 2739; V, 3199, 3200, 3305. Keator, *1736–1936 Historical Discourse*, one; *Christian Intelligencer*, October 3, 1888, 3. The New York congregation also held mid-week services, at least until 1730. *Ecclesiastical Records*, IV, 2518–2519.
11. Decker, *Ancient Trail*, 66; *Tercentenary Anniversary 1654–1954, Protestant Dutch Reformed Church of Flatlands, Long Island* (n.p.: n.p., n.d.), 22.
12. Hamilton, *Itinerarium*, 215–216. See also Boeve, "The Reformed Protestant Dutch Church of Kingston," 27.
13. In addition to information scattered in many of the works already mentioned, the writer found the following studies of special help in researching material on church services: Howard G. Hageman, *Pulpit and Table: Some Chapters in the History of Worship in the Reformed Churches* (Richmond, Va.: John Knox Press, 1962); James Hastings Nichols, *Corporate Worship in the Reformed Tradition* (Philadelphia: The Westminster Press, 1968).
14. As quoted in Dunshee, *History*

of the School of the Collegiate Church, 43.
15. Strong, *History of the Town of Flatbush*, 115–116.
16. Hageman, *Pulpit and Table*, 55.
17. *Ecclesiastical Records*, IV, 2955–2956.
18. Kalm, *Travels in North America*, II, 621.
19. As quoted in Corwin, *Manual of the Reformed Church*, 540.
20. Kalm, *Travels in North America*, II, 622.
21. *Ecclesiastical Records*, III, 2092–2093.
22. Hageman, *Pulpit and Table*, 57. The practice of having the long prayer at the beginning of the sermon did not originate until the nineteenth century. *Ibid.*
23. Andrew D. Mellick, Jr., *The Story of an Old Farm: or, Life in New Jersey in the Eighteenth Century* (Somerville, N. J.: The Unionist Gazette, 1889), 437. See also 6–7.
24. *Ecclesiastical Records*, IV, 2510; V, 3200, 3446; Benjamin C. Taylor, *Annals of the Classis of Bergen, of the Reformed Dutch Church, and of the Churches under Its Care*, (3rd ed.; New York: Board of Publication of the Reformed Protestant Dutch Church; 1857), 131; Keator, *1736–1936 Historical Discourse*, 84; *Christian Intelligencer*, September 5, 1888, 8–9; Birch, *Pioneering Church*, 80; Cole, *History of the Reformed Church of Tappan*, 16.
25. *Ecclesiastical Records*, III, 1916–1917.
26. *Ibid.*, IV, 2499; V, 3199, 3305.
27. *Ibid.*, II, 1229; IV, 2499, 2510; Keator, *1736–1936 Historical Discourse*, 84; Birch, *Pioneering Church*, 80.
28. *Ecclesiastical Records*, IV, 2500; Birch, *Pioneering Church*, 80; Keator, *1736–1936 Historical Discourse*, 84.

29. Mellick, *Story of an Old Farm*, 435.

30. When the "New Church" was completed in 1729 in New York, the consistory decided that "Men and Women shall sit separate, men by themselves, and women by themselves in the same manner as hitherto in our Old Church; and as is usual in all the Dutch Churches in Holland." *Ecclesiastical Records*, IV, 2489. Although in the following year some family pews for seating men and women together were sold in the New Church, (*ibid.*, 2516–2519), separation of the sexes in many churches lasted much longer. At Rhinebeck, New York, for example, it continued until 1768. Drury, *Reformed (Dutch) Church of Rhinebeck*, 18–19.

31. Strong, *History of the Town of Flatbush*, 92.

32. Cole, *History of the Reformed Church of Tappan*, 17.

33. Labaw, *Preakness and the Preakness Reformed Church*, 180.

34. Theodore B. Romeyn, *Historical Discourse Delivered on Occasion of the Re-Opening and Dedication of the First Reformed (Dutch) Church at Hackensack, New Jersey* (New York: Board of Publications, R.C.A., 1870), xxv.

35. *Ecclesiastical Records*, IV, 2517.

36. Birch, *Pioneering Church*, 181.

37. As quoted in Strong, *History of Flatbush*, 83.

38. *Ibid.* For costs of burial in the church yard at New York during the 1730's, see *Ecclesiastical Records*, IV, 2492–2494, 2616–2618. Some indication as to the number of burials that took place under the churches can be ascertained from the records of Barent Bradt, who served as sexton and clerk of the Albany church from 1722 to 1757. His records show that during those years, 1462 burials occurred in the church graveyard and 108 took place beneath the church. William V. Hannay, ed., "Burial Records, First Dutch Reformed Church of Albany, 1654–1862," *Dutch Settlers Society of Albany Yearbook*, VIII and IX (1932–1934), 30–69.

39. *Ecclesiastical Records*, IV, 2444. See also Drury, *Reformed (Dutch) Church of Rhinebeck*, 56; Alice Earle, *Colonial Days in Old New York*, (New York: Empire State Book Co., 1938), 297–298, *Christian Intelligencer*, January 9, 1889, 2.

40. Kalm, *Travels in North America*, II, 605. See also 629.

41. As quoted in Alice P. Kenney, *Stubborn for Liberty: The Dutch in New York* (Syracuse: Syracuse University Press, 1975), 127.

42. As quoted in Keator, *1736–1936 Historical Discourse*, 82.

43. Compton, *History of Schenectady Classis*, 18.

44. As quoted in Birch, *Pioneering Church*, 55. See also Collier, *History of Old Kinderhook*, 272.

45. Anne McVicar Grant, *Memoirs of An American Lady, with Sketches of Manners and Scenery in America as they Existed Previous to the Revolution* (New York: D. Appleton, 1846), 298. For the changing life style of Albany during these years and the reaction of the people to these changes see *ibid.*, 285–299.

46. As quoted in Lorena Cole Vincent, *Readington Reformed Church, Readington, New Jersey, 1719–1969* (Somerville, N. J.: Somerset Press, 1969), 37.

47. *Ecclesiastical Records*, III, 1689. See also IV, 2405, 2628; V, 3472.

48. *Ibid.*, VI, 4069. For some interesting discussion of this ques-

tion in Reformed circles during the early nineteenth century see *Magazine of the Reformed Dutch Church*, I (January 1827), 310–316; II (April 1827), 19–21, 23–24, 45–52.

49. *Ecclesiastical Records*, IV, 2720, 2722.

50. Wayne Andrews, ed., "A Glance at New York in 1697: The Travel Diary of Dr. Benjamin Bullivant," *New York Historical Society Quarterly*, XL (January 1956), 66.

51. Sarah Kemble Knight, *The Private Journal of Sarah Kemble Knight; Being the Record of a Journal from Boston to New York in the Year 1704* (Norwich, Conn: The Academy Press, 1901), 54.

52. Boeve, "The Reformed Protestant Dutch Church of Kingston," 18.

53. *Christian Intelligencer*, May 16, 1888, 8–9; Birch, *Pioneering Church*, 190; Pierce, *New Harlem Past and Present*, 47.

54. Earle, *Colonial Days in Old New York*, 284.

55. Keator, 1736–1936 *Historical Discourse*, 69.

56. Kenney, *Stubborn for Liberty*, 85; Earle, *Colonial Days in Old New York*, 303. For a treatment of funerals in general during the colonial period, see the recent study by Margaret M. Coffin, *Death in Early America* (Nashville, Tenn.: Thomas Nelson, 1976). Funerals in the Netherlands were also often extravagant. See Zumthor, *Rembrandt's Holland*, 158–161.

57. Andrews, "A Glance at New York in 1697," 65–66. For similar remarks about the inhabitants of Albany in 1749 see Kalm, *Travels in North America*, I, 343–345.

58. Andrew Burnaby, *Burnaby's Travels through North America*,

reprinted from the 3rd ed. of 1798, with "Introduction" and notes by Rufus Rockwell Wilson (New York: A. Wessels Company, 1904), 117.

59. Hector St. John de Crèvecoeur, *Letters from an American Farmer* (London: J. M. Dent & Sons, 1945), 49–50.

Chapter IX

1. As quoted in J. Keuning, *Petrus Plancius: Theoloog en Geograff 1552–1622* (Amsterdam: P. N. Van Kampen, 1946), 53.

2. J. N. Bakhuizen Van den Brink, e.a., *Documenta Reformatoria: Teksten uit de Geschiedenis van Kerk en Theologie in de Nederlanden sedert de Hervorming* (2 vols.; Kampen: J. H. Kok, 1960–62), I, 379–380.

3. Van Laer, *Documents Relating to New Netherland*, 2–5.

4. *Ibid.*, 36.

5. *Ibid.*, Krol's instructions are found in Eekhof, *Bastiaen Jansz Krol*, x–xii.

6. *Ecclesiastical Records*, I, 91–97.

7. Van Laer, *Documents Relating to New Netherland*, 176.

8. Eekhof, *Jonas Michaelius*, 132.

9. *Ibid.*, 133–134.

10. *Ecclesiastical Records*, I, 147.

11. *Van Rensselaer–Bowier Manuscripts*, 607.

12. *Ibid.*, 645.

13. A translation of this pamphlet is found in *Narratives of New Netherland*, 168–180.

14. *Ibid.*, 175–176.

15. Allen W. Trelease, *Indian Affairs in Colonial New York: The Seventeenth Century* (Ithaca, N. Y.: Cornell University Press, 1960), 170. The statement in *Appleton's Cyclopedia of American Biography* (6 vols.; New York: D. Appleton and Company, 1887–

89), IV, 286–287 that Megapolensis preached fluently in the Mohawk language and received many converts into the church is a gross exaggeration.

16. *Ecclesiastical Records*, I, 326–327. See also 322.
17. *Ibid.*, 398–399.
18. Safely back in France, Father Jogues wrote several letters to various individuals in New Netherland thanking them for the kindnesses shown him. In his letter to Megapolensis, "he could not refrain from offering some considerations on the Dominie's state of soul, and from urging him to return once more to the true Catholic religion of his childhood." Francis Talbot, *Saint among Savages: The Life of Isaac Jogues* (New York: Harper, 1935), 336.
19. *Ibid.*, 428.
20. *Narratives of New Netherland*, 177–178.
21. Grant, *Memoirs of an American Lady*, 117–118.
22. *Narratives of New Netherland*, 172–173. See also Eekhof, *Jonas Michaelius*, 133.
23. *Narratives of New Netherland*, 178.
24. Trelease, *Indian Affairs in Colonial New York*, 171.
25. *Ecclesiastical Records*, I, 508. See also 76–78. In 1747 and again in 1771, it was reiterated that the sacraments of Baptism and Lord's Supper could not be separated from each other in the case of adults. *Ibid.*, IV, 2954; VI, 4224.
26. *Ibid.*, II, 1233. See also 1007, 1089–1090. For Selyns' poetry, see Murphy, *Anthology of New Netherland*.
27. Tanis, *Dutch Calvinistic Pietism in the Middle Colonies*, 86.
28. Grant, *Memoirs of An American Lady*, 118n. See also Trelease,

Indian Affairs in Colonial New York, 328–329; R. Pierce Beaver, *Church, State, and the American Indians: Two and a Half Centuries of Partnership in Missions between Protestant Churches and the Government* (St. Louis, Mo.: Concordia Publishing House, 1966), 14, 18.

29. Peter Tesschenmaeker of Schenectady also carried on a limited amount of missionary work, but his career was cut short by his untimely death in 1690. He was killed during an incident in King William's War when a party of French and Indians from Montreal attacked Schenectady.
30. *Ecclesiastical Records*, II, 1087.
31. "Albany Records: Names of Members, Marriages, and Baptisms," *Yearbook of the Holland Society of New York, 1904* (New York: Knickerbocker Press, 1904), 1–106.
32. *Ibid.*, 49.
33. *Ibid.*, 66.
34. *Ibid.*, 51.
35. The Leisler Troubles are discussed in Chapter IV.
36. Although Dellius' motives in the land deals were perhaps honorable, he showed very poor judgment in the matter. In the controversy that followed his suspension, he received the support of many persons both within and outside the Dutch Reformed Church, and money was subscribed for his defense. The outcome, however, was not too satisfactory. Although the Classis of Amsterdam exonerated Dellius of any wrongdoing, the civil aspect of the case was delayed many times in England and he never received the arrears in back pay due him for his services among the Indians. For a discussion of Dellius' difficulties over

the land grants see Reich, *Leisler's Rebellion*, 140–146.

37. *Ecclesiastical Records*, III, 1867.
38. *Ibid.*, 1495.
39. *Ibid.*, IV, 2548–2549.
40. *Ibid.*, 2595–2596. See also 2760–2761.
41. *Ibid.*, II, 1065, 1087; III, 1867; Birch, *Pioneering Church*, 39.
42. *Ibid.*, 41.
43. As quoted in C. F. Pascoe, *Two Hundred Years of the S. P. G.: An Historical Account of the Society for the Propagation of the Gospel in Foreign Parts, 1701–1900* (London: The Societies Office, 1901), 68.
44. This subject is carefully documented in *ibid.*, 63–73.
45. To cite a specific example, Arent Schuyler, a member of the consistory and a heavy financial contributor to the Dutch Reformed Church at Belleville, New Jersey, stipulated in his will of 1724 that each of his two daughters would receive an Indian slave woman. George W. Schuyler, *Colonial New York: Philip Schuyler and His Family* (2 vols.; New York: Charles Scribners, 1885), II, 193–194. See also Almon Wheeler Lauber, *Indian Slavery in Colonial Times within the Present Limits of the United States* (New York: Columbia University Press, 1913), 112–117, 200–201.
46. Grant, *Memoirs of an American Lady*, 118.
47. *Ecclesiastical Records*, III, 1867.
48. Grant, *Memoirs of an American Lady*, 65, 69–70; *Dutch Settlers Society of Albany Yearbook*, VIII and IX, (1932–1934), 18, 19, 27, 29; *Two Hundredth Anniversary of the Old Dutch Church of Sleepy Hollow.* (Tarrytown, N. Y.: The De Vinne Press, 1898), 47. Increasingly, too, during the eighteenth century, the Anglican Church, working through the SPG, was sending more missionaries into the upper Hudson region. As before, this was encouraged by the English government, which because of growing Anglo-French colonial rivalry, was more anxious than ever to offset the influence of French Jesuits among the Indians.

49. *Ecclesiastical Records*, IV, 2760. Weiss expressed dismay that more was not being done, there being only one English minister working among the "wild men," with the result that "most of them [are] left to run about without instruction, like the beasts." *Ibid.* Along with his letter, he sent the Classis a ninety-six page description that he had written about the Indians, together with a painting of them, but these have apparently been lost. *Ibid.*, 2778–2779, 2809.
50. *Christian Intelligencer*, September 5, 1888, 8–9.
51. McCormick, *New Jersey from Colony to State*, 103–104; Frances D. Pingeon, "Slavery in New Jersey on the Eve of the Revolution," in *New Jersey in the American Revolution* (Trenton: New Jersey Historical Commission, 1970), 41; Edward A Collier, *A History of Old Kinderhook* (New York: G. P. Putnam's Sons, 1814), 552–559. Simeon F. Moss, "The Persistence of Slavery and Involuntary Servitude in a Free State 1685–1866," *Journal of Negro History*, XXXV (July 1950), 292. Arthur Zilversmit, *The First Emancipation: The Abolition of Slavery in the North* (Chicago: University of Chicago Press, 1967), 162.
52. For the life and ideas of Dominie Capitein see A. Eekhof, *De Negerpredikant Jacobus Elisa*

Joannes Capitein 1717–1747 ('s-Gravenhage: Martinus Nijhoff, 1917). Capitein's comments on slavery are particularly interesting because he himself was of African parentage, the first such person to be ordained into the Protestant ministry.

53. O'Callaghan, *Laws and Ordinances of New Netherland*, 60; Eekhof, *Hervormde Kerk*, II, 161; Elizabeth Donnan, ed., *Documents Illustrative of the Slave Trade to America* (4 vols.; New York: Octagon Books, 1965), III, 428; A. J. F. Van Laer, ed., *Minutes of the Court of Albany, Rensselaerswyck and Schenectady 1668–1685* (3 vols.; Albany: University of the State of New York, 1926–32), II, 431, 435–437.

54. As quoted in Henry Onderdonk, Jr., *History of the First Reformed Dutch Church of Jamaica, L. I.* (Jamaica, L. I.: The Consistory, 1884), 79. See also 44, 54.

55. Alice P. Kenney, "General Gansevoort's Standard of Living," *New York Historical Society Quarterly*, XLVIII (July 1964), 214–215; *Ecclesiastical Records*, VI, 4184; B. V. D. Wyckoff, e.a., *Historical Discourse and Addresses Delivered at the 175th Anniversary of the Reformed Church, Readington, N. J.* (Somerville, N. J.: Union-Gazette Association, 1894), 53. In 1855, *The Christian Intelligencer*, the official journal of the Dutch Reformed Church, reminded its readers that some of their own preachers in the not-too-distant past had owned slaves. *Christian Intelligencer*, October 18, 1855.

56. Eekhof, *Jonas Michaelius*, 46–47.

57. J. A. Grothe, ed., *Archief voor de Geschiedenis der Oude Hol-landsche Zending* (6 vols.; Utrecht: C. Van Bentum, 1884–1891), II, 317.

58. *Ecclesiastical Records*, I, 243.

59. As quoted in Roi Ottley and William Weatherby, eds., *The Negro in New York, An Informal Social History* (New York: New York Public Library, 1967), 11.

60. *Ecclesiastical Records*, I, 142.

61. Thomas Grier Evans and Tobias Alexander Wright, eds., *Records of the Reformed Dutch Church in New Amsterdam and New York: Baptisms from 25 December, 1639 to 29 December, 1800* (2 vols.; New York: New York Genealogical and Biographical Society, 1901–3; reprint ed., Upper Saddle River, N. J.: Gregg Press, 1968), I, 10–14; *Collections of the New York Genealogical and Biographical Society*, Volume I, *Marriages from 1639 to 1801 in the Reformed Dutch Church, New York* (New York: New York Genealogical and Biographical Society, 1890), 17, 18, 26, 29. See also Ottley, *The Negro in New York*, 8.

62. *Ecclesiastical Records*, I, 548.

63. *Ibid.*, 554.

64. That the ministers probably took a different attitude toward Christianizing the slaves in colonies belonging to the Netherlands is also indicated by the career of Dominie Lambertus De Ronde. While serving in Surinam from 1746 to 1750, De Ronde wrote "some pieces of Divine Truth" in Dutch and Negro-English for the edification of the slaves. *Ecclesiastical Records*, IV, 3109. There is little evidence, however, to indicate that he showed a similar interest in the slaves during his long pastorate at New York City from 1750 to 1784.

65. *Dutch Settlers Society of Albany*

Yearbook, VIII and IX, 43, 45, 58, 60, 116, 119, 122, 126, 127.

66. Evans and Wright, *Records of the Reformed Church in New Amsterdam and New York*, II, 17, 26, 38, 47, 58, 66, 73, 79, 92, 101, 103, 110, 123, 191, 194, 206, 284. The records of the Flatbush church for the years 1677–1757 also have only a few specific references to blacks. "Flatbush Dutch Church Records: Marriages, Baptisms," *Year Book of the Holland Society of New York, 1898* (New York: Knickerbocker Press, 1898).

67. That such information was sometimes omitted is demonstrated by the fact that on presenting their eleventh child, Thomas, for baptism on August 15, 1744, Frans and Elisabet are not listed as belonging to the servile class. This obviously was an oversight by the church clerk because the witnesses, Thomas and Maria Jacobs, are not so listed either, but are designated as such in 1743 and 1746 when they presented children of their own for baptism. Evans and Wright, *Records of the Reformed Church in New Amsterdam and New York*, II, 101, 110, 123.

68. Collier, *History of Old Kinderhook*, 552–559. But there were some exceptions elsewhere. Arendt Schuyler, for example, of Belleville, New Jersey, owned fifty or sixty slaves. Pingeon, "Slavery in New Jersey," 49.

69. *Historical Discourse and Addresses*, 53, cites Black Tony as the first slave accepted into the communion of the church at Readington, New Jersey. He was accepted about 1785, some sixty years after the church was organized. Perhaps even this landmark would have been further delayed had Black Tony not been the property of the Readington minister.

70. Godefridus Udemans, *'t Geestelyk Roer van 't Coopmansschip* (Dordrecht: Francois Boels, 1640), folio 183. On the life of Udemans and other published works by him, of which there were many, see P. J. Meertens, "Godefridus Cornelisz Udemans," *Nederlandsch Archief voor Kerkgeschiedenis*, Nieuwe Serie, XXVIII (1936), 65–106.

71. *Ecclesiastical Records*, I, 548.

72. Edgar J. McManus, *A History of Negro Slavery in New York* (Syracuse: Syracuse University Press, 1966). 71–73.

73. *Ibid.*, 70. See also John Hope Franklin, *From Slavery to Freedom: A History of Negro Americans* (3rd ed.; New York: Alfred A. Knopf, 1967), 108–109; Kalm, *Travels in North America*, I, 209.

74. *Ecclesiastical Records*, III, 1673.

75. As quoted in Marcus W. Jernegan, "Slavery and Conversion in the American Colonies," *The American Historical Review*, XXI (April 1916), 511.

76. *Ecclesiastical Records*, IV, 2953. See also 2810.

77. For some views on this see E. Franklin Frazier, *The Negro Church in America* (New York: Schocken Books, 1963), 82; Carter G. Woodson, *The History of the Negro Church* (2nd ed.: Washington: Associated Publishers, 1922), 98.

78. Eekhof, *Jonas Michaelius*, 135.

79. *Ecclesiastical Records*, II, 1118.

80. *Ibid.*, IV, 3075.

81. *Ibid.*, VI, 4078. See also IV, 2491.

82. William W. Coventry in *The Reformed Church in New Jersey*, 50.

83. McManus, *Negro Slavery in New York*, 77. For examples of mis-

treatment see *Reformed Church in New Jersey*, 50; Leslie H. Fishel and Benjamin Quarles, *The Negro American: A Documentary History* (Glenview, Ill.: Scott, Foresman and Company, 1967), 27; Marion T. Wright, "New Jersey Laws and the Negro," *Journal of Negro History*, XXVIII (April 1943), 165–166; Theodore B. Romeyn, *Historical Discourse Delivered on Occasion of the Re-Opening and Dedication of the First Reformed (Dutch) Church at Hackensack, N. J.* (New York: Board of Publication, R. C. A., 1870), 22–23; Pingeon, "Slavery in New Jersey," 41–47, 50–51.

84. According to the Puritans, the Negroes were an inferior people whom God had entrusted to the care of white men. In a catechism Cotton Mather prepared for the slaves, he taught that the Negroes "were enslaved because they had sinned against God and that God, not their masters, had enslaved them." Lorenzo Johnston Greene, *The Negro in Colonial New England, 1620–1776* (New York: Columbia University Press, 1942), 285–286. On how other religious groups viewed slavery during the colonial period see Jernegan, "Slavery and Conversion," 511, 513; Thomas E. Drake, *Quakers and Slavery in America* (New Haven: Yale University Press, 1950), 1–47; David Brion Davis, *The Problem of Slavery in Western Culture* (Ithaca: Cornell University Press, 1966), 304–306; Louis Ruchames "The Sources of Racial Thought in America" *Journal of Negro History*, LII (October 1967), 259.

85. Jernegan, "Slavery and Conversion," 504. On the lack of success by various denominations see *ibid.*, 524–527; McManus, *Negro*

Slavery in New York, 76; Faith Vibert, "The Society for the Propagation of the Gospel in Foreign Parts: Its Work for the Negroes in North America before 1783," *Journal of Negro History*, XVIII (April 1933), 171–212; Frazier, *The Negro Church in America*, 7–8; Green, *The Negro in Colonial New England*, 285–289.

Chapter X

1. See Chapter IV.
2. *Ecclesiastical Records*, I, 38.
3. For a brief discussion of the supervision of the colonial churches during the formative years see Frederick J. Zwierlein, *Religion in New Netherland* (Rochester, N. Y.: John P. Smith Printing Company, 1910), 39–42.
4. *Ecclesiastical Records*, I, 575.
5. *Ibid.*, II, 850.
6. Brodhead, *History of the State of New York*, I, 614.
7. *Ecclesiastical Records*, II, 907.
8. *Ibid.*, 1067. See also 1051.
9. *Ibid.*, 1106. In addition to questions about Bertholf's qualifications, his pro-Leislerian feelings no doubt contributed to the ill-will that Selyns and his colleagues felt toward him.
10. *Ibid.*, 1349.
11. William Banckert, a merchant of Amsterdam and a man of pietist convictions who advised the Classis of Amsterdam several times on ministerial appointments, apparently helped influence the Classis of Lingen to ordain Freeman. *Ibid.*, II, 1348–1349. See also III, 1960, 2045, 2119. Perhaps some of Banckert's interest in the colonies stemmed from his having a brother residing at Albany.
12. Maurice G. Hansen, *The Reformed Church in the Nether-*

laands (New York: Board of Publications of the Reformed Church, 1884), 218.

13. For a general discussion of this, see F. Ernest Stoeffler, ed., *Continental Pietism and Early American Christianity* (Grand Rapids, Mich: William B. Eerdmans, 1976), particularly "American Roots of Dutch Reformed Pietism" by James Tanis, 43–59. See also Nichols, *Corporate Worship in the Reformed Church*, 114–116.

14. James Tanis, *Dutch Calvinistic Pietism in the Middle Colonies: A Study in the Life and Theology of Theodorus Jacobus Frelinghuysen* (The Hague: Martinus Nijhoff, 1967). 44. See also Hageman, *Pulpit and Table*, 43–47.

15. *Nieuw Nederlandsch Biographisch Woordenboek*, III, 710. See also V, 301–303, 890; IX, 614–616.

16. *Ibid.*, VI, 108. Other early pietist preachers in this area were William Teellinck and Jean de Labadie, who served at Middleburg from 1613 to 1629 and 1666 to 1669 respectively, and Jodocus Van Lodenstein, pastor at Sluis from 1650 to 1653. Bertholf, in his decision to bypass the Classis of Amsterdam, was perhaps partly influenced by the decision of the Consistory of Amsterdam in 1691 prohibiting his mentor Koelman from preaching in that city. For another explanation, see *Ecclesiastical Records*, II, 1106–1108.

17. Tanis, *Dutch Calvinistic Pietism* 18, 27–33. As a specific example of Dutch influence at Lingen, it is interesting to note that Professor Wilhelmius was appointed to his position at Lingen by William III of Orange.

18. *Ibid.*, 2.

19. As quoted in Luidens,

"Americanization of the Dutch Reformed Church," 110–111.

20. *Ecclesiastical Records*, III, 2179–2180.

21. For a discussion of the *Klagte*, see various references to it in Tanis, *Dutch Calvinistic Pietism*. For a discussion of the opposing views of the reverends Frelinghuysen and Boel as reflections of differing views in the Netherlands, see *ibid.*, 61. In researching the story of Frelinghuysen, the writer is grateful to Joseph A. Loux, Jr., for the use of the manuscript of his introductory essay on the *Klagte* which, along with a translation of the *Klagte*, is being completed for publication.

22. Herman Harmelink III, "Another Look at Frelinghuysen and His Awakening," *Church History*, XXXVII (December 1968), 435–436.

23. *Ecclesiastical Records*, IV, 2416.

24. *Ibid.*, 2371.

25. *Dictionary of American Biography*, VII, 18.

26. For a less than favorable estimate of Frelinghuysen, see the carefully documented study by Harmelink, "Another Look at Frelinghuysen," 423–438.

27. Documents on the Freeman-Antonides dispute are found in O'Callaghan, *Documentary History of the State of New York*, III, 92–116.

28. The formation of the Coetus is discussed fully in the following chapter.

29. According to some reports, Van Vlecq returned to Holland.

30. *Ecclesiastical Records*, IV, 2572–2573.

31. *Ibid.*, 2564.

32. William J. Hinke, *Ministers of the German Reformed Congregations in Pennsylvania and Other Colonies in the Eighteenth Century* (Lancaster, Penn: Historical Commission of the Evangelical

and Reformed Church, 1951), 253.

33. O'Callaghan, *Documentary History of the State of New York*, III, 583. Adrian Leiby, *The United Churches of Hackensack and Schraalenburgh*, 4, states that Tesschenmaeker perhaps preached at one time in the English church at The Hague.

34. O'Callaghan, *Documentary History of the State of New York*, III, 583.

35. *Ecclesiastical Records*, I, 730–735.

36. *Ibid.*, 739.

37. In 1793, the German Reformed churches in Pennsylvania became independent and adopted the name "The German Reformed Church in the United States." Its indebtedness to the Dutch Reformed Church has not gone unrecognized. As expressed by one of the leading historians of the German denomination, when the German churches in the Palatinate and Switzerland found themselves unable because of war and poverty to look after their co-religionists in America and "the Pennsylvania Germans were left orphans," it was the Reformed Church of Holland that "took up their cause and became a foster mother to them." James I. Good, "The Founding of the German Reformed Church in America by the Dutch," *Annual Report of the American Historical Association for the Year 1897* (Washington: Government Printing Office, 1898), 375. One of her more recent historians stated the case even more strongly when he declared that the Reformed Church in Holland "from 1730 to 1790, was humanly speaking the only agency that kept the Reformed congregations in Pennsylvania alive during the eighteenth century." William H. Hinke, "The Bi-Centennial of the Reformed Church in the United States," *Journal of the Presbyterian Historical Society*, XII (October 1926), 329.

38. *Ecclesiastical Records*, IV, 2479–2481, 2483.

39. *Ibid.*, 2675.

40. *Ibid.*, 2752–2753.

41. *Ibid.*, 2756. See also 2920–2921; VI, 3964–3965.

42. O'Callaghan, *Documentary History of the State of New York*, III, 149.

43. *Ecclesiastical Records*, IV, 2573.

44. *Ibid.*, 2402.

45. *Ibid.*, 2702.

46. *Ibid.*, 2702–2703.

47. *Ibid.*, I, 525; III, 1661; IV, 2591.

48. *Ibid.*, III, 1719, 1858.

Chapter XI

1. *Ecclesiastical Records*, IV, 2664.

2. *Ibid.*, 2683–2684.

3. *Ibid.*, 2684.

4. *Ibid.*, 2689.

5. *Ibid.*, 2706–2710.

6. *Ibid.*, 2691–2694.

7. *Ibid.*, 2713.

8. *Ibid.*, 2723.

9. *Ibid.*, 2725–2729, 2798–2800, 2811–2819. See also Luidens, "Americanization of the Dutch Reformed Church," 95.

10. *Ecclesiastical Records*, IV, 2755, 2757. Concerning the absence of two other ministers, Van Schie of Albany and Vas of Kingston, the writer could locate no information, except that Vas' age (he was almost eighty) must have been a factor.

11. At the time of his being considered for the Long Island churches, Classis requested Van Sinderen "to lend a hand towards the Coetus of New York, and to further it as far as possible." *Ibid.*, 2894.

12. The documents of this session

are found in *ibid.*, 2974–2979, 2998–3000.

13. *Ibid.*, 3029. The controversy surrounding Muzelius is carefully treated in Cole, *History of the Reformed Church of Tappan*, 25–63.
14. *Ecclesiastical Records*, IV, 3008–3009.
15. *Ibid.*, 3101. See also 2988; V, 3412.
16. *Ibid.*, IV, 2985–2986.
17. *Ibid.*, V, 3254–3255, 3265–3266, 3272; Dailey, *History of Montgomery Classis*, 93.
18. *Ecclesiastical Records*, IV, 3043–3044, 3121–3122.
19. *Ibid.*, 3006.
20. *Ibid.*, 3064–3067.
21. *Ibid.*, V, 3152.
22. *Ibid.*, IV, 3141.
23. *Ibid.*, V, 3493.
24. *Ibid.*, IV, 2804; V, 3714; VI, 3950.
25. *Ibid.*, V, 3518–3519. See also 3532–3534.
26. Luidens, "Americanization of the Dutch Reformed Church," 95.
27. David C. Humphrey, *From King's College to Columbia, 1746–1800* (New York: Columbia University Press, 1976), 61. Chapter IV of this work, entitled "The King's College Controversy: The Dutch and Denouement," is a carefully documented study of the relationship between the Dutch Reformed Church and the debates over founding King's College.
28. *Ibid.*, 62. William Livingston's brother Philip, a deacon in the Dutch church, was an important leader of the anti-Anglican forces in the Collegiate consistory.
29. *Magazine of the Reformed Dutch Church*, II, No. 10 (January 1828), 314; Taylor, *Annals of the Classis of Bergen*, 19–20; *Acts and Proceedings of the General Synod*, I, xcvii, cv–cvii.
30. Elders were not invited to meet-

ings of the Conferentie until 1764.
31. De Ronde, however, supported the Coetus at first, but did so grudgingly under pressure from his consistory.
32. The minutes of this session are found in *Acts and Proceedings of the General Synod*, I, cxii–cxxv.
33. A fourth minister, Gerhard Daniel Kock, might also have been born in Germany. At the session of October 15, 1761, three of the eight ministers in attendance were German.
34. These were Benjamin Van der Linde, Johannes Schuyler, and Johannes Casparus Fryenmoet. Thus, Wertenbacker's explanation in his study, *The Middle Colonies*, 95, that the Conferentie was "led by a group of ministers, born, educated and ordained in the Netherlands" is too simplistic.
35. *Acts and Proceedings of the General Synod*, I, civ.
36. A few years earlier, in 1741, the Reverend Johannes Arondeus had to set sail twice from the Netherlands for Long Island. He was captured the first time by Spanish pirates and robbed of all his possessions.
37. Mancius Holmes Hutton, "Dr. John H. Livingston," a paper read to the Historical Club at New Brunswick, March 21, 1895, 10.
38. *Tercentenary Studies*, 179–182, 314–316; *Ecclesiastical Records*, V, 3645; *Acts and Proceedings of the General Synod*, I, xcix, cii–ciii; Van Gieson, *Anniversary Discourse*, 52–63.
39. *Ecclesiastical Records*, V, 3645.
40. *Ibid.*, 3566.
41. *Ibid.*, VI, 3991–3992.
42. Edelman, *Dutch-American Bibliography*, 83.
43. *Ecclesiastical Records*, VI, 3992, 3995.

44. *Ibid.*, 4134. See also Westerling, "De Nederduitsch Gereformeerde Kerk," 217.
45. *Ecclesiastical Records*, VI, 4128.

Chapter XII

1. Kalm, *Travels in North America*, I, 343.
2. Edward H. Tatum, Jr., ed., *The American Journal of Ambrose Serle, Secretary to Lord Howe 1776-1778* (San Marino, Calif.: The Huntington Library, 1940), 91–92. See also for Staten Island, Ray W. Pettengill, tr., *Letters from America 1776-1779: Being Letters of Brunswick, Hessian, and Waldeck Officers with the British Armies During the Revolution* (Port Washington, N. Y.: Kennikat Press, 1964), 177.
3. Mrs. Russel Hastings, "Peter Van Dyck of New York, Goldsmith, 1684-1750," *Antiques*, XXI (May 1937), 237; Smith, *History of New York*, 323; Benjamin F. Thompson and Charles J. Werner, *History of Long Island* (3 vols.; Port Washington, N.Y.: Ira J. Friedman, 1962), III, 157.
4. Wertenbacker, *The Middle Colonies*, 105.
5. As quoted in E. Clifford Nelson, ed., *The Lutherans in North America* (Philadelphia: Fortress Press, 1975), 14.
6. Kreider, *Lutheranism in Colonial New York*, 57. See also 58–64.
7. Leiby, *The Revolutionary War in the Hackensack Valley*, 9; Battle, *History of Bucks County*, 489; Flippen, "The Dutch Element in Early Kentucky," 145–150.
8. *Ecclesiastical Records*, II, 824.
9. *Ibid.*, IV, 2582.
10. *Ibid.*, VI, 3935–3936.
11. Zabriskie, *History of the Re-*

formed P. D. Church of Claverack, 25. It must be noted that Gebhard, although German-born and educated at Heidelberg, studied for a time at the University of Utrecht, The Netherlands, which certainly made it easier for him to learn Dutch.
12. *Ecclesiastical Records*, IV, 2340–2341.
13. *Ibid.*, 2621.
14. Kilpatrick, *Dutch Schools*, 166–215.
15. Martin Van Buren, *The Autobiography of Martin Van Buren*, ed. by John C. Fitzpatrick, Vol. II of American Historical Association, *Annual Report for the Year 1918* (Washington: Government Printing Office, 1920), 9. The Van Buren family was by no means an exception. Frederick W. Bogert, chairman of the Committee of Genealogy of the Holland Society of New York, informed the writer (June 7, 1973), "I have noted a remarkable number of intermarriages between members of Dutch families down through as many as six generations."
16. Kalm, *Travels in North America*, I, 121.
17. Grant, *Memoirs of an American Lady*, 53–54; Tatum, *American Journal of Ambrose Serle*, 91–92.
18. Kalm, *Travels in North America*, II, 626; Hamilton, *Itinerarium*, 107.
19. Kilpatrick, *Dutch Schools*, 159.
20. *Ecclesiastical Records*, IV, 2340–2341.
21. Kilpatrick, *Dutch Schools*, 155–156. The number of school-age children in New York City for the years 1700-1714 (five year averages) is given in Lawrence A. Cremin, *American Education: The Colonial Experience 1607–1783* (New York: Harper, 1970), 539.

22. *The New-York Gazette; or The Weekly Post-Boy*, April 17, 1758, 3. The advertisement was repeated throughout the month of May. The Flatbush church, however, did not even introduce partial English services until 1792, and English did not become the exclusive language of the church until 1805.

23. *Ecclesiastical Records*, VI, 4261.

24. Arthur James Weise, *The History of the City of Albany, New York* (Albany: E. H. Bender, 1884), 405.

25. Hamilton, *Itinerarium*, 86.

26. September 21, 1753, 10.

27. *Tercentenary Studies*, 61.

28. Smith, *History of New York*, 291–292.

29. William Livingston's *Independent Reflector* was suppressed at the end of 1753, after one year's existence, because of its views on church and state. In early 1754, he reprinted all the issues in a single, bound volume, together with an elaborate Preface. The above quotation is taken from the Preface, 23–24.

30. The work of the SPG among Dutch colonists is carefully treated in Nelson R. Burr, "The Episcopal Church and the Dutch in Colonial New York and New Jersey, 1664–1784," *Historical Magazine of the Protestant Episcopal Church*, XIX, no. 2 (June 1950), 90–111. See also W. K. Lowther Clarke, *A History of the S. P. C. K.* (London: S. P. C. K., 1959), 112–113, on translations of the Prayer Book into Dutch.

31. *Ecclesiastical Records*, III, 1866–1867.

32. *Ibid.*, 1553.

33. *Ibid.*, 1743.

34. *Ibid.*, IV, 2756.

35. *Ibid.*, 2920.

36. *Ibid.*, 3038.

37. *Ibid.*, VI, 3881.

38. Scattered references to the debate on the language question are found in *ibid.*, 3817–3840. See also Alexander J. Wall, "The Controversy in the Dutch Church in New York Concerning Preaching in English, 1754–1768," *New York Historical Society Quarterly*, XII (July 1928), 39–58.

39. *Ecclesiastical Records*, VI, 3838–3840, 3878–3880.

40. Several English-speaking churches were established in Holland for English-speaking soldiers serving there, as well as for English merchants and sailors, during the late sixteenth and early seventeenth centuries. One of the earliest (1586) was at Vlissingen.

41. *Ecclesiastical Records*, VI, 3879.

42. A lengthy account of his first sermon preached at New York on April 15, 1764, is found in the *Magazine of the Reformed Dutch Church*, II, no. 6 (September 1827), 161–169.

43. *Ecclesiastical Records*, VI, 3898–3899.

44. Wall, "The Controversy in the Dutch Church," 56–58.

45. "A Sermon, Occasioned by the Death of the Rev. Gerardus A. Kuypers, D. D. Preached in the Middle Dutch Church, June 7, 1833 by the Rev. John Knox" (New York: G. F. Hopkins & Son, 1833), 14. There were, however, occasional uses of Dutch at ceremonial gatherings, as on August 11, 1844, when the Middle Dutch Church was officially turned over to the federal government to serve as the city's post office. On that occasion, the Reverend Thomas De Witt, one of the collegiate preachers, pronounced the benediction in Dutch. For a time, Dutch services also reappeared for the new

wave of immigrants who began arriving from the Netherlands after about 1850.

46. The employment of a minister to preach in English did not necessarily mean that such a pastor was unacquainted with Dutch. Thus, the Reverend Basset was sufficiently familiar with the Dutch language to translate Adrian Vanderdonk's ponderous *History of New Netherland*.

47. Reynolds, *Dutch Houses in the Hudson Valley*, 297.

48. Adrian C. Leiby, *The Early Dutch and Swedish Settlers of New Jersey* (Princeton: Van Nostrand, 1964), 118; Cole, *History of the Reformed Church of Tappan*, 84.

49. As quoted in Taylor, *Annals of the Classis of Bergen*, 305–306.

50. Jonathan Pearson, *Two Hundredth Anniversary of the First Reformed Protestant Dutch Church of Schenectady, N. Y.* (Schenectady: Daily and Weekly Union Steam Printing House, 1880), 125–128.

51. As quoted in Vincent, *Readington Reformed Church*, 45.

52. As quoted from the consistory minutes of October 2, 1789 in *ibid.*, 49.

53. "The Passing of the Dutch Language," *Olde Ulster: An Historical and Genealogical Magazine*, X, no. 4 (April 1914), 113.

54. The advertisement appeared quite regularly throughout 1763 in *The New-York Gazette; or The Weekly Post-Boy* after its first appearance in the April 28 issue.

55. According to Evans' *American Bibliography*, this work, printed in 1767, was "the first book of music printed from type in America. The type for the music notes was obtained from Amsterdam." IV, 86, no. 10561. A description of the Psalm Book

and the events leading to its printing is found in Virginia L. Redway, "James Parker and the 'Dutch Church,'" *The Musical Quarterly* XXIV (October 1938), 481–500. See also *Ecclesiastical Records*, VI, 3872, 4010, 4076, 4110.

56. On the persistence of the Dutch language, see De Jong, *The Dutch in America*, 105–108.

57. *Seventy-Fifth Anniversary Historical Booklet, First Holland Reformed Church of Passaic, N. J.* (n.p.: n.p., 1946), 5; *Paterson Morning Call*, May 4, 1956, 20; *The Banner*, June 17, 1909, 389; *De Wachter*, June 3, 1931, 348.

Chapter XIII

1. *Acts and Proceedings of the General Synod*, I, 128. Actually, the term "Synod" had been used in the minutes on an earlier occasion in October 1782. *Ibid.*, 99.

2. The original articles of Dort and the Explanatory Articles of 1792 are found in parallel columns in Edward Tanjore Corwin, *A Digest of Constitutional and Synodical Legislation of the Reformed Church in America* (New York: Board of Publication of the Reformed Church, 1906), viii–lxxxvi.

3. Jedidiah Morse, *The American Geography; or a View of the Present Situation of the United States of America* (rev. ed.; London: John Stockdale, 1794), 380.

4. Luidens, "Americanization of the Dutch Reformed Church," 100–101; Clifton E. Olmstead, *History of Religion in the United States* (Englewood Cliffs, N. J.: Prentice-Hall, 1960), 140–141; Wertenbaker, *Middle Colonies*, 89; Humphrey, *From King's College to Columbia*, 60.

5. Carl Wittke, *We Who Built America* (rev. ed.; Cleveland: Case Western Reserve University, 1967), 26–29, 35, 38–39; Adolph B. Benson and Naboth Hedin, eds., *Swedes in America 1638–1938* (New Haven: Yale University Press, 1938), 52–59; Good, *Historical Handbook*, 71–72; Kreider, *Lutheranism in Colonial New York*, 57–64.

6. As quoted in McCormick, *Rutgers: A Bicentennial History*, 8.

7. Carl G. Gustavson, *A Preface to History* (New York: McGraw-Hill, 1955), 80.

8. Henry S. Lucas, ed., *Dutch Immigrant Memoirs and Related Writings* (2 vols.; Assen, The Netherlands: Van Gorcum, 1955), I, 471.

9. Howard G. Hageman, "Our Dutch Mythology," *The Church Herald*, November 29, 1974, 11.

Selected Bibliography

Books and Dissertations

Acts and Proceedings of the General Synod of the Reformed Protestant Dutch Church in North America, Vol. I, *1771–1812: Preceded by the Minutes of the Coetus (1738–1754) and the Proceedings of the Conferentie (1755–1767), and followed by the Minutes of the Original Particular Synod (1794–1799)*. New York: Board of Publication of the Reformed Protestant Dutch Church, 1859.

Battle, J. H., ed. *History of Bucks County Pennsylvania*. Philadelphia: A. Warner and Company, 1887.

Birch, John J. *The Pioneering Church of the Mohawk Valley*. Schenectady: The Consistory of the First Reformed Church, 1955.

Bridenbaugh, Carl. *Mitre and Sceptre: Transatlantic Faiths, Ideas, Personalities, and Politics 1689–1775*. New York: Oxford University Press, 1962.

Centennial Discourses: A Series of Sermons Delivered in the Year 1876, by Order of the General Synod of the Reformed (Dutch) Church in America. 2nd ed. New York: Board of Publication of the Reformed Church in America, 1877.

Cole, David. *History of the Reformed Church of Tappan, N. Y.* New York: Stettiner, Lambert and Company, 1894.

Collections of the New York Genealogical and Biographical Society, Vol. I, *Marriages from 1639 to 1801 in the Reformed Dutch Church, New York*. New York: New York Genealogical and Biographical Society, 1890.

Collier, Edward A. *A History of Old Kinderhook*. New York: G. P. Putnam's Sons, 1914.

Compton, William E., ed. *The History of the Schenectady Classis Reformed Church in America 1681–1931*. Altamont, N. Y.: The Enterprise Print, n.d.

Corwin, Edward Tanjore, ed. *Ecclesiastical Records of the State of New York*. 7 vols. Albany: J. B. Lyon, 1901–16.

Corwin, Edward Tanjore. *A Manual of the Reformed Church in America*. 4th ed. New York: Board of Publication of the Reformed Church in America, 1902.

Coulbourn, John. *A History of the Reformed Dutch Church of Claverack*. N. p.: n.p., 1966.

Cremin, Lawrence A. *American Education: The Colonial Experience, 1607–1783*. New York: Harper and Row, 1970.

Dailey, W. N. P. *The History of Montgomery Classis R. C. A.* Amsterdam, N. Y.: Recorder Press, 1916.

De Bie, J. P. and J. Loosjes, eds. *Biographisch Woordenboek van Protestantsche Godgeleerden in Nederland*. 5 vols. The Hague: Martinus Nijhoff, 1907–43.

De Jong, Gerald F. *The Dutch in America, 1609–1974*. Boston: Twayne Publishers, 1975.

DeWitt, Deweese W. *Ulster County's Reformed Church Legacy.* Kingston, N. Y.: Old Dutch Church, 1977.

Dilliard, Maud Esther. *An Album of New Netherland.* New York: Twayne Publishers, 1963.

Dunshee, Henry W. *History of the School of the Collegiate Reformed Dutch Church in the City of New York from 1633 to 1883.* 2nd ed., rev. New York: Aldine Press, 1883.

Earle, Alice. *Colonial Days in Old New York.* New York: Empire State Book Co., 1938.

Edelman, Hendrik. *Dutch-American Bibliography 1693-1794.* Nieuwkoop, The Netherlands: D. De Graaf, 1974.

Eekhof, A. *Bastiaen Jansz. Krol: Krankenbezoeker, Kommies en Kommandeur van Nieuw-Nederland, 1595-1645.* The Hague: Martinus Nijhof, 1910.

Eekhof, A. *De Hervormde Kerk in Noord-Amerika, 1624-1664.* 2 vols. 's-Gravenhage: Martinus Nijhoff, 1913.

Eekhof, A. *Jonas Michaelius Founder of the Church of New Netherland.* Leyden: A. W. Sijthoff, 1926.

Evans, Thomas Grier and Tobias Alexander Wright, eds. *Records of the Reformed Dutch Church in New Amsterdam and New York: Baptisms from 25 December, 1639 to 29 December, 1880.* 2 vols. New York: New York Genealogical and Biographical Society, 1901-3; reprint ed., Upper Saddle River, N. J.: Gregg Press 1968.

Flick, Alexander C., ed. *History of the State of New York.* 10 vols. New York: Columbia University Press, 1933-37.

Gaustad, Edwin Scott. *Historical Atlas of Religion in America.* New York: Harper and Row, 1962.

Good, James I. *Historical Hand-Book of the Reformed Church in the United States.* 2nd ed. Philadelphia: Heidelberg Press, 1901.

Grant, [Anne McVicar]. *Memoirs of an American Lady, with Sketches of Manners and Scenery in America, as they existed Previous to the Revolution.* New York: D. Appleton and Co., 1846.

Hageman, Howard G. *Pulpit and Table: Some Chapters in the History of Worship in the Reformed Churches.* Richmond, Virginia: John Knox Press, 1962.

Hamilton, Alexander. *Hamilton's Itinerarium being a Narrative of a Journey from Annapolis, Maryland through Delaware, Pennsylvania, New York, New Jersey, Connecticut, Rhode Island, Massachusetts and New Hampshire from May to September, 1774.* Ed. by Albert Bushnell Hart. Saint Louis: William K. Bixby, 1907.

Harmelink, Herman III, William W. Coventry, and Sharon Thomas Scholten. *The Reformed Church in New Jersey.* N.p.: Published for the Synod of New Jersey, 1969.

Henderson, Robert W. *The Teaching Office in the Reformed Tradition: A History of the Doctoral Ministry.* Philadelphia: The Westminster Press, 1962.

Hinke, William J. *Ministers of the German Reformed Congregations in Pennsylvania and Other Colonies in the Eighteenth Century.* Lancaster, Penn.: Historical Commission of the Evangelical and Reformed Church, 1951.

Hislop, Codman. *Albany: Dutch, English, and American.* Albany: The Argus Press, 1936.

Holland Society of New York. *Records of Domine Henricus Selyns of New York 1686-7.* New York: Holland Society, 1916.

Humphrey, David C. *From King's College to Columbia, 1746-1800.* New York: Columbia University Press, 1976.

Jameson, J. Franklin, ed. *Narratives of New Netherland 1609-1664.* New York: Charles Scribner's Sons, 1909.

Kalm, Peter. *The America of 1750: Peter Kalm's Travels in North America.* Ed. by Adolph B. Benson. 2 vols. New York: Wilson-Erickson, 1937.

Keator, Eugene H. *1736-1936: Historical Discourse of the Two-Hundredth Anniversary of the First Reformed Church of Pompton Plains, New Jersey.* Paterson, N. J.: Lont and Overkamp, 1936.

Kenney, Alice P. *Stubborn for Liberty: The Dutch in New York.* Syracuse: Syracuse University Press, 1975.

Kilpatrick, William Heard. *The Dutch Schools of New Netherland and Colonial New York.* Washington, D. C.: Government Printing Office, 1912.

Knittle, Walter Allen. *Early Eighteenth Century Palatine Emigration.* Philadelphia: Dorrance and Company, 1937.

Kreider, Harry Julius. *Lutheranism in Colonial New York.* New York: Arno Press, 1972.

Lebaw, George Warne. *Preakness and the Preakness Reformed Church, Passaic County, New Jersey: A History 1695-1902.* New York: Board of Publication of the Reformed Church in America, 1902.

Leiby, Adrian C. *The Early Dutch and Swedish Settlers of New Jersey.* Princeton: Van Nostrand, 1964.

Leiby, Adrian C. *The Revolutionary War in the Hackensack Valley; The Jersey Dutch and the Neutral Ground, 1775-1783.* New Brunswick: Rutgers University Press, 1962.

Leiby, Adrian C. *The United Churches of Hackensack and Schraalenburgh, New Jersey 1686-1822.* River Edge, N. J.: Bergen County Historical Society, 1976.

Luidens, John Pershing. "The Americanization of the Dutch Reformed Church." Unpublished Ph.D. dissertation, University of Oklahoma, 1969.

McCormick, Richard P. *New Jersey from Colony to State 1609-1789.* Princeton: D. Van Nostrand, 1964.

McCormick, Richard P. *Rutgers: A Bicentennial History.* New Brunswick, N. J.: Rutgers University Press, 1966.

McManus, Edgar J. *A History of Negro Slavery in New York.* Syracuse: Syracuse University Press, 1966.

Maynard, John A. F. *The Huguenot Church of New York: A History of the French Church of Saint Esprit.* New York: n. p., 1938.

Mellick, Andrew D., Jr. *The Story of an Old Farm: Or, Life in New Jersey in the Eighteenth Century.* Somerville, N. J.: The Unionist-Gazette, 1889.

Miller, Reverend John. *A Description of the Province and City of New York, with Plans of the City and Several Forts as They Existed in the Year 1695.* London: Thomas Rodd, 1843.

Molhuysen, P. C. and P. J. Blok, eds. *Nieuw Nederlandsch Biografisch Woordenboek.* 10 vols. Leiden: A. W. Sijthoff, 1911-37.

Munsell, Joel, ed. *The Annals of Albany.* 10 vols. Albany: J. Munsell, 1850-59.

Murphy, Henry C. *Anthology of New Netherland.* New York: n. p., 1865.

Nichols, James Hastings. *Corporate Worship in the Reformed Tradition.* Philadelphia: The Westminister Press, 1968.

O'Callaghan, Edmund Bailey, ed. *The Documentary History of the State of New York.* 4 vols. Albany: Weed, Parsons and Company, 1849–51.

O'Callaghan, Edmund Bailey, ed. *Laws and Ordinances of New Netherland 1638–1674.* Albany: Weed, Parsons, 1868.

O'Callaghan, Edmund Bailey and Berthold Fernow, eds. *Documents Relating to the Colonial History of the State of New York.* 15 vols. Albany: Weed, Parsons and Company, 1856–87.

Onderdonk, Henry, Jr. *History of the First Reformed Dutch Church of Jamaica, L. I.* Jamaica, N. Y.: The Consistory, 1884.

Pearson, Jonathan. *Two Hundredth Anniversary of the First Reformed Protestant Dutch Church of Schenectady, N. Y.* Schenectady: Daily and Weekly Union Steam Printing House, 1880.

Pratt, Daniel J. *Annals of Public Education in the State of New York from 1626 to 1746.* Albany: The Argus Company, 1872.

Pratt, John Webb. *Religion, Politics, and Diversity: The Church-State Theme in New York History.* Ithaca, N. Y.: Cornell University Press, 1967.

Raesly, Ellis Lawrence. *Portrait of New Netherland.* New York: Columbia University Press, 1945.

Reich, Jerome R. *Leisler's Rebellion: A Study of Democracy in New York 1664–1720.* Chicago: University of Chicago Press, 1953.

Reitsma, J. and J. Lindeboom. *Geschiedenis van de Hervorming en de Hervormde Kerk der Nederlanden.* 5th ed., rev. 's-Gravenhage: Martinus Nijhoff, 1949.

Reynolds, Helen Wilkinson. *Dutch Houses in the Hudson Valley before 1776.* New York: Dover Publications, 1965.

Riker, James. *Revised History of Harlem (City of New York) Its Origin and Early Annals.* Rev. ed. New York: New Harlem Publishing Company, 1904.

Schotel, G. D. J. and H. C. Rogge, *De Openbare Eerdienst der Nederl. Hervormde Kerk in de Zestiende, Zeventiende en Achttiende Eeuw.* 2nd ed. rev. Leiden: A. W. Sijhoff, n. d.

Smith, George L. *Religion and Trade in New Netherland: Dutch Origins and American Development.* Ithaca, N. Y.: Cornell University Press, 1973.

Smith, William. *The History of the Late Province of New York, From its Discovery to the Appointment of Governor Colden, in 1762.* 2 vols. New York: New York Historical Society, 1830.

Stiles, Henry R. *The History of the County of Kings and the City of Brooklyn.* 2 vols. New York: W. W. Munsell, 1884.

Stoeffler, F. Ernest, ed. *Continental Pietism and Early American Christianity.* Grand Rapids, Mich.: William B. Eerdmans, 1976.

Stokes, Isaac N. *The Iconography of Manhattan Island, 1498–1909.* 6 vols. New York: R. H. Dodd, 1915–28.

Strong, Thomas M. *The History of the Town of Flatbush, in Kings County, Long Island.* New York: Thomas R. Mercein, 1842.

Sutphen, David S., e. a. *Historical Discourses [on the]... Reformed Dutch Church of New Utrecht.* N. p.: The Consistory, 1927.

Sweet, William Warren. *Religion in Colonial America.* New York: Charles Scribner's Sons, 1949.

Talbot, Francis. *Saint among Savages: The Life of Isaac Jogues.* New York: Harper, 1935.

Tanis, James. *Dutch Calvinistic Pietism in the Middle Colonies: A Study in the*

Life and Theology of Theodorus Jacobus Frelinghuysen. The Hague: Martinus Nijhoff, 1967.

Taylor, Benjamin C. *Annals of the Classis of Bergen, of the Reformed Dutch Church, and of the Churches under its Care*. 3rd ed. New York: Board of Publication of the Reformed Protestant Dutch Church, 1857.

Tercentenary Committee on Research. *Tercentenary Studies 1928: Reformed Church in America*. N. p.: Published by the Church, 1928.

Thompson, Benjamin F., and Charles J. Werner. *History of Long Island*. 3rd ed. 3 vols. Port Washington, N. Y.: Ira J. Friedman, 1962.

Thompson, Henry P. *Into All Lands: The History of the Society for the Propagation of the Gospel in Foreign Parts, 1701–1950*. London: Society for Promoting the Christian Gospel, 1951.

Trelease, Allen W. *Indian Affairs in Colonial New York: The Seventeenth Century*. Ithaca, N. Y.: Cornell University Press 1960.

Two Hundredth Anniversary of the Old Dutch Church of Sleepy Hollow. Tarrytown, N. Y.: The De Vinne Press, 1898.

Van Gieson, A. P. *Anniversary Discourse and History of the First Reformed Church of Poughkeepsie*. Poughkeepsie, N. Y.: Published by the Consistory, 1893.

Van Laer, A. J. F., ed. *Documents Relating to New Netherland 1624–1626 in the Henry E. Huntington Library*. San Marino, Calif.: The Henry E. Huntington Library and Art Gallery, 1924.

Van Laer, A. J. F., ed. *Van Rensselaer Bowier Manuscripts Being the Letters of Kiliaen Van Rensselaer, 1630–1643*. Albany: University of the State of New York, 1908.

Van Troostenburg de Bruyn, C. A. L. *De Hervormde Kerk in Nederlandsch Oost-Indie onder de Oost-Indische Compagnie, 1602–1795*. Arnhem, The Netherlands: H. A. Tjeenk Willink, 1884.

Vincent, Lorena Cole. *Readington Reformed Church, Readington, New Jersey, 1719–1969*. Somerville, N. J.: Somerset Press, 1969.

Weis, Frederick Lewis. *The Colonial Churches and the Colonial Clergy of the Middle and Southern Colonies, 1607–1776*. Lancaster, Mass.: Society of the Descendants of the Colonial Clergy, 1938.

Wertenbaker, Thomas Jefferson. *The Founding of American Civilization: The Middle Colonies*. New York: Cooper Square Publishers, 1963.

Weslager, C. A. *Dutch Explorers, Traders and Settlers in the Delaware Valley 1609–1664*. Philadelphia: University of Pennsylvania Press, 1961.

Wilcox, John C., ed. *The Old Church on the Green*. Hackensack: Published by the Congregation, 1964.

Wright, Louis B. *The Cultural Life of the American Colonies*. New York: Harper and Brothers, 1957.

Year Book of the (Collegiate) Reformed Protestant Dutch Church of the City of New York, vols. 1–10. New York: n. p., 1880–89.

Zabriskie, F. N. *History of the Reformed P. D. Church of Claverack: A Centennial Address*. Hudson, N. Y.: Stephen B. Miller, 1867.

Zumthor, Paul. *Daily Life in Rembrandt's Holland*. Translated from the French by Simon Watson Taylor. New York: Macmillan, 1963.

Zwierlein, Frederick J. *Religion in New Netherland*. Rochester, N.Y.: John P. Smith Printing Company, 1910.

Articles

"Albany Records, Names of Members, Marriages, and Baptisms." *Year Book of the Holland Society of New York, 1904*. New York: Knickerbocker Press, 1904. 1–106.

Beaver, R. Pierce. "American Missionary Motivation before the Revolution." *Church History*, XXXI (June 1962), 216–226.

Burr, Nelson R. "The Episcopal Church and the Dutch in Colonial New York and New Jersey 1664–1784." *Historical Magazine of the Protestant Episcopal Church*, XIX (June 1950), 90–109.

Corwin, Edward Tanjore. "The Ecclesiastical Condition of New York at the Opening of the Eighteenth Century." *Papers of the American Society of Church History*, 2nd series, III (1912), 81–115.

De Jong, Gerald F. "Dominie Johannes Megapolensis: Minister to New Netherland." *The New York Historical Society Quarterly*, LII (January 1968), 7–47.

De Jong, Gerald F. "The Formative Years of the Dutch Reformed Church on Long Island." *Journal of Long Island History*, VIII (Summer-Fall, 1968), 1–16; IX (Winter-Spring, 1969), 1–20.

De Jong, Gerald F. "The *Ziekentroosters* or Comforters of the Sick in New Netherland." *The New York Historical Society Quarterly*, LIV (October 1970), 339–359.

De Vries, George, Jr. "Church and State in New York: An Historical Account." *The Reformed Journal*, November 1975, 18–21; December 1975, 25–28.

"Flatbush Dutch Church Records: Marriages, Baptisms." *Year Book of the Holland Society of New York, 1898*. New York: Knickerbocker Press, 1898. 87–152.

Frantz, John B. "The Awakening of Religion among the German Settlers in the Middle Colonies." *William and Mary Quarterly*, XXXIII (April 1976), 266–288.

Good, James I. "The Founding of the German Reformed Church in America by the Dutch." *Annual Report of the American Historical Association for the Year 1897*. Washington: Government Printing Office, 1898. 375–384.

Hannay, William V., ed. "Burial Records, First Dutch Reformed Church of Albany, 1654–1862." *Dutch Settlers Society of Albany Yearbook*, VIII and IX (1932–1934), 1–145.

Harmelink, Herman, III. "Another Look at Frelinghuysen and His 'Awakening.' " *Church History*, XXXVII (December 1968), 423–438.

Hinke, William J. "The Bi-Centennial of the Reformed Church in the United States." *Journal of the Presbyterian Historical Society*, XII (October 1926), 325–338.

Hinke, William J., ed. "Church Records of Neshaminy and Bensalem, Bucks County, 1710–1738." *Journal of the Presbyterian Historical Society*, I. (May 1901), 110–134.

Hinke, William J. "Rev. Paulus Van Vlecq." A paper presented at a meeting of the Bucks County Historical Society at Doylestown, Pennsylvania, January 16, 1917, and published in *Bucks County Historical Society Papers*, IV, 1–15.

Jerengan, Marcus W. "Slavery and Conversion in the American Colonies." *The American Historical Review*, XXI (April 1916), 504–527.

Johnson, Edward Payson. "Christian Work among the North American Indians during the Eighteenth Century." *Papers of the American Society of Church History*, 2nd series, VI (1921), 3–41.

Johnson, Edward Payson. "Early Missionary Work among the North American Indians." *Papers of the American Society of Church History*, 2nd series, III (1912), 13–39.

Kenney, Alice P. "Private Worlds in the Middle Colonies: An Introduction to Human Traditions in American History." *New York History*, LI (January 1970), 4–31.

Labaree, Leonard W. "The Conservative Attitude toward the Great Awakening." *The William and Mary Quarterly*, 3rd series, I (1944), 331–352.

Oppenheim, Samuel. "The Early History of the Jews in New York, 1654–1664." *Publications* of the American Jewish Historical Society, XVIII (1909), 1–91.

Redway, Virginia L. "James Parker and the 'Dutch Church.'" *Musical Quarterly*, XXIV (October 1938), 481–500.

Shewmaker, William Orpheus. "The Training of the Protestant Ministry in the United States of America, before the Establishment of Theological Seminaries." *Papers of the American Society of Church History*, 2nd series, VI (1921), 75–197.

Wall, Alexander J. "The Controversy in the Dutch Church in New York Concerning Preaching in English, 1754–1768," *The New York Historical Society Quarterly*, XII (July 1928), 39–58.

Westerling, H. J. "De Nederduitsch Gereformeerde Kerk in de Provincien New York en New Jersey onder het Engelsche Bewind," *Nederlandsch Archief voor Kerkgeschiedenis*, Nieuwe Serie, XVI (1920–21), 209–212.

Wilkenfeld, Bruce M. "The New York City Common Council, 1689–1800." *New York History*, LII (July 1971), 249–273.

Index

273

Index